S0-DJE-987

the Church of God movement
HERITAGE SERIES

Diary of
A. J. Tomlinson
1901–1924

WHITE WING PUBLISHING HOUSE
CLEVELAND, TENNESSEE 37312

Compiled by Dr. Hector Ortiz,
International Director Center for Biblical Leadership
And Adrian L. Varlack, Sr., Church Historian
Church of God of Prophecy

Published by *White Wing Publishing House*, Copyright ©2012
Church of God of Prophecy Cleveland, Tennessee.

ISBN 978-1-889505-91-6

> *"If you would understand anything, observe
> its beginning and its development."*
>
> —Aristotle

It is our sincere pleasure to make the *Church of God Movement Heritage Series* available to you. We trust it will enrich your understanding of the past, as well as enlighten your vision for the future as you read about our history and the people who formed it.

It has been our desire to keep this series as authentic as possible. For this reason, what you are about to read has not been rewritten or updated. We have changed nothing more than minor spelling or punctuation errors. Otherwise, the content is exactly the same as the original. We believe this will enhance your experience as you read and study our rich history.

We do hope you enjoy reading this series.

In Christ,

Gene Browning

Director
White Wing Publishing House

Notation

You will see throughout this manuscript the use of an abbreviation, D.V. This abbreviation stands for Deo volente, the latin term for *"Lord willing."*

PREFACE

Today it is common knowledge that the fresh outpouring of the Holy Spirit in our age flowed out of the wellspring of the Azusa Street revival and the ministry of William Seymour. That fountain continues to flow powerfully on every continent of the world through millions of adherents. And most who have studied the history leading to the Azusa Street revival know about Topeka Kansas and the school where Charles Parham was teaching about the Holy Spirit and how Seymour learned sitting outside the class listening through a window. Several students received the full Holy Spirit Baptism there.

Yet many do not know about the robust outpouring of the Holy Spirit in the late 1800's in the mountains of North Carolina in a revival at Schearer's School House. At that meeting nearly one hundred received the full Baptism of the Holy Spirit and fire. Just a few years later, A. J. Tomlinson would participate in leadership with ministers from this outpouring to launch the family of ministries using the name 'Church of God' around the world. Chronologically, many refer to this revival in North Carolina and the movement that sprang up from there as the original spark of the full Baptism of the Holy Spirit in our age.

Today more than one hundred years later we can affirm that this work of God was in fulfillment of Peter's message on the day of Pentecost, and his reference to Joel's prophecy from God, "in the last days I will pour out my spirit over all the earth." In this significant work of God, A. J. Tomlinson stepped on the scene and was used of God to lead significantly. It is fortunate for we who read this diary today that he was a man who was passionate to record what God was doing in his time. It is our prayer that the pages of this diary will usher each reader into an age of deep significance and into the lives of ministers and ministries that God was using to light the original spark of Holy Spirit revival fire which would spread to consume the earth. May God use these pages to ignite fresh sparks in each reader for further Holy Spirit renewal today.

Randall E. Howard
General Overseer
Church of God of Prophecy

FORWARD

The Center for Biblical Leadership in collaboration with the Historical Series is pleased to present this comprehensive volume of the Diary of A. J. Tomlinson. This first volume of his diary is to hear A. J. Tomlinson in his own words, his style of writing, his life, his trials, his love and passion for the Lord he so deeply loved. This volume has been duly compared with A. J. Tomlinson's hand written diary to ensure we are hearing his words. In recent years historians have taken another look at A. J. Tomlinson and have revisited some of his writings as well as some of his actions as a Pentecostal leader. We are pleased that some scholars are beginning to review Tomlinson's life and give him a better read without some negativism that was written about him by some individuals. As all great leaders, he had his faults and his errors, but his enduring legacy of his outstanding work outshines and outlives any misstep that he made in his lifetime. The Church of God of Prophecy is honored to have him as their founding father.

The Church of God of Prophecy has never produced a diary of A. J. Tomlinson, and after so many years, it was felt that the time was right for us to take his handwritten diary and let it speak as he wrote it. A diary is a person's most personal thoughts of their journey in life. As one reads his words, one is moved as A. J. Tomlinson was a man sent from God. He was not perfect; who is? We witness his spiritual growth, maturity, his change of doctrinal views and his hunger for a deeper walk with his Lord. We witness his moments of great victory, times of sickness and his determination to trust God for his divine healing, his trials, his moments of depression, and the great victories that God wrought in his ministry.

As one reads Tomlinson's Diary, one senses his love for God in his often vigils of prayer, his hunger for the gifts of the Spirit, his often travels by faith without means, and how God provided. His love to win the lost is witnessed as he often walked twenty plus miles in a day with no place to sleep and without food. Tomlinson meant business for his Lord and his life is proof of his unflinching commitment to spend and be spent.

A. J. Tomlinson left a print on the sands of time that is captured in the following portion of his prayer "O heavenly, heavenly Dove, we want to speak good to thee, we want to speak good of Thee always . . . keep us for we are not able to keep ourselves without thee."

Hector Ortiz, D.Min.
Director of the Center for Biblical Leadership
May 31, 2012

FORWARD

Ambrose Jessup Tomlinson's hand-written Journals (five in all) were lodged in the Library of Congress of the United States, Washington, DC, by his son, Homer, in October of 1952. The note on the front page of the copy of the first book of the microfilmed version of the handwritten diaries (microfilmed 1990) obtained from the Library of Congress (LOC) reads,

Tomlinson, Andrew [sic] Jessup, Bp., 1865–1943
Diaries, 1901–1943
Clergyman. Manuscript diaries of Bishop A. J. Tomlinson of the
Church of God of Prophecy; also, copy of the published version of these
diaries (3 v., 1949-1955).
82–95745

We note that the LOC's recording clerk made an error in rendering A. J. Tomlinson's first name as "Andrew" when in fact it is "Ambrose." This error notwithstanding, we are absolutely certain that the copies of the five journals reproduced for us by the LOC on microfilm and printed under supervision in hardcopy form at the Dixon Pentecostal Research Center, are in fact authentic copies of the Journals of Ambrose Jessup Tomlinson (1865–1943) written by his own hand. The microfilm and hard copies are now at the Church of God of Prophecy (CGP) Archives.

Tomlinson's secretary of almost 25 years, Lille Duggar, made the following pertinent observations about the writing style he used in his Diary:

> [Bishop] A. J. Tomlinson had his own way of expressing himself.
> If some of his expressions contained in his writings seem a little
> odd, just remember that is the way he wanted it. And if certain
> words are spelled one way one time and another way another
> time, it is because he often spelled words as the Bible [KJV]
> spells them.
>
> Quite often he put "oh" in his writings. Sometimes he used "oh"
> and other times "O." The Bible uses "O" a great deal and Brother
> Tomlinson said he liked to see the big "O" by itself even though it
> is not correct to use it as he did. . . He gave very little attention to
> paragraphing and seldom separated his thought contained in an
> entry into paragraphs. He was great for doing things that did not
> concern others as he wanted to do them, even if his way did not
> conform with [sic] what was considered correct."[1]

Except for several typos and a secretary's usual corrections of her supervisor's obvious misspellings, we found Duggar's typescript of the Journals (CGP Archives) faithful to the LOC copies of the originals. This is consistent with her observations quoted above. All review work, comparisons, and compiling, were done under the direction of Dr. Hector Ortiz, International Director of the Center for Biblical Leadership (Church of God of Prophecy) by the Faculty and Staff of the Center. The Journals are being published as one Diary, in two Sections. This Section covers the years 1901–1924. It is the intention that the Journals will be translated into several languages as time and funds allow.

Adrian L. Varlack Sr.
Church Historian/CBL Instructor

---

[1]*A. J. Tomlinson*, Lillie Duggar (Cleveland: White Wing Publishing House and Press, 1964, xiv.

CONTENTS

1901

Thursday, March 7

Went to see about contracting for a farm of 600 acres for an industrial farm. The price give, [*sic*] I commenced to view the farm.

Friday, March 8

I spent nearly the whole day in viewing the farm. Was very favorably impressed with it. In evening I was almost overwhelmed with the love and providences of God. The land was priced at $3,500. I had not a penny to spend for a farm, yet I had inspiration and joy in my soul as I acted as if I was going to buy.

Saturday, March 9

I was informed by the cooks that our food was short. I had near $20 in my possession but could not spend it for food, as it had been given me for building purposes.

Sunday, March 10

My fast day. I was told the bread stuff was all consumed at breakfast. 12 children and 9 grown workers to support. All are cheerful and happy. James H. Withrow and his wife and two Bible students were sent forth as the "Foxes" on a missionary tour. I am reading "Life of George Muller" and seeking the kingdom. I am waiting to see what the Lord will do.

March 11

God sent me $2.12 besides some receipts, showing a friend had paid bills for me to the amount of $1750 which had not been presented to me. While praying and meditating upon the purchase of land for our industrial work, etc., these words kept ringing in my inner ears, "Will not the God of the whole earth do right."

March 16

We have not enough food to last over Sunday. Every penny gone. The children and all are very happy and industrious all day. In evening we repair to P. O. and fully expect means from somewhere to supply our needs. God was faithful and our needs are once more supplied.

Sunday, March 17

A blessed day for all. Sunday school and preaching. Prayer in one house and singing in the other at night.

Monday, March 18

Writing copy for Samson's Foxes. Must now repair to P. O. and store to secure food for breakfast tomorrow. God is supplying us just day at a time, but my soul is happy.

March 19

The house is full of life and industry. Had the privilege of practicing the Bible again today. "Give to every one that asketh and from him that would borrow of thee turn not thou away." Gave to a Mr. Brown and loaned to Mr. Carter. Praise God for this privilege.

March 25

The day and week begun with a special burden and prayer on my heart for $5,000. After a special outpouring of the Spirit in our Sunday meeting yesterday. I could not take my breakfast as usual. At night we had special prayer and after prayer I read the words of Jesus that we received the petitions we desired because we keep His commandments. I then turned, guided by the spirit, and read where Jesus washed the disciples feet and said "ye ought to wash one another's feet." I had never obeyed this commandment. I at once laid aside my coat, girded myself with a towel, poured water into a basin and washed the feet of the brethren present. Praise God. Other members of our household became more zealous to keep the commandments.

March 27

I repaired to the woods early this morning to fast and pray, spent the day alone with God, with a prayer continually on my heart for $5,000 to purchase a farm where we can have for our industrial school work, etc. Have been secluded all day. God gave me as a text to start with when I fell upon the ground in the woods, John 14:11-15. I am resting upon that promise tonight. God sent me as an earnest through the mail this evening $1.20. Praise God for His blessed presence with me and the security I feel in Him tonight.

April 2

Have spent three whole days in absolute fasting and in prayer. The cry of my heart is for the $5,000 which means the purchase of the farm.

Sunday, April 7

Some new faces in attendance at our meeting today.

April 10

Corn for horses failed yesterday but God so arranged that our horses worked for a neighbor yesterday and earned their board. This morning I sent for six bushels of corn for which I have to pay $4.20. I only have 72¢ left for postage, food for the day and other incidentals. No human being knows the pressure I am under, and I can seek help of none but God. If He don't come to my rescue I am totally ruined. 25 mouths to feed, Samson's Foxes to mail, which are now several days tardy. But God being my helper I will pray and trust and if I fail I will go down trusting God. God's Word is true and I am determined to trust Him by His grace.

April 10, time evening

The pressure is great. No mail all day, Money reduced to 20¢. I hear the cooks say they are puzzled about anything to get for supper. I am searching to see if there is an "Achin" in the camp. I know my faith is being developed for it is being tested seemingly to the very last notch. I feel clear before God. My soul is happy. The Spirit witness so He is at home in His temple. My heart crys out, O God, give us the farm. O God, give us $5,000 at once. Family all seem to be contented and happy. Praise God.

Sunday, April 14

Money all gone not even enough to mail a letter. Have received nothing for several days. My faith is being greatly tried. I engaged two bushels of corn yesterday to be delivered in two or three days. Am expecting to pay cash for it. Our Sunday school went off as usual. I had been waiting on God all morning for a message for the meeting. Could get nothing. Meeting commenced. I felt all broken up and completely dependent on God. Read a few verses where Jesus was comforting His disciples. Took it to ourselves. Were somewhat comforted and knelt in prayer. God blesses our souls. God gave a message from the life of Joseph. Application was made to ourselves. The Holy Ghost and fire fell upon us and we had an old fashioned Pentecost. Though our food is nearly gone, yet we have the blessed evidence that God is with and has not forsaken us. Praise God. The responsibilities are great, the pressure is heavy, but my soul is happy as I lean hard upon the everlasting arm. I believe He will see us through same way as he did Joseph, as He did Muller, as He has in time past. My heart still crys out for the farm, where we can make a garden of Eden where God can come and talk with us in the cool of the day and we will not be ashamed and hide as Adam did, but only be too glad to meet Him. O God, give me the five thousand dollars for Jesus' sake.

April 15

A friend gave us some dried fruit and some onions, which served nicely with our cornbread for two meals. Some friends in Ohio, moved by the Holy Ghost, sent us a P. O. M. O. for $8.95—$3.25 to be used for food, etc., and $5.70 for the building. Praise God, thus He supplies our needs when we are faithful and obedient.

April 16

God sent us $1.10 which is very acceptable at this time. God is again smiling upon us and showing us some favor after the refining and purging process. My heart goes out in prayer for God to keep me humble so that I may be in a condition to receive from His all bountiful hand from day to day.

April 23

This is a day of deep trial. Spent my last money for half a bushel of meal. Living now for several days on cornbread and potatoes. Corn for horses nearly gone and corn costs 75¢ per bushel. We are in God's hands, subject to His providences. I feel like saying this evening, "Though he slay me, yet will I trust Him." O God, keep me humble and true in these trying days.

April 24

This morning the pressure is very heavy, still no money even to mail a letter. I would like to mail our paper but will await God's time. The text that is on my heart this morning is this, "The trial of your faith, being much more precious than gold though it be tried in the fire, might be found unto the praise and honor and glory at the appearing of Jesus Christ." This is a time of deep heart searching among the workers.

April 24, 3:00 P. M.

The cooks say all the food was consumed at dinner and nothing left to prepare for supper. I am waiting to see what the Lord will do. I am very busy with my office work. The men are at work on the farm. The women are about their house work. Children at school. In our prayer service at nine this morning the Holy Ghost gave me new light on Romans 7:25. With my mind I serve the law of God or the law of heaven, but as I am yet in this world, my flesh, that is my body is subject to the law of sin, that is, instead of living in perfect purity and eating the fruits of the garden, I am compelled to act in a large measure as people under sin, and while I don't eat the flesh of animals, thereby causing them pain, yet my shoes are made of leather and I don't yet see anything to take its place. So in this and other similar things I serve the law of sin which causes destruction, but with my mind I serve the law of God and hope for the time spoke of in Isaiah 11 where nothing shall be destroyed in all God's holy mountain. My heart crys out today, Lord Jesus, come quickly, even so come Lord Jesus.

April 24

Nearly supper time, nothing yet received, no mail. For more than a year, have gotten letters nearly every day and many of them containing money, but now for several days mail has stopped, and everything seems to be closing up. God has a motive in it. The trial of our faith is precious. I am looking for a flood of letters and large amounts of money if we can fast it through, without a murmur. Blessed be God who only doeth wondrous things.

April 24

After Supper. Supper time came, the bell rang as usual, we took our places at the table, I saw a very little bread, a little gravy and a little salad. I did not turn up my plate, thinking I would go hungry rather than have any one else fail to have plenty. As time went on more was placed on the table until all had enough. I don't know where it came from but I praise God for it. Don't know what breakfast will be, but tomorrow has not yet come and sufficient unto the day is the evil thereof. My soul is happy tonight. The Lord is with me. Praise His blessed name.

April 25

The Lord gave us three meals today, although they were scant, yet we have got through without suffering or murmuring. Got a card from Wisconsin stating that the writer wished to send us $5.00 and wished to know how to remit safely. Praise God for this token of the watchful care of our Father.

April 26. God has taken us through and given us three meals, but no money except some postage stamps. I had written a number of letters and God supplied the stamps.

April 27

God sent me more postage stamps and supplied us with cornbread and potatoes for the day and over Sunday.

April 28

Our Sunday school and meeting well attended. God met with us and blessed our souls. A brother gave me 10¢ for the paper.

April 29

Sold a Bible for 150, but early in the morning I was led mysteriously and unthoughtedly to take some papers out of my vest pocket and among them I found a dollar bill which supplied the amount needed to mail the paper to the balance of the subscribers. Praise God who only doeth wonderful things. The trial of our faith is more precious than gold, so tis trial of faith for food is better for us than money to buy it. It would seem that our children should have a more suitable diet than cornbread and potatoes, but God knows best and I am submissive to His blessed will. Late in evening God gave me $1.10 through the mail.

April 30

An old lady 84 years of age has just come in says she wants to stay with us a few days, she wants to be where she can hear the name of Jesus honored and enjoy the songs of Zion. Brother Will Ballew started this morning for Atlanta, Georgia after we prayed and bid him God speed, we sang "God be with you till we meet again," 4:00 P. M. Just received a card from Brother Ballew, he is traveling in victory. The report just comes from the cook not enough meal for bread for breakfast. No money came. I don't know what to do. I am leaning hard upon God. Surely He will not fail us. The pressure is very great indeed. Corn out for horses also. Paul says, "Owe no man anything," I can't go in debt, God, what will I do? Please hear the groans of my heart and supply in your own way. The word says "All things are yours, and ye are Christ's, and Christ is God's." I will reach out and take it by faith, this is all I can do. God have mercy.

May 1

God awoke me early this morning and led me out and as I returned from my walk, I met a man who owed me and he gave me $1.16. Then I came on and a good brother gave me some corn for the horses and would receive no money for it. Then at breakfast the announcement was made, no food for dinner. While eating a messenger came calling me to the bedside of a sister who was sick, not able to rise. Brother W. and I with our wives went in answer to the call, leaving nothing for the cook, to get for dinner. We anointed and prayed for the sister who was instantly healed and arose and dressed. When we were about to go, she said there was a sack of meal out there in the hall, half of it is for you. I hesitated about taking it until I was convinced that it was God's plan to supply our needs at this time. A sister present also said she had some potatoes for us. So our needs are supplied for the day again. Cornbread and potatoes, thank God. The men and horses are very busy in the field and the children in school. I feel they must be fed and God has shown that He has not forsaken us. Praise His dear name. A. M. Evening—Three meals today. Praise God. O this wonderful strain in the trial of my faith. God have mercy and come to my rescue. I know He will not forsake me so I am restful.

May 7

For the past seven days God has given us food for just about one meal at a time. Praise His dear name. I am now becoming so accustomed to this kind of a life that I am getting so I don't mind it when we don't have anything to cook. Cornbread is our principle diet but no complaint. Our garden stuff is growing nicely so we have some salad and soon other vegetables will do to use. Praise God for the trial of my faith which is more precious than gold. Our work is prospering even if we are very close in food and other needs. Children are doing well in school. God must supply nourishment for their brains in a miraculous way for we have had no diet for the brain nor nerves for some time. We are not to live by bread alone, but by every word that proceeds from the mouth of God, so He gives us strength for our labor and good health.

May 9

This is our day of prayer. I confess as the war looms up before me, lack of means to meet demands and push the work I am almost in despair, but in Jesus' name I refuse to despair. Just after prayer service which lasted two hours, I feel much encouraged and built up in faith. I was led in my prayer to thank and praise God for the sack of flour He was going to give us today. I have no money to buy it so I await results. Time now near noon. Time night: Father sent us the sack of flour. Praise His dear name. I received through the mail stamps and money $11.44. Praise God for the tests and for faithfulness and for deliverance. Hallelujah.

May 11

This morning Brother W. and wife started out again on a mission trip with Matt. 29:20 as their commission sent burning into their hearts by the Son of God. The message was given by the Holy Ghost in our prayer service before they started. Praise God for the privilege of having workers in the field. Praise God also for a triumphant victory in the way of means again. We have been without a penny a good deal of the time for near three weeks. I now have in my possession all told $24.71. I am sure it came in answer to prayer. It came from four or five different states. The farm work is moving on nicely under Brother A. W. and helpers. I am so glad we have had the test that was more precious than gold. Bless God. Amen. The paper is again slow in coming from the press, but I'm asking and trusting God to stir up the printer.

Sunday, May 12

Mrs. Ballew started to meet her husband in Atlanta where he is working for God. The Sunday school lesson was the great commission, last verses of Matthew. The subject was enlarged in the meeting which was today held in the afternoon. The Holy Ghost put a great yearning in our hearts to go and teach and preach the gospel that souls might be saved.

Monday, May 13

I went to Murphy and got the deed to Zion Hill recorded, deeded to God Almighty.

Tuesday, May 14

God is very real to me today. He gave me a special lesson which will be given in Samson's Foxes, Vol. 1, No. 6, June, 1901. Praise God who only doeth wondrous things. He gave us today all told from different points in the U. S. $24.62. How it pays to be true to God during the trials and tests. He said to me today, I am with thee, etc. Isaiah 41:10.

May 18

Today God gave us a barrel and a half of flour and some other articles of food. Blessed be His precious name.

May 20, 12M

Just closed our regular midweek prayer service. God met us and blessed our souls and gave us real prevailing prayers in the Holy Ghost for money for the buildings that are so much needed. God has been supplying us with food in His own miraculous way and I feel that we have been just as thankful for it as when we had to get enough for a meal at a time. Praise God for victory and a spirit of perseverance. We are not free from trials and tests of faith hardly a moment but God giveth grace to overcome.

May 31

Opened a box containing nice clothes for the children. Came from Ohio. My heart was greatly touched as I felt this was an evidence again that God wished us to continue this work. A lot of nice books received also.

June 12

Returned this morning from Dillsboro, N. C. where I have been in making arrangements for the advancement for our work in Haywood and Macon Counties. Found several bills to pay. Brother McGraw and wife arrived here this evening from Texas and cast their lot with us to help in the work. A box of goods from dear Mother Cress of Talmage, Kansas was unpacked amid tears of joy and praises to God. The value of the goods near $100.

June 13

I was able to pay every bill, thank God.

Sunday, June 16

In our service the Spirit led us to teach divine health as seen in the atonement. Afternoon had special prayer service for $7 specially needed to pay some freight on some goods, dishes, glassware, etc. at R. R. station.

June 17

The berry crops are now coming in and we are having plenty of good wholesome diet. Thanks be unto our God who supplies all our needs by Christ Jesus. I have a special burden today for a convenient house or store room where we can place our books on sale, also for means to commence our school house and the main Mount Zion building. O God, send the money.

June 20

Our special prayer day again. God gave us a good service and prayers in the Holy Ghost. Two barrels of dishes were unpacked after supper amid great rejoicing, sent us from Chicago, Ill. God by His providences is still pushing us on in this work. A box of valuable books was also received from friends in Pennsylvania.

June 21

Today I have the privilege of giving eight dollars and ninety cents to a person who has been an outspoken enemy to our line of teaching. Sickness has reduced him to poverty and he now needs help. The dear Lord has given me more money than this through today. Praise His dear name. How He blesses my soul today.

June 21

A barrel and box of dishes were unpacked amid praises to God and rejoicing in the Holy Ghost.

June 27

Nothing of special note has taken place for a few days except another box received containing bake pans, dippers, spoons, dishpan, teakettle, etc., and a barrel of flour. God is still supplying our needs. God met with us again today in our special prayer service.

June 28

School closed today in the little box house. We are hoping and trusting for a new house for school next term.

June 29

Sent about 600 Foxes out today. God gave us a special meeting tonight. The baby Jessie was very ill, seemed to be going down fast. We rallied our forces and met the enemy, conquered by the blood.

Sunday, June 30

The baby played some today. God gave us a very precious meeting.

July 1

No money received for few days, only about 10¢ and some bills to meet probably tomorrow. God abideth faithful.

July 9

Praise God we have met every bill as it was presented except 38¢ for S. S. supplies, but that will be cancelled soon by God's help. We had a very special meeting last night, which lasted until 2:00 A. M. today. Baby Jessie was again seized by the enemy and almost passed away but we rallied our forces, confessed our sins, begged forgiveness of each other and God marched out and again met the enemy and routed the death angel and she is yet alive and seems much relieved. Praise God.

July 10

Baby Jessie was again taken worse and her parents and myself and wife covenanted to fast and pray as David did until she was either well or gone to heaven. About sundown she left us and as we did all we could and turned every stone we knew we are in victory crying, "Thy will be done."

July 11

We spend the day in preparation for the funeral which is to be about 12 miles away.

July 12

Nearly all in our home attended funeral services. The service was not spent mourning and eulogizing the dead but the preaching was directed to the living and plain Bible truth. God gives the dear young parents grace and victory.

July 13

Sister Woodward arrived this evening, don't know yet what God means by sending her here but she feels she has a mission to fill here for the Lord. She came from Brother Knapps at Cincinnati, went there from Pittsburg, Pa.

July 20

Brother Withrow and Brother McGraw left today for the Percimon Creek country on an evangelistic trip. Sister Woodward is teaching music. I still have severe trials for means to run the business. We are compelled to live very economical. Some money still coming in for building purposes. I am greatly exercised for means to build the school house at once.

July 25

This is again our special day of prayer. I can't describe my feelings. I feel that I am almost alone. I feel that my experience is recorded in Psalms 22. Two persons here who say God sent them here and I do not doubt it, disagree much with our teaching. I feel that all "shiloh" is at my back pushing me on and I dare not go back on the teaching I received at Shiloh. Brother Overstreet, husband of our school teacher, arrived here yesterday. We gave him a nice informal reception at their new home where they commence house keeping. The prayer of my heart is, O God, keep me true in these very trying times. The devil is trying very hard it seems to get all three of our children in different ways. I am very much concerned about it.

July 29

Brother Arthur Withrow and wife moved to themselves and now have the responsibilities of home life. The saints gathered there tonight and had special prayer service with them. Brother J. H. Withrow and family are too moving to themselves. Sister Woodward has gone to stay with Brother and Sister McGraw, and I an [sic] my wife and children are again to be alone (in Father's cottage) after two years and one half of constant living with from two to thirty in our home or where God's providence placed us. How we appreciate it for we feel that it is God's will. All our people are victorious and we are living harmoniously in "common". We now have five families living in common and others expected soon. O God, give us wisdom to continue to direct this movement. Mrs. Burroughs left today to join her husband in Indiana.

August 1

The message given me this morning by the Holy Ghost was "Go deeper." In our regular Thursday prayer service today God applied it wonderfully to every heart and the result was grand. We received the witness that we had prevailed with God for the building money so we stepped over today and thanked God for it and for wisdom to use it instead of asking for more. The Holy Ghost fell upon us as at the beginning of this work and gave us an old time baptism of blessing. Glory to God. I confess I feel the freest that I have since last winter about the time we fell into that severe trial with Mr. B. and his wife. God shows His smiles of approval in the arrangement of the families in homes to themselves. O, glory to God. I must not fail to hearken diligently to that still small voice.

August 2

Today is largely spent in wrapping "Samson's Foxes" for the mail. We are doing our cooking on a little oil stove but we are happy with even this much.

August 10

I am specially exercised with a deep desire for wisdom to train up our children on Bible lines. I am advancing in wisdom and ability to enforce Bible light as I get it. I see laws given that I never saw before. God help me to see more as fast as needed. We have begun to practice the two meals a day system of eating this week. God is blessing this to the good of our souls. There are some bills falling due today. I suppose $10 or $12, and this morning I have only about $1.50. Father will have to come to our rescue or I will fail to keep the demand "Owe no man anything." God help us now, right now for Jesus' sake. Evening: God sent me $3.80 and I find our bills I was expecting to come in today did not all come, so I have just about enough to square off. Praise the Lord forever and ever.

August 13

Quite a persecution raised against us in the secular press as well as among the people. Brother McGraw was accosted and shaken up slightly by toughs. Threats are being made but we are laying low at Jesus' feet, awaiting developments, but at the same time moving steadily on with our work.

August 15

The Spirit was blessedly in our prayer service this morning. Soon after the close I was called to the front door and I there met a Baptist minister by the name of Davis and one of his brethren. I politely shook hands with them and invited them into the house, but they declined. They seemed to be somewhat agitated and quickly produced Samson's Foxes. The minister asked me if I claimed it as my publication. I said "yes sir." He desired to show me some of the false statements in it concerning the condition of 25 of the southern people of the poor whites. I listened with but very few words for several minutes while he called me a fraud, deceiver, hypocrit, [sic] liar, etc. He finally run down with his tirade of abuse, after he repeatedly said our work would have to stop, I asked him if he was through. He said he was. I said I would not offer any defense but gently and tenderly invited them in and we would pray about the matter. They refused and railed upon me for the insult as they seemed to take it as such. Then I asked that we might shake hands, they hesitated again, but I insisted saying that I had nothing but love for them for all they had said. I told them I would pray for them and asked them to kindly pray for me. They finally took my extended hand and departed. One of my coworkers kindly advises me to leave the town but I am refusing to go. I am here to give my life for this people if needs be until I am delivered by God Himself. We are going on with our work, although, they said they were determined to stop us and to stop our supplies from the north. Poor things, they do not realize that they are fighting against God and that their task is such a hard one. God pity and forgive them, they know not what they do.

August 18, 1901

Yesterday morning a man called at my home, called me out and asked me to walk out with him as he desired to talk with me. I went very carefully in God. He turned and began a great tirade of abuse, cursed me to everything he could think of. Done all he could to get me to take my part and resent him so he would have a chance to commence a fight. I took it all quietly without a ripple in my soul. He went off, threatening and cursing. I went to my office; three of my men came in. I talked some to them, we knelt and prayed. While on our knees the Spirit whispered, "depart." We committed all to God, prayed for our enemies. When we arose, I told them I thought I had best absent myself from home for a while. I began to get ready and before I was wholly ready a messenger came in saying they were forming a company of men to wait on me. I hastily kissed my wife and children good by and slipped out to the woods and hills. Praise God, like Jesus, Paul and others I was permitted to escape their cruel hands, and when it was dark I slipped around the town and walked ten miles through mud and rain to the house of a friend. He a poor man, the kind of people we are trying to help, and the kind the upper classes? are determined we shall not help. I arrived here about midnight, the night was very dark, I fell in ditches, waded water,

and these words kept ringing in my ears, "Vagabond in the earth."
"Hunted down like a sheep—killing dog. The friends gave me a
kindly welcome and a hard bed, but the best they had, and it was
greatly appreciated. They are so poor they can hardly live, but are
very kind to me. They have not knives, forks and spoons sufficient
to set the table, so the children ate with their fingers and the
good house wife ate nothing. My heart sinks within me as I see
the poverty and ignorance that I am yet unable to avert but glory
pours into my soul as I resolve to make a mightier effort than ever
to lift these poor whites from their ignorance and poverty. I am
waiting here today for further orders by the Spirit.

Monday morning, August 19, 1901

I am out early for Murphy to take the train east. Three times I
unthoughtedly opened my Testament and every time to Acts 21
where Paul was pressed of the Spirit to go on toward Jerusalem. I
don't know all it means.

August 22, 1901

I arrived at Whittier, N. C., 80 miles from Culberson, yesterday
noon, made my way down the river and over the mountain to the
lowly house of a friend, Brother Yarboro. They received me very
kindly. I received a letter from my wife yesterday stating that
after I had gone, a gang of toughs came to our place, rocked the
houses, broke out windows, cursed and threatened, I thought if
they would do all that in my absence, what would they have done
if I had been there. I thanked God that it was no worse. I spent
yesterday P. M. in writing letters, sending instructions home, etc.
I am treated very kindly here, but expect to go on to Waynesville
30 miles east soon. I am not discouraged about our work at
Culberson. I am only inspired to more energy. Don't know yet
what I will do. Have no light to return. It rather looks like I would
go on east.

August 25

Waynesville, N. C. I with dear Brother Yarboro arrived here
yesterday after a few days of special providences. We met one, Mary
Ault, a holiness Bible woman, who was very much encouraged by
our presence. With her in meeting one night. She with a brother
of the neighborhood were much dejected, however, when we made
known to them that the Spirit bade us go on. At Waynesville we
are received very kindly. I have met a first cousin to my father,
Jerome Tomlinson. He and his wife were much pleased to meet me.
I am sure God has led me this far. I am today fasting and specially
waiting on God for special guidance for tomorrow.

Monday morning, August 26, 1901

Addressed a small company last night. Received some financial encouragement. I am waiting further directions of the Spirit.

Tuesday, August 27, 1901

I am today shut in an upper room alone with God awaiting special directions. My cousins are very kind to me. How my heart yearns for the poor children back in the mountains. The text still rings in my ears, "Open thy mouth, judge righteously and plead the cause of the poor." Brother Yarboro has left me and gone on to his colportage work. I don't know how long the Lord will shut me in here. Later, I confess it seems very strange that I have no liberty to leave this place. I received letter from wife saying they are putting in foundation for school house. So the work is going on.

Wednesday 28

I arose with a strong desire to push our work. Later, I am greatly exercised in prayer, it just seems to me that all will be a failure if God does not come to our rescue soon. I am still held here at Waynesville. Evening. Received a special invitation about noon to call on a lady of wealth at 4:00 P. M. I called, had a very pleasant time for a few minutes, she subscribed for the paper and expressed a desire to contribute something for the work a little latter [*sic*]. I am waiting. God is moving.

Tuesday 29

I am greatly exercised in prayer for God to let go to Shiloh, Maine for a few days at least.

Friday, 30

Came to Asheville, N. C. Found two men greatly interested in our work. They promised to push the work in this city.

Saturday, 31

Came to Morganton. Brother Baker met me at train and kindly drove me out here to his home in the country. How I enjoy it after being in city for several days.

Sunday, September 1

Went to a Sunday school. Had the privilege of preaching to a small audience and at night again to a larger company.

Monday, September 2

Went to Morganton, received quite a number of subscriptions to Samson's Foxes, and succeeded in finding a man who is greatly interested to push the work in his town. I am now back at my friends house in country.

Tuesday, September 3, 1901

I came to Salisbury and called upon a cousin who refused to give me a place for the night even before I asked for it. A city of about ten thousand and I could find no one worthy so I came on to Thomasville. Got there after dark and was refused a place to stay by three men. I offered a hotel keeper money but he refused. I staid on his porch until midnight and he finally told me I could lay on an old hard sopha with an old dirty straw pillow. I thanked God for that much.

September 4, Wednesday

I started off this morning on foot for a town about 6 miles across the country, but as I was on the way the Spirit turned my course and led me on and on to the home of my brother-in-law's brother. Arrived here about noon, having been without food for about thirty hours. This friend is worthy and received me gladly. Icy feet are sore, limbs and body very weak, shoes considerably worn and only 20¢ left.

Thursday, September 5

I arose after a good night's rest very much refreshed. After breakfast I went to the woods and prayed, after I returned I got in a very trembling condition, with a fear of failing or disobeying God. I finally felt a kind of drop or letting loose in my soul. I hardly know what it meant, but this evening I repaired to the woods again to pray and I was made to know I was becoming too much burdened and occupied with our work at Culberson, and I felt a kind of burden that was not pleasant as I would plan to raise means for it, so I consecrated it to God and told Him it was His work and I could not carry it any longer. I was not able and I was becoming hardened by it, so I turned it over to fail or go on as it pleased God. My honor, reputation, the cause and all went into a pile together. I don't know what will be, I am here in Randolph County, North Carolina with only 20¢, but nobody but God knows it and I asked God to specially help us to keep my needs a secret from all people. O God, keep me true to this consecration and let me be free. I told the Lord I could stay here for Him as well as any where but it seemed the next station I should reach was Boston, Mass. I don't know why but I felt very much like I should go to Shiloh, Maine, and yet I feel now to be content to remain here until God's providences arrange for my departure. I expect to go to a prayer meeting tonight. I will try and be perfectly submissive to God in all things.

Sunday, September 8

Jacob Robbins took me to a meeting. They gave me the stand. I preached, after which two came to the altar for salvation, claimed what they sought. Meeting broke, one half dollar was slipped into my hand. Preached again tonight to about 200 people.

Wednesday, September 11

This week I have been helping Brother Robbins cut fodder. I went to Quaker meeting where there were only four grown folks and two children assembled. This afternoon I repaired to woods and poured out my heart to God. I am so wonderfully burdened with a desire to go on to Shiloh, at once. I am now at a place for decision, either to return to our mission or go on to Boston. I have no money for either. I have not heard from home for a week. I confess I am in great distress, but I tell the Lord to turn on the heat, if this is only for refinement.

Friday, September 13

I heard from home yesterday. They are well but hard put to it for bread. I have reached a decision to go on to Shiloh, Maine as soon as I can from here. I have spent nearly two whole nights in prayer and one day fasting. I feel much easier since the decision is made. I am now waiting for God to give me the money. He will surely do it.

September 14

Saturday, President McKinley died this morning from the effects of a wound received at the hand of an assasin. "Beginning at Jerusalem" keeps ringing in my ears.

September 15, Sunday

I preached at same place that I did last Sunday. After meeting God gave me money to the amount of $3.15. Praise His dear name.

Monday, September 16

Had a letter from wife. She says they still have bread and able to pay for lumber sawed, or nearly so. Praise God, the work still moves on.

Tuesday, September 17

I am in a great strait. I confess I have to almost continually keep asking God for grace to keep my head above the waves of fear, impatience and discouragement. I don't want to murmur or complain as the fire is heated more and more. The mission work is progressing very well in my absence.

Sunday, September 22, 1901

After a few days of haste and special providences of God, my birthday finds me on the Atlantic Ocean aboard the "Howard" speeding away toward Boston, bound for Shiloh, Maine. God has heard my cry and giving me the desire of my heart, and His providences are very favorable so far. Praise Him forever.

September 28, 1901 Saturday

I arrived here at Shiloh, Maine September 24. All O. K. or victorious. About 3:00 P. M. of same day I was taken with a hard chill which lasted until I was piled up in bed for some time. That night to my utter astonishment I found I was sick and helpless. I called for the "elders" they anointed me and prayed. I was then taken from Shiloh extension and brought to "Bethesda" where I have been ever since. For about 12 hours the second day I suffered untold agony, nothing could relieve me. They prayed, they whispered all in vain until God said enough. The precious blood availed when God got ready and said "enough." I am out a little today. Praise God for raising me up. I have missed four days of the convention but I have had something better for myself.

October 1, Tuesday

I was baptized by Mr. Sandford in the Andrascogin River. Into the "church of the living God," for the evangelization of the world, gathering of Israel. New order of things at the close of the Gentile age.

Saturday, October 5, 1901

I have victory, for our work in the south and I feel that I must return there soon in the power and authority of the almighty God. I am now waiting the hand of providence to supply the means.

Wednesday, October 9, 1901

Yesterday a friend and myself left Shiloh for the south. Are now at Tannton, Mass. with a friend of his. A letter from wife states that they are having some trials for bread, etc. I will soon be there with them again, D. V.

Saturday, October 12, 1901

We are today in Trenton, N. J. Expect to remain here over Sunday. The Lord has given us a nice upper room furnished where I am fasting and waiting on Him today. Hide me away in thyself, Lord.

Friday, October 18, 1901

Left Trenton today on foot for Philadelphia.

Saturday, October 19

Left Philadelphia. Stayed in Salvation Barracks last night.

Sunday, October 20

Stayed in barn last night. Traveled through Delaware on foot.

October 21

Stayed in barn last night.

Sunday, October 27, 1901

I had the privilege of a good talk on our mission work. I am here with a family in the country. Don't know yet how long God will have me here. I am very anxious to get back home, but am content to abide God's time.

Sunday, November 3, 1901

The man who started to the south with me he proved himself to be disloyal to the truth. I rebuked him sharply and the past week he left me without even saying goodby. I found this morning that my only white shirt I had with me is missing from my valice and I suppose he has taken it. The Lord have mercy upon him and yet reward him according to his works. I feel that the "pillar of cloud and fire" will begin to remove from here in about a week. I am shut in here with God getting plans for our work in the south,

November 16, 1901

I arrived home today or rather this morning 2:00 A. M., after many tests of faith for means to get through. I find a spirit of compromise in the workers here. But God helping me I will never yield to it.

December 4, 1901

We have been having some confession meetings and we are having a general sifting. One person has been asked to leave the work. Others are searching their lives. Brother Overstreet is specially exhorting every one to be true to God's apostle. We are having a financial strait but we hope to be relieved soon as all things are sifted and purified. The school which is being held in one room of Zion Cottage No. 1 with 23 scholars is prospering.

December 11, 1901

Last night while wife and I were sitting in our room after all the household had retired, a volley of bullets came crashing through the wall of the house, rattling about us like hail. No one hurt. They shot through the wall and door of Brother McGraw's house but they were unharmed. I am told that my life is in danger every day I remain here, but I must be true to God. I cannot leave here until God says go and providences favorable.

December 12, 1901

Brothers McGraw and Withrow departed today, leaving the work, discouraged. They expect their families to follow soon. With our workers deserting us we scarcely know what to do, but we are leaning hard upon God and trusting Him for wisdom, guidance and protection. Brother and Sister Overstreet are still faithful and true. We believe God will send us other workers. Many encouraging letters are being received and some bearing money.

December 14

Dark rainy day. I had a great battled [*sic*] against the rulers of the darkness of this world. I was tempted to even hate God, my nearest friends and others and disbelieve the Bible. I called my wife and daughter, Halcy, to my rescue. We wrestled with God for about two hours before the darkness gave way. O how I feared I would fail God in these hours of trial and purging. Thank God for the knowledge I had so I would not yield to temptations. A few lines from the pen of Bishop J. C. Ryle, "Godliness rewarded hereafter." gave me much help. I feel like inserting it here. "If ever there was a case of Godliness unrewarded in this life, it was that of John the Baptist. Think for a moment what a man he was during his short career, and think to what an end he came. Behold him that was the prophet of the Highest, the greater than any born of woman, imprisoned like a malefactor! Behold him cut off by violent death before the age of 34, the burning light quenched, the faithful preacher murdered for doing, his duty, and this to gratify the hatred of an adultrous woman, and at the command of a capricious tyrant!

"Truly there is an event here, if there ever was one in the world, which might make an ignorant man say, 'What profit is it to serve God?'

"But this is the sort of thing which shows us that there will one day be a judgment. The God of the Spirits of all flesh shall at last set up an assize, and reward every one according to his works. The world shall yet know that there is a God that judgeth the earth.

"Let all true Christians remember that their best things are yet to come. Let us count it no strange thing if we have sufferings in this present time. It is a season of probation. We are yet in school. We are patience, long suffering, gentleness, meekness, which we could hardly learn if we had our good things now. But there is an eternal holiday yet to begin. For this let us wait quietly. It will make amends for all. "Our light affliction, which is but for a moment, worketh for us a far more exceeding and eternal weight of glory." —Bishop J. C. Ryle. Then some Scripture texts were given and my spirit is much revived at noon. I still say with the Psalmist, "Though he slay me, yet will I trust him."

December 30, 1901

Myself, wife and children are now alone, living in Father's house. We are not lonely since the other folks all left. God is caring for us. We are contemplating buying this property. Will perhaps decide today. God forbid that we should make any mistakes. We are seeking special wisdom and guidance every day. Brother John Ballew was the only one who met with us to worship yesterday.

1902

January 22, 1902

The dear Lord enabled me to give Brother Ballew $500 cash and receive the deed to about 75 acres of land, etc. here. We are now settled and by God's grace we will continue our work.

January 26

Our worship for three successive Sundays has been specially sweet and owned and blessed of God. A Mr. Bell is here from Mississippi. We are somewhat perplexed about some bills that are due and we are not yet able to meet them. Surely God will come to our rescue soon as He has in the past. We have 620 subscribers to Samson's Foxes. While God has shown us favor by giving us a place, yet we are somewhat cramped for want of means to push the work, yet I do not say this to complain or murmur but rather to state a fact.

February 18

God has given us some means so we have reduced our debts some for which we are thankful, but we still need $56.00 at once. Robert Barker, an orphan boy of 16 years who has been with us a few days, was admitted into our home yesterday and was gloriously converted.

July 27, 1902

I have been so pressed with work that I have neglected keeping a correct diary. Many things have transpired since the last date written. Brother and Sister Overstreet left us. Brothers Mitchell and South came, also Brother Eads and family with printing press. We now have four orphans besides other children, fourteen in all. Total number in household about 20. We have just finished tending our corn crop. God is still sending means. We seem to be pressed of the Spirit to resume building on Zion Hill. What a great undertaking. More than I feel able to carry, but God is at the head. I feel somewhat heavy in spirit today. I can't write what is on my heart. The burden of the work is heavy upon me. O Lord, what shall I do? In some respects the work looks encouraging but the responsibilities are great, and cares and burdens in one sense havy, [*sic*] but trusting God all is light.

August 4, 1902

After dinner I and wife and three children Halcy, Homer and Iris, also James South, J. W. Bell, John Crisp, Jessie Johnson, and four orphan children we have went up to Zion Hill and commenced to clear away the brush, measure and stretch lines for building, dig for basement, etc. God has given us some means for the house and pressing us to go on with the work. We all knelt in prayer and uncovered our heads while we read Ps. 48:2; Obed. 17:21 and a few other Scripture verses. In the evening we received $8.25 cash in hand and a promise of $10 soon. All glory be to God. Amen.

August 11

Put stone cutters at work getting marble for wall of basement. Received money sufficient to meet expenses of the day.

August 18

Seven men now at work. Expenses for labor only, $5.60, besides other incidentals. A lady in New Castle, Pa., Mrs. Julia M. Cline, covenants to pray with me every Monday at 8:00 P. M. specially for this work and means to meet expenses. I will D. V. ascend Zion Hill tonight to open up the battle. Got very, very encouraging letter from Mother Cress with $13.85 and freight bill for boxes of books and clothing 630 pounds. Praise God.

September 11

Two bad boys persuaded our Columbus boy to run away. I could not go after him but wife, Brother South and two older boys went, but failed to find him.

September 12

I got up, started without breakfast, tracted and followed him to Ducktown, recovered him and returned. Walked over thirty miles.

September 18

Mrs. Overstreet having disappointed us about teaching, we are yet without a teacher, but leaning hard upon God and His Word. I am laboring under great discouragements, but Christ is my King and the Comforter is at home. Running sores are breaking out on my body and I feel to be in a kind of a dreamy state of mind. Brother Withrow came again nearly a week ago.

1903

Elwood, Indiana, May 10, 1903

I must confess I have been laboring under peculiar difficulties and
have not had sufficient inspiration to write in my diary for quite
a while. I with my family left North Carolina late in November,
1902 and came to this city. I obtained employment the next day
after arrival as machinest in glass factory. I have been enabled to
get down into the every day life of the laboring factory men which
has been of vast importance to me in many particulars and I trust
will result in good to some of them. I am now privileged to attend
a convention where G. D. Watson is in charge. Last night the first
service, a question arose in my mind as to whether I had yet been
overshadowed, or covered over, or had put on the outer garment
viz. divine love. Col. 3114. Today the question arises as to whether
I want to die for Jesus. I have been willing to die, but now it
comes with force, do I want to die for Him? I go down before God
for all He wants in me.

May 27, 1903

I left Elwood, Indiana for Culberson, N. C. Purchased $50.00
worth of Bibles at Cincinnati.

June 13

I was ordained a minister of the gospel of the Holiness Church at
Camp Creek, N. C.

July 8

Wife and children arrived here at Culberson, N. C.

August 14

Just arrived home from Tennessee where I have been in revival
work for three weeks, About 30 professed salvation besides quite a
number renewed and blessed. I have preached about 45 sermons

since I arrived in North Carolina this time. We have purchased a printing plant at a cost of about $125. Hope to be able to publish our little paper again soon,

December 9

I can't write all that has taken place since the last date. I have been in revival work nearly all the time. Quite a number of souls have been blest. On the 3rd instant I officiated at the wedding of X. C. Murphy and Mrs. Shearer. Last Sunday our meeting was distrubed [sic] and broken up at Camp Creek, Cherokee County, N. C. by Ross Allen, a ranter. The next day he was arrested and after trying every way we could to get him to promise to let us alone, all in vain, he was tried, convicted and sentenced to jail for an indefinite time. I offered to pay him out and let him go free if he would only promise to let us alone, which he would not do. I was so sorry to send the poor fellow to mail [sic] but it seemed it was the only way to deal with him, and we felt one man had better suffer than for a number of souls to be lost, which he was standing in the way of. Sister Mattie Briggs is here now teaching. I have been selected pastor of these congregations for 1904. One at Union Grove, Tenn., one at Luskville, Tennessee, one at Camp Creek, N. C. I came home last evening to stay for two weeks to edit and print our paper "The Way," and do some writing, etc. Also to prepare for a Christmas convention in Tennessee.

1904

Feb. 19, 1904

I am home again after an extended tour and work among the churches in Tennessee. I have preached about 35 sermons this year, besides visited a number of families, anointed 5 with oil for healing, organized one church, assisted in editing and printing the paper, The Way. The R. R. has granted me a clergy permit for all this year. I am sure I belong to Jesus. I love Him. I will expect to leave home to travel my circuit again Feb. 25. Have four points to make before I return again.

March 8, 1904

I have just returned home from my circuit. Traveled about 160 miles, held 12 meetings, preached 9 sermons, gave several Scripture lessons.

April 3, 1904

Just returned home again after about 160 miles travel. Preached 8 sermons.

April 6

I am at home, very busy writing and work in printing office.

March 12 and 13

Preached three times in Georgia.

March 19 and 20

Preached twice in Georgia. A fuller account given in the April number of The Way.

April 9

Went to Ducktown. I preached one sermon. Brother Lemons gave Bible lesson on Sunday. We walked home 16 miles. We distributed tracts. etc.

May 2, 1904

Just got home after being away nearly three weeks. Took my family with me this time. Preached 14 sermons and baptized 6 persons. Large attendance at some of the meetings. On Sunday, April 17, we had an all-day meeting, baptizing, communion and feet washing. Several hundred people there all day.

May 9, 1904

Just returned from Georgia where I have been over Sunday. Preached 4 times.

May 15

Preached in our home neighborhood.

June 6, 1904

Just returned home again after being away for 18 days. 13 sermons. Sunday, May 29, all day meeting. It was estimated seven or eight hundred in attendance. Baptized 7 persons. Anointed and prayed for one child who had fits in North Carolina.

June 13, 1904

Just returned home from Camp Creek where we had meeting on Sunday 14 miles out in Mountains. Preached two sermons. Was called to Georgia last week to anoint a man and pray for his healing.

June 21, 1904

Just returned home from Jones and Baldknob, Georgia. There over Sunday. I preached 5 sermons. Some professions and four baptized. Will be off for Tennessee in a few days, D. V.

July 5, 1904

Just returned home from Tennessee. Preached at Luskville, Union Grove and Drygo. 9 sermons. Went to Chattanooga and to Dalton, Georgia, bought a gospel tent, $97. Some other expenses, $101 in all to get back some way.

July 7

Attending a meeting at Culberson. Printed The Way.

July 19

Just returned from Camp Creek where we had meeting ten days, preached 22 sermons and baptized two. Other good work done.

August 4, 1904

Just arrived home last evening from Drygo, Tenn., where we held ten days meeting. Some converted, some received the Holy Ghost. I baptized five. Preached 19 sermons. I missed one night meeting on account of sickness. We used the tent there. Put Brothers Murphy and Ellison in deacons place for trial August 1, to ordain later.

August 17, 1904

One Funeral Sermon. Just returned home last evening from Jones, Georgia where we held a tent meeting 11 days. Preached 23 sermons. Some converted, some baptized, some got the Holy Ghost.

September 6, 1904

Just returned home from Luskville, Tennessee where we have been holding a meeting in tent for 15 days. A very hard battle but 4 professions and quite a number renewed and blessed. I preached about 25 sermons. I am home now for a few days to print and publish the paper.

September 15 and 16

Preached 2 sermons in the Baptist meeting house at this place— Culberson, N. C.

October 1

Returned home on account of being unable to continue preaching at Union Grove, Tennessee where I preached two sermons.

November 9

Preached 5 sermons in October and up till this date in November in Tennessee, North Carolina and Georgia. I am arranging to move to Cleveland, Tennessee and take charge of churches at Drygo and Union Grove and mission work in Cleveland.

November 24

Had Thanksgiving service at Union Grove, Tenn., dinner and good time. I preached one sermon.

November 26

Bought a house and lot in Cleveland, Tenn. Went from there to Drygo, Tenn., where I preached two sermons.

November 30

At home getting ready to move.

December 6

Left Culberson for Cleveland. Wife was very sick but she got through and got better toward night.

December 8

I came to Cleveland to make ready for my family. Homer came on the tenth. Wife and daughters came on the 13th.

December 18

I preached at Union Grove, came home this evening.

December 21

I am writing, fixing up office and things about the house now for several days. Our things are not all here yet. Hope they will be soon.

December 29

We all went to Drygo neighborhood on the 24th, stayed until yesterday. Preached three sermons. Had a good time.

1905

January 1, 1905

The old year is gone. I have tried to do my best and can look back over the past year with no regrets, that is, I feel I have done the best I could under the circumstances. I went out from here about 15 miles last evening and organized a Sunday school and preached one sermon today at Drygo.

January 2

I am up this morning long before day to read my Bible and to get ready for the business of the day in the printing office, etc. Children start to school.

January 8

Went to Union Grove last night, preached one sermon today and came home. I am very busy these days printing office preparing the paper for publication.

January 15

Preached at Drygo one sermon.

January 21

Preached at Andy Lawson's at night.

January 29

Preached at Union Grove one sermon. Still working in printing office every day.

March 15

I went to Atlanta, Georgia March 4 to attend a Holiness convention. Bud Robinson and Will Huff were the preachers. I arrived home about midnight Saturday, March 11, and in answer to a telegram I went on next train to North Carolina to preach a funeral sermon. Preached Sunday and Sunday night March 12. Got home last night.

March 19

Preached at Drygo last night and today.

April 3, 1905

I arrived, home today after an absence of 12 days. Preached 11 sermons, 2 in J. H. Simpson's house, 3 in Simpson's Chapel, 1 at Brother R. G. Spurling's residence, these in Tennessee also one at Ducktown, Tennessee, Jones, Georgia 3, and one at Culberson, N. C. Anointed nine with oil.

April 10, 1905

Just returned home from Union Grove where I preached two sermons and had victorious meetings.

April 15

I leave home today for about a two week's trip, more evangelism. I leave Brother Stewart to run the printing office. Brother Stewart came here on April 5, 1905.

April 28, 1905

I just returned home from Georgia after an absence of two weeks. Preached four sermons at Drygo and three in Georgia. Worked six days on church house. On this trip on account of missing connection with trains, etc., I walked about eighty miles. The dear Lord has been providing for my family while I have been away.

April 30

Preached at Wildwood one sermon.

May 13

Went to Drygo, Tennessee one week ago today. Had meetings over Sunday. I preached two sermons. We commenced our tent meeting the night of the tenth. I have preached four sermons up to date. I go D. V. this afternoon to Union Grove, and leave the meeting here with Brother Lemons.

May 15

Returned from Union Grove where I preached four sermons and delivered a Sunday school address.

May 18

Preached 8 more sermons at tent. Brother and Sister McCanlass came this evening.

June 2

I have just gotten home after preaching 9 sermons at Simpsons Chapel, Spurling, Ducktown, Isabella, Jones Georgia and went to Culberson, N. C., then back to North Carolina again in search of Luther Bryant. The meeting here in tent has been progressing nicely under the management of Brother McCanless. 60 professions already. Praise the Lord.

June 6, 1905

Came home last evening from Drygo where I preached five sermons. The meeting here is still in progress. Over 80 professions and the tide is still rising.

June 9

I preached last night and the night before. Brother and Sister McCanless not able to preach . . . I go to Wildwood to preach tonight.

June 13

I filled my regular appointment at Union Grove the 11th instant where I preached two sermons. We have stopped our meeting at tent until tomorrow night. 9:30 p. m. Just got in from street meeting. Brother Lemons and myself held on public square in Cleveland. God helped us preach.

June 19

I filled my regular appointment at Simpsons where I preached two sermons. Got home last evening in time to attend the tent meeting

June 27, 1905

We closed the tent meeting night before last. I preached four sermons last week. We closed having a general good time.

June 28

Homer and Iris went to Drygo yesterday. Wife goes today, D. V. Brother and Sister McCanless went away this morning. Brother Lemons went home Monday. Brother Stewart and myself will remain here a few days, then go to Drygo, D. V.

July 4

Came home yesterday from Drygo. We had fine meetings Brother Lemons and Brother Spurling preached. I directed the services. I preached one sermon. Had the bread and wine and feet washing on Saturday afternoon. Sunday afternoon was the Children's Day exercises. Everything was a success from first to last. I am sick, not able for work, and oh, the work there is to do. But I must be patient.

September 5, 1905

Well, I am at home again after an absence of almost two months, except a few hours one time. July 8, went to Union Grove where we held meetings for three weeks. Quite a number of renewals, conversions and several professed sanctification. I baptized 19, 23 received into the Church. The most wonderful meeting I was ever in. People fell in the floor and some writhed like serpents, some cried out until they were released from the devil, some fell in the road, one seemed to be off in a trance for four or five hours. The Church seemed to be greatly edified and blessed. I think it was July 27 we went to Simpsons Chapel and were there eight days. Some good work done, some renewals, but we were compelled to go on to Jones, Georgia August 5, where we held for about two weeks. Some professions, both of religion and sanctification. A very good work was done. I baptized two and two were received into the Church. We then came to Drygo where we held for two weeks and two days. Some renewed, some professions of religion and sanctification. I baptized ten, nine received into the Church. Now I am home to work here in Cleveland for two weeks or more. I suppose I preached near 100 sermons in the 60 days.

October 7, 1905

Quite a lot of things have taken place since I last wrote. I preached one sermon in the Cumberland Presbyterian house, then Brother Charles Stalker came and preached four sermons there, then they very kindly invited us to discontinue there, so Brother Charlie went to Ohio, and on Saturday, September 16, we pitched our tent and commenced meeting on Saturday night without any seats. We have had meeting every night since and some day meetings. Brother Lemons, Sister McCanless and myself have been preachers. Saturday, the 23rd, I went to Wildwood and had three services there, then worked here ever since. We have had several professions and renewals. The Lord is working with us. We have also issued the last of The Way, September being the last. We have disposed of the publication, having the Church Herald sent in its stead. I also went to Drygo on the first of October, preached once. I go to Union Grove tomorrow. Brother John Lawson brought a cow and gave it to us this morning. God is so wonderfully helping us and providing in His way. How softly and carefully I am walking before Him. I feel He is doing much more for me than I deserve. I am having some expenses that I am falling a little behind with and I can hardly ask for the means to help me in that as I see Him doing, as I said, more for me than I deserve.

Sunday, October 8, 1905

I went to Union Grove and preached one sermon. A dozen or more came to the altar. Quite a giving way to God. I came back home and preached in tent at night to a very large congregation, I suppose more than 500 people. I was so affected for souls that I stopped a time or two and wept in the stand. At the close, quite a number came to the altar, and there was such a crowd and so many came that some who did come could find no place, so got lost to view in the crowd and I guess fell back. Monday night I preached again at tent, one came to altar and got blessed. Tuesday night was rainy and only a few came out, but I delivered the message He gave me. The Lord is still providing. A sack of bran came for the cow. We don't know who sent it. A sack of flour came yesterday, we found it sitting on porch is all we know about it. A nice glass pitcher was given last night by D. N. Coffman. Money is given very often.

October 16, 1905

We closed the tent meeting last night with good interest, although the weather was damp and cool. One profession and others at altar. The Lord sent us a load of hay for the cow. Had a healing service here for Brother Murphy.

October 25, 1905

The Lord has been providing for us in His own way. I have been preaching at Wildwood. 5 sermons. Continue there this week as far as I know. I was called to visit Brother Murphy yesterday. He has been very low since we anointed Him, but has refused all remedies and his faith is yet strong in God. He is one among thousands who stands for the Bible truth and would rather die than to disobey the Bible and thus grieve the Holy Spirit. Oh, for our people to have faith in God.

November 10, 1905

Had several meetings at Wildwood. Preached at Drygo Saturday night, November 4, and Sunday night, November 5. Also at Mount Harmony on Sunday, November 5. I go to Union Grove today for a few days meetings. Brothers Mitchell and Way came to Cleveland.

November 3 1905

I fasted 72 hours and prayed and read, beginning October 30 for the work in general.

November 22, 1905

Preached several sermons at Union Grove with good results. Some professions. Had to leave meeting one night on account of taking sick. Next morning Brother Lemons anointed me and prayed and in a little while I got up, went to meeting and preached an hour. Praise the Lord for healing. My year being out I was voted in for another year unanimously as pastor at Union Grove. Anointed and prayed for two who were sick. I am home now only for a few days.

November 24

I preached at Wildwood last night to a very appreciative audience of about fifty in a cottage. Several manifest a desire for prayer.

December 15, 1905

I and my family left home November 25, went to Simpsons in McMinn County. I officiated at marriage of Henry McNabb and Minnie Simpson, November 26. We went on to Georgia and North Carolina on the 27th. We had a great time on Thanksgiving Day at Culberson, N. C. We with Sister McCanless had several meetings in Baptist church house. We left Culberson December 5, went to Camp Creek, N. C., got home December 9. I was home only five hours and off for Union Grove where I preached two sermons visited and prayed with eight or ten families. Came home again December 12.

December 17

Was at Wildwood last night and today. Preached two sermons. After dinner several gathered in where I had taken dinner and a meeting followed where one was converted and a backslider reclaimed. It was told me that the woman that was converted came out from the mountains and heard her first gospel sermon that day. Glory to God. This morning I felt a special burden for souls in Central America and I am not sure yet but Father may have called me to that field as I was at prayer out in the woods. As the call seemed to come, I said, yes Father, and entered into groanings that could not be uttered which lasted for several minutes. The country and people are unknown to me, but I'll go if God sends me.

December 19

I have worked at home for two days, but I expect to be off tomorrow for North Carolina and on to Georgia to preach Jesus.

1906

January 6, 1906

I am again at home after the trip to North Carolina, Georgia
and the mountains of Tennessee. I preached 14 sermons in all.
Three this year. Traveled 70 miles this year. Visited some of the
very poorest of homes in the mountains. Saw the effects of the
work of the Spirit in many ways. Shouting, leaping, clapping the
hands, jerking and hand shaking. Brother Bryant was with me in
Georgia and Brother Lemons met me at Coco Creek, Tennessee
and accompanied me until we separated at Athens. We were called
to the bedside of a young man to pray for him and we went after
a meeting at night about three miles over the mountains. Brother
Lemons was so faint from exposure, he had to lay down and rest
two or three times on the way.

January 10, 1906

Have returned from Drygo, where I preached two sermons and
one at Mount Harmony on Sunday night, Traveled about 33 miles.
Had prayer meeting at our house last night. Brothers Mitchell and
Murphy here.

January 15, 1906

Returned home today worn out and sick. I preached three
sermons and delivered a Sunday school address at Union Grove,
Saturday night, Sunday and Sunday night. Preached one sermon
at Harmony Grove Sunday afternoon. I traveled about 25 miles.

January 16

Brother Lemons anointed me last night and I am better today.

January 22

Just returned from Wildwood where I preached three sermons,
and traveled 14 miles.

January 30

I arrived home about midnight last night from Camp Creek, N. C. We held a Church assembly there. I acted as ruling Elder and made the minutes of the proceedings. Preached two sermons, anointed five persons and traveled about 163 miles. The meeting on the whole was noticeable for the love to one another and the unity. Sunday we observed the sacrament and washing of feet, and this meeting was freighted with the power and presence of the Holy Ghost. Every one who engaged and most of those who were spectators were bathed in tears showing the sacredness of the occasion.

February 7

Returned home last evening from Drygo. Preached two sermons there and one at Mount Harmony. Traveled about 40 miles. I had a very difficult time preaching on Sunday morning. I felt like my efforts were a failure, but I did the best I could. I visited the sick and prayed with them and quite a number of other families.

February 8, 1906

Held a meeting at Mr. Smith's a mile out of town last night. Preached one sermon,

February 12

Just arrived home from Union Grove. Preached four sermons there and one at Harmony. Traveled about 32 miles. The Lord gave me good liberty and some who had never heard me before seemed very much affected at Harmony. I feel very much worn and fatigued after so much labor in one day and the responsibility.

February 15

Held a meeting at Mr. Smith's last night. Preached one sermon. I have now secured a Church house here in Cleveland on Middle Street where I expect to open up the first of next month. The prayer of my heart is that God will help to accomplish great good here.

February 17 and 18

At Wildwood. Preached 3 sermons. Traveled about eight miles. While there closing up the last service Brother Bryant from North Carolina came in to my surprise. After meeting I learned he came after me to go to North Carolina to anoint and pray for Brother Murphy who was very sick.

February 21

I just came home from the above trip. Anointed Brother Murphy and left him last night at midnight much better. I went to bed early expecting to get up at midnight and start for home, but it got to raining so bad and being seven miles from R. R. it became a question as to whether we (Brother Lemons and myself) should venture out or not as we had no way to go but on foot. But I could find no rest in my spirit, and the more I prayed the more unrest I felt until I decided to come. Father held the rain up but our pine torch went out while in the woods and it was very dark. We hurried on in the dark the best we could, falling into gullies, one about waist deep. Arrived at station all right but the agent could not sell us tickets, so we had to board the train without them, expecting to have to pay full fare as it was not expected that the conductor could recognize our clergy permits. However, the kind conductory after an explanation on our part, wishing to help us out made a rate, but after consideration I asked the conductor if he would have to use deceit in making his reports to help us that way. He replied in the affirmative, upon which I said we would feel better just to pay full fare, so he would not have to lie to accomodate us. He thanked us very politely and accepted the money. I did not have sufficient money to take me home, but Brother Lemons supplied the lack. I had to walk eight miles from one R. R. to another in the rain. Part of the time it was so dark I had to crawl across the cattle guards. I am now at home but very tired. I told Father on the way that I would willingly endure all this hardness if He would only give me great power in preaching and confirm my work with signs following. While I walked and prayed on this line the dear Spirit manifested Himself so sweetly, upon which I said I believe You will do it, Lord. I traveled on this trip about 154 miles. When I left home I did not have enough money to take me through, but as I was hurrying to the train with what I had trusting God for all, a gentleman handed me some saying, "a certain gentleman sent it to you." Praise His precious name. I am billed for a meeting out in the country tonight. Lord help me.

February 22
Preached one sermon last night, one mile out of town.

February 28
I left home on the 23rd instant, went to North Carolina, thence to Georgia where I preached two sermons and held three meetings. On Sunday night two women came to the altar, one soon received the blessing of sanctification. The other one sit up and I asked her how she was getting on and she said she had no hope, but felt she was lost and that there was no salvation for her. I prayed for her several minutes and rebuked the devil in Jesus name and then asked her how she was and she said she now had some hope of becoming a Christian. I resumed my prayer again for several

minutes more. After a while I felt the joy come into my soul and soon she was up shouting the victory while I remained there on my knees praising the Lord. Brother Bryant who was with me did excellent service in prayer and faith against the power of the devil. I returned home last evening after traveling about 214 miles.

March 2, 1906

Yesterday I cleaned up and fitted up a meeting house where we opened last night for services for a year. Tuesday and Thursday nights and the fourth Sunday and at night each month. Fair attendance last night for the first and the Lord gave me good liberty while I preached one sermon. It is on Middle Street here in Cleveland. I am writing letters today. Recently some good friends in Kansas led by Mama Cress sent us a lot of nice things—me a suit of clothes, overcoat, shirt, three collars, one tie, pair of gloves, money purse, six pairs of socks and Mary some clothes. The Lord is so good to us. Sending aid to us while we work for Him. Praise Him. Dear Mama Cress sent me a fine Bible, just the kind I have been praying for for over a year. I think the Lord aims for me to preach on for a while and I am going to do my very best by His help. I'll be off again tomorrow, D. V.

March 5, 1906

Came home this morning. Preached two sermons at Drygo and one at Mount Harmony. Traveled about 38 miles.

March 6

Preached tonight at our mission here in Cleveland.

March 9

Preached last night in our mission here. The Spirit was with us and He gave me free and easy delivery. There is a steady increase in attendance. Praise the Lord. I go to Union Grove this evening, D. V.

March 11, 1906

Came home today from Union Grove. Preached four sermons there and one at Harmony. The S. S. talks I make and three sermons a day besides almost exhausts me. But I promised the Lord that if He will help me like He did yesterday, with such joy and victory, that I'll preach as long as I live. I always have good large congregations out there at Union Grove. Traveled about 32 miles.

March 13

Preached one sermon in Cleveland tonight.

March 15

Preached one sermon in Cleveland tonight. Did not have quite as much victory as usual.

March 19

I went to Wildwood Saturday evening. Had a little meeting Saturday night and Sunday. But few came out and I had no spirit to preach, although I talked some the best I could.

March 20, 1906

I got an organ put in our mission here in the city to cost $25.00 and we pay for it at 50¢ per week, or rent it as long as we want it at the same price, 50¢ per week. I preached at the mission tonight as usual. Three came to the altar. First altar call I have made. God give us souls.

March 23

Preached at the mission last night. Nine came forward to altar. Two claimed to have got the blessing they sought.

March 27

Came home yesterday from an Island in the Big Tennessee River where I held meeting over Sunday and organized a Sunday school. Delivered one Sunday address and preached four sermons. Traveled about 52 miles. Brother Mitchell left for home in Ohio this morning. Preached here in Cleveland tonight.

March 29

Preached here in Cleveland tonight.

April 2

Just came from Drygo where I preached two sermons and one at Mount Harmony. Traveled about 38 miles.

April 3

Had a good talk meeting at the mission tonight.

April 5

I preached at the mission tonight.

April 9

Just came home this morning, preached two sermons at Union Grove, 9 at the altar. One sermon at Harmony and about ten or eleven at the altar. I went to Brother J. H. Simpson's at

Charleston and stayed last night. He was in bed suffering very much. I prayed for him and he became easy and rested till about night. During the time of his severe suffering I was awakened I thought by Sister Simpson, but she said it was not her, so it must have been an angel of the Lord, for I seemed to hear the words distinctly to get up and come in and pray for Jake for he is suffering severely. I arose and dressed and went in and he was suffering severely so I prayed for him again and he eased off while I prayed, then went to sleep and slept till morning. Praise God. I traveled about 30 miles on this trip.

April 11

Preached a short sermon at our mission last night. Got our tin spouts repaired today.

April 12

I followed Brother Kincade in a short sermon at the mission tonight.

April 13

Preached one sermon at Oak Grove tonight. Two miles out of town. The Lord gave me good liberty. Four miles. I am repairing our windows and having some house repairing done. The tin and plaster patching.

April 14

Preached at Oak Grove tonight. Four miles.

April 15

Preached at Oak Grove today. Four miles. Preached here in Cleveland tonight. Nine at the altar, one profession.

April

Had our chimneys repaired at top today. Repaired porches and worked about the house.

April 20

Had meeting last Tuesday night and last night at mission. Preached last night. Four at altar. Some shouted. I start this morning for North Carolina in answer to a telephone message to pray for sick.

April 23

I returned from the North Carolina trip Saturday evening. Traveled 150 miles. Anointed one. She seemed much relieved and blessed in her soul. Preached two sermons here yesterday, and visited five families. Seven at altar and two professions last night. Meeting called for every night this week except Friday night. God help me and give me strength.

April 24

Had a glorious healing service down on South Ocoee Street last night. Preached on divine healing. Anointed two. God gave me great liberty and victory.

April 25

Had meeting last night at the mission. I gave opportunity for all to talk and some took advantage and used too much time for the best. I am asking God to help me to know just how to manage such people. I am working hard every day painting the house and moving meeting every night. I preached in North Cleveland tonight to a small audience.

April 26

Preached in our mission tonight.

April 30

Just came home from the Island where I preached one sermon. Brother Lemons was with me. We went by way of Chattanooga. We had the privilege of being in a part of two meetings in Chattanooga. Traveled about 150 miles.

May 5

Preached at the mission tonight. Brother Bryant and family came last night and I spent the day with him looking for a home for him. I had a peculiar experience about a dun for $2.45 that I thought I paid when I bought the goods. I surely did for I don't make a business of making debts, but I expect I'll have it to pay to satisfy the parties. I'd rather pay it twice than to leave any chance for reflection. I must abstain from all appearance of evil.

April 9

Been helping Brother Bryant get a place. Went to Chattanooga for him. Went to Drygo last Saturday. Preached one sermon. Just got a place for Brother Bryant last evening. Helped Brother Murphy's some moving some too. Meeting at mission last night. I am very close financially but the Lord will help me out.

May 16, 1906

I am very tired tonight been painting. Went to Union Grove and Harmony last Sunday as usual. Brothers Bryant and Lemons were with me. I preached two sermons. The Spirit made both very impressive. The one at Union Grove was on divine healing. I believe the Lord helped me to preach healing stronger than ever before. The message was delivered wholely in the Spirit. God help me to continue faithful and keep humble. I was very much impressed that I was preaching to some one at Harmony who was probably hearing the last message before going to the judgment. Preached last night at the mission here in Cleveland. Got some Rose Comb R. I. Red eggs to eat.

May 18

Preached last night at mission. I am sick today but not discouraged.

May 22, 1906

Preached last Saturday night at Oak Grove. Brother Lemons preached for me Sunday and at night. Halcy commenced work in Woolen Mills yesterday. Preached at the mission tonight. I am still painting my house as I have time. Last Saturday morning after breakfast found us without food for next meal. I told wife the Lord would help us and He did. I went to post office and there was $2.00 for us. God has given us more since then. We had been so close for a few days and I finally learned that $5.50 had been detained at Saint Louis which had been started several days before to us from Texas. Praise God. O, wonderful Jesus. Amen.

May 24, 1906

Yesterday I was called to anoint two and pray for them. One is up and all right today, have not heard from the other. Was up all last night with Brother Murphy. He is near death. I am very much grieved because he has resorted to physicians instead of God, after being healed several times before by the Lord. I preached at the mission tonight.

May, 28

Brother Murphy died Saturday night. We took him to his old home and buried him yesterday. I preached and conducted his funeral service at Henegars Chapel. Traveled about 30 miles. Mrs. McCanless conducted the meeting here at the mission in my place and she did the preaching again last night. Several at the altar, I went to minister some help and sympathy to a sick man here in town today. Took him some food tonight, but he was suffering so severely he could not eat until we prayed for him. The suffering stopped, his soul was blessed and he sat up in bed and ate, Said it was the first he had wanted for a week and that had tasted good. We left him resting sweetly. To the Lord be all the glory. Amen and amen.

June 2

Mrs. McCanless has been preaching at the mission at night this week. Have anointed two since last writing with good results. I go to Drygo D. V. this afternoon.

June 5

Went to Drygo, preached two sermons. About 32 miles. Wife and Mrs. McCanless go to Drygo today to spend the week in visiting families.

June 6

I am still painting our house. Mrs. Murphy is keeping house while Mary and Homer are away. Halcy working at Woolen Mill. Preached at mission last night. Had a glorious meeting.

June 7

Worked hard all day painting. I was so tired I could hardly go to meeting and could hardly stay when I got there, I thought about excusing myself and coming home, but the Lord sustained me and gave me much liberty and victory while preaching and in prayer.

June 12

I went to Union Grove Saturday evening, did not preach any this trip. Was physically unable. Sister McCanless preached on Sunday. Brothers Bryant and Lemons helped me out in the other meetings. I have been sick ever since I came home. Could not go to meeting tonight.

June 18

About well again. Preached at the mission last night.

June 21

Preached at mission tonight.

July 6, 1906

Have not been able for much service for some little time. Am well again now. Preached at the mission last night. The last service. The house was sold and we gave possession with good feeling. Carl Stalker came here June 30, 1906.

July 16

Preached at Oak Grove yesterday. Go to Union Grove D. V. tomorrow to commence a revival there.

July 25

We are here at Union Grove in the midst of a revival. Three definite professions. Preached about six sermons. I can't write the particulars now.

July 27

Up this morning full of love. Had a great meeting last night. I preached. Have been ten professions. One came in the altar and went and hunted up a sister to pray for her. She did not get through but it was a good step.

July 29

Yesterday God gave me a glorious message and allowed me to soar away in the Spirit while delivering it. At the close a precious brother gave a good testimony but was carried over the line and spoiled the service. I refuse fanaticism so I closed the service rather abruptly to speak to him to save him and the meeting. Thank God he heard me and now appears very teachable. God gave us a precious service last night. I was used as the messenger. Large audience. They were held attentively by the Spirit until the altar call was made when 17 or more fell at the altar and the wails and groans and crys for mercy reminded one of the groans and wails of the damned. I believe two professions. Awful conviction. Shouts and screams and three or four stretched on the floor, at times it almost seemed they were almost dying. Dear Brother Bryant was so under the burdens that he fell two or three times and suffered untold agonies. I was able to help him to our boarding place late in the night. This morning at break of day I was aroused by a brother calling my name and saying he could hold it no longer. He wanted to tell me he was sanctified. He is bearing the fruits of one having the experience. This is Sunday. Three services to hold. The cry of my heart is, "Lord help use and keep thy hand upon us and the people and have thy way."

July 30

Praise God. A large crowd gathered yesterday and the Lord gave me a burning humble message which was given out in glorious humility and victory. When we made the altar call 15 came in. Some got through. Preached again last night to a small audience caused by rain. 9 came to altar. Only three in the house who did not come. Heavy burdens on three of the brethren today. One woman left the house to go and make restitution. Others made confessions. We are quite sure others will have to make confessions and restitution before they get through. Brother Bryant is sick and his wife is sick and sent for him and I don't know what we will do.

August 1

I preached Monday night, also last night. The interest seems
to be increasing. Yesterday we set the altar, had no preaching,
but witnessing and the people came to altar at intervals during
the service. Last night after I preached I made the altar call and
climbed up on the pulpit and sat there and watched the people
as they came and filled the altar. The Lord gave victory. One lady
arose from her seat, went and confessed to some in congregation,
then fell at altar.

August 3

I preached Wednesday night. Closed the meeting here at Union
Grove last night. Go home today, D. V.

August 6

Came home from Drygo where I preached two sermons on
Sunday. Anointed one and another a few days ago.

August 20

Just closed an eleven days meeting at Oakland with about 27
professions and some sanctified. Organized church. Baptized
seven. Preached ten sermons. Just been home a few minutes. Will
go again to another place in a few minutes. Organized Sunday
school. Infidel converted and burned his books.

August 28

Have preached six sermons since last writing, and organized
another church. Went back to Oakland for Sunday and will
probably go back there tonight for a few meetings again. It is
reported that there was a large crowd awaiting there again
for us last night but the rain hindered our going. There is no
chance for rest.

September 15

Came in from Drygo day before yesterday where I held 12 days
tent meeting. Was at Oakland a few days before going. I left
Brothers Bryant and Lemons there while I went to Drygo. I have
preached 23 sermons. Tent is pitched at Oak Grove now where I
commenced last night for another series. Preached the funeral of
a little girl this morning. Brothers Bryant and Lemons are now at
Chattanooga. Brother Carl Stalker left for Ohio the 7th instant.

September 18

Having good meeting at Oak Grove. Some professions. Preached five
sermons. The Lord has been wonderfully helping me to lay out the
truth. Brother Lemons is with me now. Brother Bryant was with me

yesterday. The Lord is revealing our inheritance among them that are sanctified. The gifts of the Spirit or at least it looks that way now.

September 24

Still having good meetings. Some are getting sanctified. Some professions. Had three meetings yesterday. God wonderfully helped me to lay out the truth and glorious results followed. Have preached about 8 sermons since last writing. Am at home today. Meeting again tonight.

September 26

Meeting still going on at Oak Grove at night. Four professions last night. Preached two sermons since last writing. Preached two more sermons. Preached one more sermon.

October 2

So much rain we gave up our tent meeting last Sunday. Tent is still up, we may have some more meetings there yet. Brother Lemons and I visited a sick lady and while there a visiting sister was converted.

October 4

Did a washing today for my wife and preached a funeral sermon.

October 13

Pitched our tent here in town.

October 14

Preached in tent at night. Brother Lemons filled my place at Union Grove today. Was called out at midnight to go and pray for a sick child. After praying and anointing it I could just see it get better and is now all right.

October 16

Preached at tent at night. Special season of prayer followed from 9 to 10.

October 18

Preached at tent at night. Altar service followed.

October 19

A son came to our house about 6 p.m. Mary wants to name him Milton. Brother McCanless preached for me at tent. Brothers Lemons and Bryant both left me to engage in other work, leaving the responsibilities of tent, etc. on me. I felt a little lonely and burdened about it at first but it is alright. Brother Trim is with me and rendering good service. I am compelled to discontinue work at tent now until I go to country for meetings over Sunday.

October 21

I write at 11:30 p.m., since coming home after a wonderful day's work to me. I preached last night at Oak Grove and preached one sermon there today. Preached one sermon to a large crowd at lake where I baptized three. Then came home and preached tonight at tent to a large congregation. God gave me the hearts of the people to a great extent. Quite a number of strong men came forward, begged me to pray for them and said they were going to pray for themselves until they got saved. Three professions, besides the women, beside a good work done. Wife is getting along pretty well, baby too.

October 22

Preached at tent tonight in tears and prayed with much weeping under a great burden feeling that souls would be lost.

October 27

Preached last night at tent, five professions. Preached one other time not recorded. I now go to Oakland for tonight and Sunday. Brother Bryant gone to Georgia. Brother Lemons and Brother Trim remain here.

October 29

I went to Oakland Saturday evening and preached three sermons, baptized 5 and received 9 into the fellowship of the church. I also preached here in tent last night. One profession. The weather is cold for tent but the people come and we work right on.

November 5

Put the tent away for the winter on the 2nd instant. Too cold for meeting. Had a glorious little service in a cottage last night on Central Avenue. 9 at altar. 5 said they received what they sought for. The real power fall. I preached. Anointed one for healing a few days since.

November 7

I preached one sermon night before last at a cottage meeting here in town. Was called yesterday to pray for sick. Go D.V. this afternoon to a new place for a revival. I go with victory if I go.

November 14

Providences were against my going to the above place so I went to Union Grove again for over Sunday. I preached two sermons. They chose me again to serve them as pastor for another year. God help me to do them good.

November 28

Returned home last night from Culberson, N.C. I was at Jones, Georgia and preached two sermons. We had sacrament and feet washing there on Sunday and I felt I must go to Culberson on Monday morning. I went and found that dear old grandpa Hyatt had died the day before and they wanted me to conduct the funeral service. I preached the funeral sermon at the graveyard. The Lord gave me great liberty and victory in the discourse so that some were weeping and others shouting. The daughters of the departed rejoiced. The same night I was called up about 1:30 A.M. to go and pray for a sick sister who was taken suddenly ill. I prayed for about two hours and could not reach complete victory from some cause. I prayed again the next day but was obliged to take the train and leave her sick. I must say, too, that I was chosen pastor at Jones, Georgia, for another year.

December 7

I went to Drygo last week, had meetings and helped Brother Lemons build his house. Preached five sermons. Was called to go and pray for a sick man last night which I did, he said he felt very much helped. Had a telephone put in our house the 30th of November. It is much help to us.

December 11

Returned home today from Union Grove where I preached two sermons.

December 17

Preached three sermons at Oak Grove Saturday night and Sunday and here in town last night. The Lord is still with me.

December 27

Went to Jones, Georgia, had meeting over Sunday. Preached two sermons. Preached one funeral sermon on Christmas day about five miles out from Cleveland. Meeting at our house three or four times lately.

December 31

Preached Saturday night and Sunday morning at our own house, two sermons. This closes another year's work. I did the best I could although it is not as much as I would like. Preached 196 sermons, anointed 17 for healing, all but one got well and he resorted to medical aid. Baptized 15 and traveled about 2,646 miles. By the help of the Lord I want to do more the coming year. I am praying for more power and ability in every way including means for expenses so I will not have to spare any time from the Lord's service from lack of means.

1907

January 1, 1907

Preached a funeral sermon. Mary has been very sick but the Lord had mercy on us and healed her.

January 7

Went to Drygo last Saturday. Held a sacramental and feet washing service. Preached three sermons.

January 17

I have been deprived of writing for ten days. On the 9th instant I went to Union Grove to attend the annual Assembly. While there I delivered 6 discourses and preached two sermons. I filled executive office and directed the services during the whole four days. I am sure God gave me special ability by the Holy Ghost. The workers were all full of love and submission, I anointed and we prayed for ten persons while there for healing. God honored His word and sent blessings. I came home Monday morning. A lady who was here was very sick. I anointed and we prayed for her and she was up and felt well she said in about an hour. There was a telegram awaiting me when I got home to go to Georgia to conduct funeral services, about 100 miles away. I took the next train, walked eight miles to the other R. R. in the dark, arrived in time, arrived at my destination the next day about 10:00 a. m. Preached the funeral sermon and another at night. I arrived home again last evening about worn out. I anointed two while gone this time.

January 21

I preached at Oak Grove Saturday night and again yesterday. I felt that I could not preach so I just stood up and was a channel through which the Lord poured the message for an hour. It was really wonderful to myself. Had cottage meeting at our house last night. I preached a little sermon. I anointed two. One yesterday and one two days before. Brother Lemons called me over the phone today to come to Chattanooga tonight for meeting, but I have not gone.

January 23

I was called up last night near midnight to go and pray for and anoint little Bessie Simpson. I was called for her again today. Both times she seemed much relieved. I received a call this evening to preach and conduct funeral services tomorrow.

January 24

Preached a funeral here in town.

January 30

Came home last evening from Georgia where I went last Saturday. Preached two sermons and one funeral sermon. Was called to stay at a place on account of sickness on Monday night in a little log hut, very open and weather very cold. Small place, only two beds and we had to take it by turns going to bed. I had walked ten or twelve miles that day, conducted the funeral service and done without dinner, but the Lord sustained me. Homer has been very sick but the Lord had mercy on him and he is now in school, but his hearing is not good yet. We are counting on God to restore it perfectly.

January 30

We were called to J. H. Simpson's where I preached one sermon and anointed one. The Lord graciously came down and poured out His blessing.

January 31

Was called with others to pray for the sick. I did the anointing, only one. The Lord very graciously poured out His blessing upon us.

February 11

Went to Union Grove day before yesterday, Saturday, for meeting over Sunday. Came home last night at midnight to attend a funeral today. Was called to pray for and anoint the sick as soon as I got home. I preached four sermons at the Grove. God was with me and blessedly helped in power and delivery.

February 18

Have been called up several times lately in the night to pray for and wait on the sick. Saturday night I was called up about 11 o'clock by a young man who was so under conviction that he could not go to sleep. I invited him in and gave him religious instruction and prayed for him. He said he was willing to do anything to get right with God. He gave me a box of cocane which had been a curse to him. I put it in the fire. He said he had some straightening up to do and promised to do it and go all the way so I bid him good night and he departed. I preached at Oak Grove yesterday and preached last night at a cottage in a suburb of this city. We are planning and arranging to build a church house here in town as soon as possible.

March 5

On February 20 I went to Chattanooga to engage in revival meeting. Preached 8 sermons and anointed one. Anointed one since I came back. Was called home the night of March 1 to preach a funeral which I did the next day. Then I went to Drygo in the evening for over Sunday where I preached three sermons. I received a phone call this morning telling me that I made an enemy because I spoke against Christians belonging to secret lodges. I am sorry the brother is so offended but according to the New Testament I must advise Christians against fellowshipping infidels; drunkards, thieves and murderers. Then I regard the secret part very close akin to the beast of Revelation, the mark of which is in the forehead and In the hand. 2 Cor. 6:14-17; Rev. 14:9-11. Then they have a form of worship (godliness) but deny the power thereof. 2 Tim. 3:5. From such we must turn away. The brother that was so offended is not a member of the Church. Brothers Trim, Lemons and Bryant are at Chattanooga yet. I hope to hear from them today, I must add a word for the glory of God in regard to the way He supplies my needs. I was to go to Chattanooga. I got my baggage hauled to station. I had no money. I asked the bill. "Nothing" was the response. I hastened to postoffice and in my mail was a check for $5.00. My family too was about out of supplies. I hurried home, gave wife $4.00 and took the other dollar and went to Chattanooga. After I got on train and became quiet as I mediated about the goodness of God, I rejoiced in my spirit as the tears rushed to my eyes as I thought how wonderfully God supplied me again; not knowing the parties that sent the money but expecting it from some where.

March 11

I have just returned from Chattanooga where I have been again for a few days. Preached four sermons. Some good work done. One soul gloriously saved but some how I have come home with a heavy heart from some cause, feeling the need of more power. God help me.

March 20

Have been called to pray for the sick. Have anointed four. Preached at Oak Grove last Sunday. Meeting at our house S. night.

March 26

Came home from Jones, Georgia where I held meetings over Sunday. Preached three sermons. Was at Culberson, N. C. yesterday. Anointed three for healing here in town last week.

April 1

Yesterday being the fifth Sunday I was home all day. We have been out of money for several days; our food supplies run short, but we had a good Easter dinner and while we were thanking God for his blessings $2.00 arrived from California. Then we shed tears of gratitude and praised God. This life of faith, Oh how glorious, when we just know it is God who supplies us. Preached funeral sermon here in town March 21. I got Brother Bryant to go and fill a call at Tellico Plains over Sunday so I could get to be at home one Sunday again. I am papering our house. Some of rooms have never been papered.

April 15

Have held some prayer meetings and preached three sermons since I last wrote. Have been fixing up our house. Came back from Union Grove today where I have been over Sunday. Preached three sermons and had pretty good meetings. Weather has been very cold for a week. All the fruit is killed. Lots of leaves in the forests look like they have been scorched. March was very warm, but April is cold.

April 22

Quite a number of us town folks went out into the country two miles to a school house and had meeting. I did the preaching. Had a good prayer meeting at our house last night conducted by Brother Trim. Quite a crowd for a cottage meeting. It is raining today. I was called by telephone to go out in the country about 12 or 13 miles pray for a sick man who is dangerously ill. I expect to start in a few minutes even if the weather is very unfavorable. Lord be with me and help me.

April 27

I was called out about 12 miles to preach and conduct a funeral. Received a message to go out about four miles for a meeting tonight and tomorrow.

April 29

Preached at Oakland yesterday. Preached last night at a cottage meeting here in town.

May 7

I was at a place called Zion Hill over Sunday, about eight miles out and had meetings. Preached three sermons.

May 13

This is Monday morning. Preached one sermon at Union Grove yesterday. Came home last evening so I could be here this morning to assist in the commencement of the building of Brother Bryant's house and the meeting house.

May 20

On the evening of the 16th instant I officiated in the marriage of a couple at our own home, Warmack and Woods. Yesterday, Sunday, I preached at Oak Grove, probably for the last time. Prayer meeting at our house at night.

May 21

I am working every day now on our meeting house. Commenced roofing today.

May 29

Working on meeting house every day, visiting the sick at night. Anointed one.

June 3

Held meeting at our house last night. I preached. Visited the sick some yesterday.

June 14

Returned home today from Birmingham, Alabama, where I have been for a week in a meeting with Brother M. M. Pinson. Glorious results. Speaking in other tongues by the Holy Ghost.

June 17

Held an all day meeting yesterday at Blue Springs, five miles out of town. Engaged in the sacrament and feet washing. Quite a large crowd. Dinner at the grove. Out doors grove meeting. Brother Lemons, pastor, was there, but he asked me to do the preaching. Three sermons with glory in my soul.

June 25

Came home last evening from Jones, Georgia where I was over Sunday. I only preached two sermons this time. have anointed four for healing since last report.

July 2

On the 28th ultimo received a very pressing call to the mountains on account of the sickness of a young man. Providences hindered my going the next day, so the next day following I with Brother Bryant boarded the train, riding to the end of the route, we then commenced the ascent up the mountain roads and trails walked a distance of five or six miles, came to the little settlement of timber (Tie, wood and log) cutters. We passed three or four little low plank houses, (saw one man who had cut himself with the axe so he could not work) the next house they said was where the sick man was. Just room enough between the mountains for an ox wagon and once in a while a little extension where the houses were built. We came to the house, greeted the family, who were very "proud" to see us. I sit down by the side of the bed and was keeping the flies off the sick man when he came to himself he recognized me but by the time Brother Bryant had spoken to him he was gone again. This was the last time he ever seemed to notice anything. We held meeting with the family and friends who came in and the next morning the man died. We shaved, washed and dressed him and held the funeral service and were compelled to leave before he was buried. Then came a race for the train which was to leave the station five or six miles below at 3:55 p. m. We walked and run and spoke hurriedly to the men as we passed them with their big ox teams harnessed to sleds, hauling timber down the mountains to the R. R. below. We came the "near way" which took us over very high steep mountain, the descent side was so steep that we must be very sure footed for one miss step and we were in danger of tumbling to the bottom or be jammed up against a tree or rock and very badly bruised if not killed. We had asked the Lord for strength and help to make the trip and so we got through all well except very hot as it was a very hot day. The rude huts, the rough home-made bedsteads, the stone fireplaces and stick and clay chimneys reminds one of colonial days. I can't describe the rough fare and the kind hospitality there is among these mountain people. We took with us two large S. S. picture rolls and four large print Testaments and a few small Testaments. There were all distributed and gave so much joy and comfort. The only trouble was, we did not have near enough picture rolls. If the Sunday _____ A prayer for more. I preached two sermons besides the funeral sermon. I am very much worn and tired today but am arranging for tent work.

July 3

Pitched the tent in South Cleveland and commenced meeting the same night. Brother J. H. Withrow is helping me besides Bryant, Trim, Simpsons and others. Preached the introductory sermon.

July 4

Meeting afternoon and night. I preached at night to a full tent. Good start for meeting.

July 9

This is Tuesday. I am fasting today. Have had meetings right along since they started. Brother Withrow gave out and went home last week. Very sorry he could not stay. Have delivered seven sermons. Preached three times on Sunday and seven professions, but the labor and strain was almost too much for me. 0 God, for more strength to work for Thee.

July 11

Preached one sermon last night, and one the night before at tent. Night before last there was 16 in the altar and we had a fine meeting last night. The wicked spirits seemed to press hard upon us at the last and made it very hard. This afternoon I preached a short sermon and again one at night. We had a glorious service and the Lord gave us eight professions after they cried with loud voices and gave up sin.

July 17

My time has been so occupied with the meeting, etc., that I could not write all the happenings. Missed having meeting Friday and at night on account of rain, but Saturday night the revival fire was not abated but rather increased. I preached and 8 professions. Sunday I preached three searching sermons and there were fifteen professions besides the other good that must have been done. Some spoke with other tongues Sunday afternoon. Monday night I preached with victory but the altar service was hard and no professions. Yesterday and last night Brother Spurling was with us and did the preaching. I followed and made the altar call in the power of the Spirit. A young lady who had been saved went to her father and spoke to him about his soul but, he thrust her away, and took his little ones and left apparently in a rage. I immediately Sister Simpson dropped on her knees and sent a volley of petitions up for him. I also was seized with a spirit of prayer for him and the agony was severe, my bowels were much pained as I was drawn and bent almost double. Conviction and power fell and people tumbled into the altar and some professed before we concluded the altar invitation. Six professions. Brother Bryant was not able to be with us but the Lord was with us.

July 18

Held two meetings yesterday and last night. Brother Spurling did the preaching. I made the altar call and 12 or 15 came and some professed again before I had concluded the call. Seven professions.

July 19

Eight professions last night at the meeting.

July 20

Meeting at tent last night, four professions. I did the preaching.

July 21

Meeting at tent last night. A wonderful meeting. Shouting, praying, weeping, singing, embracing, showing much love, people getting reclaimed, fired up and converted. Nine professions.

July 22

Yesterday was the most wonderful time in my experience. I preached about one hour and a half, after which 18 joined the Church and were given the right hand of fellowship amid great rejoicing with tears and shouts, etc. I exposed sin and denounced it in high places and exhorted Christians to separate themselves completely from all ungodly organizations and obey Jesus and the Apostles' doctrine only. Solomnly [sic] charged them, to never stain the Church or bring reproach on Christ's cause by any act of failure in any way. 2:30 P. M. Experience meeting followed by repairing to the water where I baptized eight. Very large crowd to witness the sacred service. The highest pitch of the revival was reached last night. 14 professions and I have no better way to describe the scene than the 8th of Acts. Attendance very large. A mass of happy people working with seekers, praying, singing, shouting, reeling like drunken men, screaming for mercy until one after another was delivered. The Holy Ghost was in charge and I had only to watch and see that no disorder or wrong spirit came in. One man was dismissed who claimed to be a Christian but he was located by the Spirit and this was without a break or jostle in the work and but few knew anything about it. What a scene. I cannot describe it. We rest until tomorrow night, when we expect the work to continue under the direction of the Holy Ghost.

July 24

Meeting again last night. Brothers Spurling, Lemons and Trim left Monday for their respective places of labor. Brother Bryant is with me. I preached last night after the altar was filled and 12 professions followed. The revival fire is still burning and the tide running high, No abatement from Sunday night. God help me to keep humble and in my place so the holy Ghost can continue His work.

July 25

Preached two sermons yesterday and last night. The altar was quickly filled and there were seven professions although it was one of those hard services unaccounted for.

July 26

Preached two sermons yesterday and last night. 6 professions. Good work done by the converts. O, such drunkenness on the Spirit. Glorious victory and success.

July 27

Preached last night. Two professions. I was very much exhausted on account of continuous labor. This morning I don't feel able for service but I trust God to carry me through. The continuous strain and labor for 24 days has been almost too much for me. But souls are still going down to hell and I do so much need more physical strength to continue the work of rescuing souls.

July 28

Preached last night. I was very much worn by constant toil day and night but God took me above all exhaustion and helped me with power and demonstration of the Spirit to unfold the Scripture, after which a number came to the altar and quite a number affected by the gospel and there were 6 professions.

July 29

I believe yesterday and last night until near midnight was the greatest day of my life. Preached three sermons and baptized nine. But I am completely exhausted physically. No not but what I am up at 5:30 and attending to some business but I am very much worn. God made me equal to every emergency. I had the whole work, that is there were no ministers to help me, but such victory and boldness at every service and in the water. Yes, I preached a short sermon at the water. Received 14 into the Church. All glory to God. Conviction feel heavy at the tent and at the water. Strong men could hardly hold up under the power of God.

August 6

I was compelled to lay up and rest last week, so there was only one meeting held during the week until Saturday night. I was then scarcely able to get to the tent, but God took me above in the service as I preached so I felt much better at the close. Two professions. Sunday or yesterday I preached four sermons. Last night the tent and surroundings were crowded. The Lord led me to expose false prophets and strike sin in high places. It was sure sharp and cutting but I showed how the Christ I was representing could take away and cleanse from all sin. One profession, several at the altar. Meeting announced for tonight but it is raining. I must say that I baptized one yesterday.

August 7

Meeting last night. I was there but not well and Brother Bryant preached. One profession. I feel much better today. I was accosted on the street this morning on account of a challenge I had made about being free from sin though the power of Christ. He said he did not believe that a man could live without sin in this world and accused me of sinning every day. I told him kindly that I was living free from sin and asked him if he could find a blot on my life. He said he could not, but he did not believe, etc. But I told him kindly that his unbelief did not change the Bible nor the lives of those who were free from sin. He referred to what I had said that preachers or any one who sinned were on their road to hell. I told him I gave my judgment on that from a Bible standpoint. "He that sinneth is of the devil." I asked him if those who were of the devil were not on their road to the devil's country. He was about through as it seemed a crowd had gathered and another man came in and took me to the seventh of Romans, the which I was very much delighted with. For I told him that was evidently Paul's experience while yet under the law. He said no, that was his experience as a Christian. I said if you construct it in that way, then the sixth and eighth chapters contradicts that chapter, for they both teach freedom from sin under the law of Christ and this makes the Bible contradict itself and that being the case we had just us well throw the whole thing away. He said that would not do and I concluded by saying to the crowd that if my critics and objectors can get more souls saved and produce more fruits of service to God then I can I'd like for them to get at it and one said, "for you want to get the world saved as soon as possible," and I said, "yes, and any way it can be done." The Lord gave me real victory and I count it a victory for the Lord right on the streets. Glory. I want to always be ready for emergencies.

August 8

Preached a funeral sermon yesterday and preached at tent last night. Held the last service at the tent tonight. Had a number of bold, fiery testimonies. Good meeting.

August 10

Took down the tent yesterday. Took it to Blue Springs and put it up and had meeting last night. I preached the introductory sermon. I came home this morning, am to go to Union Grove this evening to commence a revival there. I leave the tent with Brother Lemons.

August 19

Just returned from Union Grove where we held revival for eight days. I preached 11 sermons. 14 professions and others helped. One received the baptism of the Holy Ghost and spoke with other tongues. Brothers Was Simpson and Tallent continue the meeting and I go to Blue Springs tonight D. V. to assist Brother Lemons with tent.

August 22

Came home from Blue Springs today. Closed meeting last night. Preached four sermons. The outside people were so against us that we could do but little but help the saints. Five I think claimed sanctification.

September 6

I have been in Georgia and North Carolina and out from Cleveland since last writing. Preached 6 sermons. In North Carolina to get to the train we had to walk about seven miles over a mountain trail which led through wild looking places where we were told there were rattle snakes and copperheads abounding; but we were not molested. The mountains over which we passed were very rugged and steep. Brother Lemons missed his footing one place and fell down the mountain several feet, but although he was bruised some he received no serious injury. I slipped at the same place but by sufficient activity saved myself from falling.

September 9

Came home from Union Grove where I have been over Sunday. Preached one sermon.

September 16

Varnished church house last week. Led prayer meeting in South Cleveland Saturday night. Went to Oakland yesterday, preached two sermons. Preached funeral of a little child today.

September 21

Went to Chattanooga last Tuesday to buy lamps for meeting house. Been painting meeting house this week. I performed marriage ceremony of Jesse Trim and Viola Lemons at night.

September 26

I have just got in from completing the new church house and cleaning up around it. 5:30 P.M. Have just taken off my old work clothes and put on nice ones and knelt down and prayed and thanked God. I can see the top of the house from where I am sitting in my room at home. The carpet will probably be here to put down tomorrow. We are going over to try the new lamps and trim them up tonight.

September 29

The long-looked for day for the dedication of the new church has come and gone. Three services today. I preached the dedicatory sermon, made the statement and cost which was $1,093.67 and took up collections which amounted to $453.80. Then I offered the dedicatory prayer about 4 o'clock p.m. Then Brother Spurling preached at night. The whole day has been a real victory and success.

October 1

Had meeting yesterday and last night and the same order today. 7 professions. Crowd increasing. Interest growing. I preached today one sermon. One spoke in unknown tongues.

October 5

Have been running meetings every day and night. People getting saved from sins or sanctified at nearly every service. The house was crowded tonight. Preached three sermons. 9 more professions, several renewed and some sanctified. 16 professions this week.

October 7

Organized a Sunday school yesterday at new church, with 92 scholars enrolled. Brother Lemons preached the sermon afterwards. 2 professions. I preached last night to a packed house. They sit around me on platform so thick that I could scarcely move when I made the altar call it was quickly filled with seekers. So crowded we could only work with much difficulty, but there were two professions and several sanctified. No meeting today nor tonight except the S. S. committees meet tonight.

October 9

Preached last night and tonight. Two sermons. One profession. Several at altar. Preaching was with great victory and liberty. Some shouted while I preached. Others shouted while I made altar call. House about full.

October 10

Held meeting yesterday and last night. I preached at night. Several at altar. One profession. I preached with great grace and demonstration.

October 11

Held meeting today and at night. I preached at night. 1 profession and 2 sanctified.

October 12

Put up stoves in meeting house today. Brother Bryant went to Tellico Plains and Brothers Trim and Corbit Simpson to Union Grove for meetings over Sunday. I have to continue here at Cleveland tonight and over Sunday alone except the Church.

October 14

Preached Saturday night and yesterday and last night, Three sermons. Superintended the S. S. and directed the Bible study. The S. S. has increased to 124 scholars the second Sunday,

October 17

Delivered a lecture or sermon to the church last night on their duty about giving. We are going to put in practice the New Testament order—1 Cor. 16:2; 2 Cor. 9:5-8.

October 20

Conducted the S. school, preached two sermons and conducted a Bible study.

October 25

Last Monday I left home, bound for the back mountains and the regions of Jeffries Bell. I arrived home last night. I walked about 60 miles. Found people very destitute of both the gospel and this world's goods. A great field of labor, much of it unoccupied by a gospel messenger. I preached two sermons.

October 28

Superintended the Sunday school yesterday, preached two sermons and led the Bible study. Brother Bryant was at Jones, Georgia for me.

November 4

Led the prayer meeting last Wednesday night. Conducted the Sunday school and Bible lesson yesterday and preached two sermons. Had good meetings,

November 9

I have spent some time this week in building a chicken house. Led the prayer meeting at the church and teachers meeting. Brother Bryant went today to Tellico Plains and Brother Lemons holds the meetings at Union Grove tomorrow.

November 11

I preached two sermons yesterday here at Cleveland and conducted Sunday school and Bible study. At 11 o'clock preaching eight came to altar. 6 professions. After preaching at night one profession. A missionary from Turkey was with us at the meeting at night and gave us a short talk.

November 19

Just came home last night from the Tellico Mountains where I have been for a week holding meetings. Some good work done, the Spirit was present every service, but one service in a special manner. While I was preaching some laughed, about all cried and one fell off his seat and just fellowed out in good fashion. Every one present touched. I think every one in the house came to the altar. I was very calm but surely the signs of God's presence was manifest. I preached 10 sermons on this trip. I am in a quite financial strait just now but I believe God will help me out some way.

November 25

I acted as superintendent of the Sunday school, held the meeting, conducted the Bible study and held the meeting at night at the new church house yesterday. Preached two sermons. I am still in a close place financially but I am still prayerful and hopeful. My heart is groaning, "Lord help" nearly all the time.

November 28

National Thanksgiving Day. Held a service in the church house here in the city. I had charge. After a number of songs and testimonies I preached a short sermon on the sacrament after which we engaged in the same. After that I preached a short sermon on feet washing and then we engaged in that sacred service. Afternoon we went to Lake Wildwood and baptized two. Had meeting again at night. Short talks by a number.

December 7

Next day after Thanksgiving I went to Turtletown, Tenn., held a meeting, the next day to North Carolina. Had a sacrament and feet washing service on Sunday, the next day in company with Brother Alex Hamby I went about fourteen miles back farther in the mountains and held a few meetings. I came home night before last. I held five services on the trip and preached five sermons.

December 8. Sunday night, 9:30

Just got home from meeting. I acted as superintendent of Sunday school, preached at 11:00 A. M. and preached again at 7:00 p.m. The services were impressive and I believe some good was accomplished. In the Bible study one man who had not been there before showed a contentious spirit but later on he calmed down and did not cause any trouble, except some of us was wrought on by the Spirit of discernment but we worked very easy and but little disturbance was realized by the class. At night we had a service on Pentecostal lines. Several of us tarried after dismission and some expressed the receiving of great blessings from God. My work today has been pleasant and very satisfactory, though I would love to have seen greater results. God surely helped me to preach. I am tired and worn in body, but my soul is aglow with the love of God. Preached two sermons. Brother Lemons went to Union Grove and Brother Bryant to Hill View. Brother Trim was at Drygo last Sunday.

December 15

I conducted the Sunday school at 9:30, preached at eleven. Conducted the Bible study at 2:30 and preached again at night. The Lord was blessedly with me, three came forward for prayers and quite a number came seeking the baptism of the Holy Ghost.

December 19

Led the prayer meeting last night. Married a couple this evening. Ed Dixon and Minnie Penland.

December 22

Conducted the Sunday school, the service for worship, the Bible study and the meeting at night. Preached two sermons. At the eleven o'clock service at the close of the sermon nearly all who claimed religion came into the altar and some fell under a travail of soul, I with others. A powerful time in prayer for a little while. The text was James 5:16 on prayer. Nearly all who were not religious asked for prayers for themselves. Last night the subject was the pentecostal experience. The Lord was with us. We expect to protract the meeting this week.

December 26

Held meetings day and night all the week so far. The Holy Ghost has flashed the light upon us wonderfully. I have done all the preaching. Preached eight sermons up to 3:00 P. M. today. Yesterday the church and Sunday school gave us a pleasant surprise in the way of Christmas gifts. Rocking chair, provisions and money. Nearly $25.00. I suppose 75 or a 100 came in on us carrying their gifts. We crowded them into the house and had a few talks, viz. presentation speeches and one of acceptance and appreciation and a prayer.

December 30

Held meetings day and night. Conducted the Sunday school, meetings and Bible study yesterday. Four professions last night.

1908

January 1, 1908

Held meeting at the meeting house last night till after midnight.
God helped me to preach and there were two professions.
Preached three sermons since last writing. This makes 203
sermons in the year 1907. I am praying that I may be able to do
much more this year for Jesus than any year in my life. May God
grant this prayer.

January 6

I went to Union Grove Saturday night to be there for Sunday
meeting. I had to walk four miles through the rain and mud
and dark except carried a lantern. I preached one sermon and
returned home for meeting here at night. Brother Jesse Clark
preached a good sermon. Three professions. Good interest in the
whole congregation.

January 13

Our Assembly consumed the last three days of last week.
Saturday night. Brother Cashwell preached and on Sunday,
yesterday, at nearly the close of his discourse the Spirit so
effected me that I slid down off of my chair on to the floor or on
the rostrum and as I went down I yielded myself up to God and
after a considerable of agony and groans my jaws seemed to be
set, my lips were moved and twisted about as if an examination
of them was being made, after that my tongue was operated on in
like manner, also my eyes, several examinations seemed to taken,
and every limb of my body was operated on in like manner, then
my whole body beyond my control was rolled and shaken and
finally while lying on my back both of my feet were raised right up
in the air several times, then I felt myself lifted as in a great sheet
of power of some kind and moved in the air in the direction my
feet pointed. As I lay there great joy flooded my soul. My hands

clapped together and I glorified God without any effort whatever on my part. At other times the most excruciating pain and agony but my spirit said yes to God at every point. My mind was finally carried to Central America and I was shown the awful condition of the people there and after a paroxism of suffering the Holy Ghost spoke through my lips and tongue beyond control which seemed to me the very language of the Indian tribes there. Then after a little rest I was carried in mind to all of South America, and of all the black pictures that was surely the blackest, then my mind settled on Brazil, then after another paroxism of suffering the Spirit spoke again in another tongue, then after a little relaxation I was shown Chili, with the same effects and results, then in like manner Patagonia, down among those illiterate Indians, each place I was shown I gave assent to go to them. From Patagonia to Africa and on to Jerusalem and while there awful suffering in my body. I never can describe it. After every paroxism of suffering came a tongue. From there way up to Northern Russia, then to France, then to Japan, then I seemed to get back to the United States, but soon I was taken away up north among the Esquimaux. While here the language seemed to be a little like the bark of a dog. Then some where in Canada. Then I came back to Cleveland and seemed to be asked if I was willing to testify or speak on the public square of the city, without any effort my spirit seemed to give consent, then to Chattanooga and then my mind seemed to be carried along the rail road to Cincinnati right on through the city and on up to my old home in Indiana. Then to Westfield, then to Hortonville and Sheridan came up and a little meeting house away back in the country from Sheridan where I held a meeting ten or twelve years ago. I must say too that some where in the experience I came in direct contact with the devil and while in this state came the awfullest struggle of all and while talking in an unknown tongue to me the Spirit seemed to envelope me and I was taken through a process of casting out devils. They went. Also the 16th of Mark came up, these signs shall follow, dwelling on casting out devils, speaking in tongues and taking up serpents. I seemed to try to get to healing the sick but could not quite get to that. Numbers of people came before me whom I could see coming, among them was my wife and children. I seemed to see us all on a missionary journey. Glory to God. I must not fail to tell about the song I sung in unknown tongues. Oh it was glorious. This was really the baptism of the Holy Ghost as they received Him on the day of Pentecost for they all spake with tongues. With all I have written it is not yet told but judging from the countries I visited I spoke in ten different languages. It seemed that the Spirit was showing me these countries with a view to taking me there. Each place I was lots of people coming to the light and baptism. I could see multitudes coming to Jesus. I don't know if God wants me to go to these places or not, but I am willing to go as He leads.

January 14

I was called to attend the funeral of Effie Peck, about nine miles out in the country. Preached with ease and I believe with good results.

January 20

We have been continuing the meeting ever since I last wrote. Saturday night the house was full. Last night was packed and many had to leave because they could not get in. Yesterday afternoon in the service an M. E. Preacher withstood Brother Cashwell to the face about the tongues but it all worked out for good. He made a fool of himself and showed it to the entire audience and the affair won hearts to the truth. We raised $37.04 for Brother Cashwell. I preached at night,

January 21

Held two meetings. I preached two sermons.

January 21

I preached at night.

January 26

I must say that last Sunday we were called to the bedside of a little girl of eleven years who was sick of pneumonia fever. We anointed and prayed for her and we held on to the promise in the fifth of James until she was converted healed and today she was in Sunday school and meeting. The congregation was small today on account of rain and smallpox scare but God gave a good meeting. I preached the sermon.

February 11

Have been at Union Grove two or three times and to Drygo as many times assisting in meetings and went one trip to McMinn County. Preached twelve sermons. Anointed some who were healed. I probably go to Rome, Georgia tonight for a meeting. Glory.

February 21

I just arrived home from Rome, Georgia last evening. Had a good meeting although the weather was bad and the people did not come out very freely. My ministry evidently was somewhat appreciated for they gave me about 23 dollars. I preached 12 sermons. The altar was filled with seekers nearly every service.

February 24

I preached yesterday and last night here in Cleveland. Two
sermons. For about two hour at home before I went to the night
service I was specially exercised in prayer and weeping and
groaning. I preached in tears on eternal punishment and made an
altar call and broke down again in agony and blinding tears and
after coming to myself again and on looking up I saw the altar filled
with seekers. Some were weeping others crying to God for mercy.
At least two professions. The meeting held until 10:30. Before I
dismissed the main audience I asked all to stand who wanted
prayers, I suppose about fifty arose. Some very much affected.

February 25

I was called yesterday to go out 16 miles to anoint and pray for a
sick child and after prayer he got up and got a piece of bread and
went to eating and playing. I heard from him today and was told
that he did not act like there was anything the matter with him.
Last night we had a meeting at the church here in town. Called
it as a solemn assembly to weep and pray over the lost and those
who had been overcome by the powers of the devil. I preached.
Some at altar very much affected.

March 1

I preached two sermons here at Cleveland. Two seekers at altar at
night. Sister Julia Simpson broke down in weeping, groaning and
agonizing prayer similar to my experience last Sunday night.

March 4

Have just returned home from Chattanooga where I preached four
sermons. Some healed, one burned his tobacco. A number of seekers
for pardon, sanctification and the baptism of the Holy Ghost.

March 9

Just came home from Union Grove where I went Saturday
evening. Preached two sermons. Disfellowshipped 9 for disorderly
walks. Halcy went with me. A number at altar as seekers.

March 15

Preached here at Cleveland today and tonight. Two sermons. Led
Bible lesson afternoon. A number at altar today as seekers. One
reclaimed tonight.

March 16

Had a cottage meeting tonight out in town and one profession.
The manifestation of the Spirit was noticeable. One old lady over
100 years old shouted all about over the room. Another old lady

lying on the bed not fully recovered from a broken limb spoke in tongues as the Spirit gave utterance. Others spoke of receiving great blessings and showed signs.

March 22

I was called to Chattnooga last Friday where I held four meetings Friday and Saturday. Went to Rome, Georgia Saturday evening and held meeting at night and three on Sunday. Just got home this evening. Preached 7 sermons. Anointed one and one healed without anointing. I am very tired, and worn but God gives grace and glory.

March 27

Preached funeral of a little child here in town.

March 29

I conducted the temperance exercises at the Sunday school here at Cleveland and preached the temperance sermon. I went out about 8 miles in the country to Piney Camp Ground and preached at night to a well-filled house. I was elected pastor for the church at Oakland, or rather Blue Springs.

April 5

I went to Blue Springs last evening, held one meeting. Preached one sermon. Came home this morning, went to Sunday school, taught my class, then preached the sermon at meeting. Was called to attend a funeral at one O'clock, held a short service but they put off the funeral service until tomorrow. Preached a funeral at three o'clock. Came home and then preached at the church again at night. This is now 10:20 at night. I feel very much worn but God gives grace and strength. Two at the altar tonight.

April 6

Preached at a funeral service, The Holy Spirit was present with power to apply the truth and the service was very impressive. The Holy Ghost gave me a little outline of the message only a few minutes before time for the service. The Holy Ghost did the work. He shall have all the glory for all that was done.

April 7

Preached about four miles out in the country tonight. Walked in home and have just got here at 11:30 tonight.

April 8

Prayer meeting last night. I preached. I have been helping Brother Bryant paint his house. I am now fixing to fence our lot across the street.

April 14

Went to Union Grove last Saturday. Held meeting Sunday and baptized five, came home and held the meeting here Sunday night. Preached three sermons. A Mr. Rogers was here when got home Sunday evening, for healing. We prayed for him and did all we could for him but he was unwilling to meet the conditions and the poor man went back to Chattanooga today not much better. So sorry for him.

April 19 Easter

I went to Chattanooga last Thursday. Called on Brother Rogers, found him submitting to God and getting better. Praise God. Came home Saturday. Preached two sermons. Today and tonight I preached two sermons. I performed the marriage ceremony of a couple here at my house today. Led the Bible study this afternoon and taught a Sunday school class this morning. A number at the altar tonight, I am tired in my body but have blessed victory in my soul. All glory to Jesus for all.

April 26

Preached two sermons last night and three today. One funeral sermon.

May 2

Just came home from Chattanooga where we have been all week putting up a tent and starting meeting. We got tent up and hoodlum boys tore it very bad so we had to take it down and repair it. Held two meetings in it. I preached last night and started home. I was running to catch car in the dark and fell and missed the car so I was late to station, the train had gone so I came early this morning. I go back again today.

May 4

I was called home again today from Chattanooga on account of wife being ill. I preached three sermons yesterday and one night before last. Several at altar every service. The meeting is commencing with good interest.

May 18

I have been holding meetings in tent at Chattanooga ever since last writing, assisted by Brothers Trim and Lemons, until I came home day before yesterday. Preached 18 sermons. Several professions of religion and sanctification. Four received the baptism of the Holy Ghost and spoke in tongues. Some very wonderful manifestations of the Spirit. A breeze, as a rushing wind was felt by some. Some layed under the power for hours. I myself was controlled and wafted about by the Spirit two or three times. Spoke in tongues in prayer on one occasion. Some spoke in tongues and sang also, some saw visions, some played unseen instruments. The manifestations of the Spirit in me was more than I can explain. I feel like great things are to be done soon and that we are now only in our infancy in this wonderful work.

June 6

I returned to Chattanooga May 19 where I continued work in the tent. I was called to Charleston May 21 to preach funeral of Brother Lemons little baby boy three years old, Seth R., I returned to Chattanooga again the next day where I have been laboring ever since. I came home last night at midnight to be ready to attend services here tomorrow. I preached funeral of a baby in Chattanooga June 2. The meetings there have continued with good interest and much blessing. A drunken woman converted and sanctified. People converted, sanctified and baptized with the Holy Ghost and spake in tongues. Preached 23 sermons.

June 7

Preached two sermons last night and today here at Cleveland. Spoke at children's meeting at night. At the close of the discourse today I made an altar call and six or eight came forward. I was very much exercised in prayer end weeping. The seekers were very much wrought upon by the Spirit.

June 22

Have been in tent meeting at Chattanooga since last writing. Closed there the night of the 17th after a siege of seven weeks. About 20 received the baptism of the Holy Ghost and spoke in tongues. Among the number were three little girls, 10, 9 and 7 years of age. Quite a number were converted, reclaimed and sanctified. I baptized 11 in a beautiful little lake. One little girl only about nine years old. Others are yet expecting to be baptized. The signs are blessedly following the preaching of a full gospel. Signs and wonders have been wrought by the blessed Holy Ghost to glorify Jesus. The gospel was given out with power. I cannot describe the demonstrations. I myself was caught up by the Spirit and spoke in tongues numbers of times as the Spirit gave utterance. People would stay for hours and sit on the rough board seats with no backs when they could hardly be kept an hour on nice comfortable pews in the churches. God's power is wonderful. Glory to His name. I preached fifteen sermons, two more here and 1 funeral yesterday afternoon, George Freeman's little Raymond at Union Grove. I am expecting to go to Chattanooga again tomorrow.

June 29

I came home from Chattanooga Saturday where we had the large tent up and I left Brothers Lemons and Trim to hold the meeting there. preached three sermons here yesterday. One at the funeral service of Mrs. Newberry. I go to Madisonville today, D. V. to assist Brother Bryant in meeting in small tent. Jesse Clark helped him pitch it and start the meeting.

July 5

I returned home yesterday from Madisonville where I preached six sermons. The people, it was told us, made it up and agreed among themselves that they would not attend the meeting so we decided to close the meeting and moved tent to another place and I and Brother Mitchell came home. I preached here last night and today and at night again. Three sermons.

July 18

On the 8th instant I went with Brother Bryant to hold tent meeting at the Red Knobs where I stayed until the 15th. I came home over night and went to Chattanooga the next day, came home again last evening and will be off again today for the Red Knobs D. V. Preached 15 sermons. Brothers Lemons and Trim at Chattanooga were arrested for making so much noise after ten o'clock at night. Compromised by agreeing to move the tent when they did. The meeting there is going on with good interest.

July 19

I started yesterday to the Red Knobs but my train was late and when I reached Athens the other train was gone so I came back home and held the meetings and Sunday school here. After the sermon at night I made an altar call and about twelve came to the altar and four professions. I feel like God's providences arranged for me to be here to get these souls saved. I preached the two sermons.

July 28

I just returned from the meeting in the Red Knobs last evening. 34 professions and some sanctified. They cut our tent down one night, cut eighteen ropes but we tied it up again and went on as though nothing had happened. I preached 12 sermons. I go to Chattanooga this evening if nothing happens.

August 4

Returned home this evening from Chattanooga to commence tent meeting here. We closed meeting down there and organized last night with 49 members, with quite a number of others expecting to come in soon. I preached last Sunday under the power of the Spirit to about 1,000 people and God wonderfully confirmed His word with signs following. Glory! What followed is almost indescribable. Shouts, speaking in tongues, sister played organ controlled by the Spirit. I was enveloped in a kind of sheet of power and controlled and they said my hair stood straight up on my head. Glory. It is wonderful. Since our meeting commenced there the first of May until the close last night there has been about 75 who received the baptism of the Holy Ghost and spoke in tongues which is the Bible evidence. Glory. Brother Lemons and Brother Bryant are at Union Grove at a meeting. Preached 10 sermons since last report. Last Sunday evening I preached to about 5,000 people on a lake shore where we were baptizing. Brother Trim did the baptizing.

August 9

Held meeting in the church house here since Wednesday night. Brother White is with me, Brothers McCarson and McDaniel here today. We had an overflow meeting tonight. The altar was filled and the Lord swept down and gave three the baptism of the Holy Ghost. Fear, consternation and amazement fell upon the congregation. About seven or eight seemed to have fallen under the power. One little girl saw visions. A glorious victorious meeting. Sister Clyde Cotton is here helping. I have preached seven sermons.

August 10

We pitched tent here in town but did not get it ready for meeting so had the meeting in the church house, I preached and made the altar call and 18 or more came forward. Two received the baptism of the Holy Ghost. Baby was one of them. They spoke in tongues and two or three of us workers were exercised in the same way. Sister Cotton played the instrument under the power of the Spirit. God is glorifying His Son Jesus. Glory.

August 11

Commenced meeting in the tent tonight. About 500 people at first service. Brother White led the discourse, I followed and preached and called the altar services. 3 converted and two baptized with the Holy Ghost. Brother McCarson led the singing. Good meeting.

August 12

Held meeting in tent afternoon and at night. I preached one sermon and made the altar calls. Two baptized with Holy Ghost.

August 13

Held meetings. Glorious. Three converted, one baptized with the Holy Ghost.

August 15

Held meetings yesterday and today at tent. Five converted and four baptized with the Holy Ghost and spoke in tongues. I preached tonight to about 1,200 people. About fifty piled into the altar. Glorious service.

August 16

Held meetings about all day. Just got in now at 11:50 at night. Much good seemed to be done. 6 professed religion. Some opposition. I am threatened but not fearful. After some others gave short talks I preached and the altar was filled and some could not get in but asked us to pray for them. They told me they thought there were 1,500 or more people out at tent. One old man was saved at just about ten o'clock. Before I preached a Baptist preacher from Knoxville took my stand and for a few moments claimed that his body sinned but his soul was pure, and poured out a volley of words holding up for a sinning Christian life, but when it came my time the Lord helped me to cut him all up with the Word and I asked him to go to the altar and get salvation. I guess about 50 at the altar.

August 17

We had a glorious little service at our house A. M. Three received the baptism of the Holy Ghost. Meeting at tent afternoon and at night, I preached at night. A number came to the altar. Three received the baptism of the Holy Ghost, Homer was one of the number, and four professions. I was told that some men tried to run from the tent and fell outside under the power. Tonight was the greatest meetings and most powerful and a sweep of the Holy Ghost came down in the most wonderful way with manifestations and miracles, of any meeting I was ever in. I have just got home and it is now 2:50 in the morning. I preached by request of some business men in the city from 1 Cor. 14:27-33. God sure gave me liberty and honored the message. Glory to Jesus forever.

August 19

Storm tore out tent considerably so we could not have meeting afternoon, but we were ready for night. Brother Lemons preached and I made the altar call and 30 or 40 piled in and four professed and one received the baptism of the Holy Ghost. One also received in cottage meeting about noon. I'm told a warrant is taken for my arrest but I hardly think so.

August 20

Held meetings in my house and two meetings in tent. I made the altar calls. Seven professions and five received the baptism of the Holy Ghost at night. The mayor of the city served a paper on me this morning asking me to close the meeting at about 10:00 o'clock or be arrested. We prayed earnestly and I told the officer about the matter and told him I could not go away and leave seekers in the altar and that I would not be compelled to close at any certain time. Tonight the officers came and plainly threw open the privilege for us to hold the meetings as long as we want to and we should have their protection. God gave great victory. Over 60 piled into the altar.

August 21

Had a wonderful meeting at our house this morning. Three received the baptism of the Holy Ghost and one profession. Wife was one who received. Storm interfered with meetings at tent some but I preached two sermons and several in altar.

August 22

Held prayer service at our house A. M. Arranged tent for meeting P. M. Tonight it was packed again, and when I made the altar call it was well filled. I suppose about 50. Five professions and one baptized with Holy Ghost. A strong robust man fell off his seat just like he had been shot during the altar services.

August 23

Held three meetings in tent besides Sunday school. I followed the preachers and made the altar calls. I might say I preached three sermons. About ten professions and one received the Holy Ghost. Some said there were about 2,000 people out tonight.

August 24

Had meeting in my house A. M. Rained so we did not have much meeting at tent P.M. until night. I preached but I believe no one got through. One little girl saw visions. We had some very sore trials to overcome today but I am victorious. Glory.

August 25

Had a good service at our house this morning. One received the baptism of the Holy Ghost. At tent afternoon three received the Holy Ghost and the meeting continued right on till the night meeting. One woman was under the power for about six or seven hours. At night followed the regular discourse with a short sermon and made the altar call. Altar filled, one converted and one received the Holy Ghost. I received a challenge from a minister in town to debate the question of the baptism of the Holy Ghost. I don't know what I will do about it.

August 26

Held service at our house and at tent. Wonderful meetings. Nine baptized with the Holy Ghost and ten professions of religion.

August 27

Held services at our house and at tent. Seven professions and one baptized. This was a very peculiar experience. I am told we are gaining favor with the people rapidly. Large numbers are believing and teaching but only a few getting the experience. I have just got in from meeting now at 2:15 at night.

August 28

Held services at our house and at tent. 12 professions and 10 baptized with the Holy Ghost. I preached at night and made the altar call and possibly 65 or 75 came to the altar. One man fell under the power and was carried into the altar and he was a leader in the Baptist church in the city but he got the baptism of the Holy Ghost and arose speaking in tongues. He stood and gave a message in tongues for some time and continued under the power for hours. The most wonderful meeting yet. Numbers were stretched out under the power on the shavings. Conversations were carried on in tongues by two or four girls for hours and sang the most heavenly music I ever heard. To describe the meeting would be impossible. It is now 2:45 at night and I came away and left one at the tent under the power still. Oh, it is indeed wonderful what God is doing.

August 29

I arose early this morning and after breakfast I lay down to rest a little and was called to go down, a gentlemen wishes to see me. I hastened down and he at once stated his business. He wanted to be saved. We prayed for him until he was converted, then until he was sanctified and then he was filled with the Holy Ghost. By that time others had come and more fell under the power and another got the baptism and one or two converted. A wonderful meeting. Then Brother Lemons and myself had to go pray for a sick boy who was relieved almost instantly. Then meeting at tent P. M. And again at night. I preached at night I suppose to 1,000 people. The altar was filled quickly when I gave the call. A wonderful time again. Six, I believe, received the baptism today and about nine or ten professions. About 500 hands were held up for prayer. Glory to God, it is indeed wonderful. One man fell outside the tent and got the blessing. The signs and glory is wonderful.

August 30

Well this has been a great day. I preached three sermons. I was told today that I preached to 5000 people last night but tonight it was much more. We were crammed in so tight we could scarcely work in the altar. 14 received the baptism all day and three professions. Every service was full of victory. Glory.

August 31

Meeting in tent going right on. I preached tonight. Three received the Holy Ghost and four professions.

September 1

Meeting at my house and twice at tent. I preached two sermons. The one at night I cried it through. The altar was about filled at both services but only four or five professions.

September 2

Meeting afternoon and at night. I preached at night and the altar was crowded but nobody got through. Large crowd.

September 3

Held prayer service at my house and two services at the tent. I preached at night. Three received the baptism of the Holy Ghost and four professions. Numbers of seekers.

September 4

Held meetings yesterday and last night and tonight. I preached tonight. Several at altar.

September 6

Held meeting at tent A. M. and at night. I baptized 33 in a pool about a mile cut of town. I preached one sermon.

September 7

Held meetings at tent and each time after a number of testimonies, altar calls were made and the matter did not have to be pressed very strong to get it filled with seekers. Five received the Holy Ghost and 1 profession.

September 8

Held meeting at tent afternoon and at night. Two baptized with the Holy Ghost and two professions. I preached at night.

September 9

Held cottage meeting and meetings at tent P. M. and at night. I followed Brother Spurling and preached some and made the altar call. Six professions and one received the baptism of the Holy Ghost.

September 10

Held meeting at tent afternoon and at night, A wonderful meeting at night. No preaching. A special time of weeping fell on some of the workers during the testimony service and I called for a special, concert intercessory prayer which lasted for several minutes, and a little later at an opportune time I stepped up on the altar and as I did so I seemed to see a kind of blue vapor or mist settle down on the congregation and people turned pale and as I made the altar call 75 or 100 piled in very quickly. Numbers fell prostrate under the power but only four succeeded in getting the full baptism of the Holy Ghost and seven professions. But the fire is spreading more and more in every quarter of the city and for miles in the country. God help me to keep low and humble right down in the dust.

September 11

Meetings at tent afternoon and at night. Big crowd at night. I preached. Five professions and four received the baptism of the Holy Ghost.

September 12

Held meetings at tent afternoon and at night. Big crowd at night. I preached and made the altar call. Two received the baptism of the Holy Ghost and two professions. I was told tonight that above the tent last night was seen by more than one a streak of fire or light, and that the people were stirred up about the meeting for fifteen and twenty miles in nearly every direction. Glory. It is the Lord's work and indeed wonderful.

September 13

Great work today. I conducted all the services except the Sunday school and made the altar calls, but others did the preaching. Six received the baptism of the Holy Ghost and three professions. Wonderful meetings and large crowds. Glory, glory, glory.

September 14

Well this is after midnight again after a day of toil, praying for sick, working in the meetings, etc. Three professions and two baptized with the Holy Ghost. I preached a little sermon and made the altar call.

September 15

We held cottage meeting A.M. Meeting at tent afternoon and at night. I preached with wonderful victory at night and made altar call. Three received the baptism and three professions today. This is after midnight again. Glory! Glory!! Glory!!!

September 16

At our prayer service at 10 A. M. a spirit of intercessory prayer came on me and lasted I suppose nearly an hour with the awful agonizing groans and crys that are peculiar to such experiences. My body was exercised a good deal by the Holy Ghost, also prayed in unknown tongues. During the time the same spirit fell on a number of others in the room. It was indeed a wonderful prayer service. Meeting as usual at tent afternoon and at night. One profession and two received the baptism with the Holy Ghost. I preached two sermons and made the altar call.

September 17

Held cottage meeting., anointed one for healing. Meeting in tent afternoon and at night. Six professions. I preached at night and made the altar call. One of the city preachers lectured in the court house tonight against the doctrine I am preaching at tent but I had the crowd, or at least the tent was full as usual.

September 18

Meetings today as usual. While I was preaching tonight a lady fell under the power in the congregation and received the baptism with the Holy Ghost. Numbers of strong men and some women came into the altar when I gave the invitation. Quite a number were down under the power speaking in tongues, praising God and greatly shaking, etc. etc. Two received the baptism and about four professions. The whole congregation seemed much affected.

September 19

Three meetings today. I suppose over 2,000 people out tonight. Altar crowded but not so much apparent results as at other times. Two received the baptism. One man came fifty miles to get religion. He got it today but he don't want to leave without the Holy Ghost. This meeting is a general talk for miles every direction. Preached once.

September 20

This has sure been a busy day for me. I preached a funeral at nine o' clock this morning, again at 11:30 at tent, at the baptizing pool at 2:30 and at tent at night again. Four sermons, prayed for the healing of one, baptized 25. The power of God was manifest wonderfully at the water. Several thousand there. Thousands at tent at night, too. Two received the baptism with the Holy Ghost and two professions. People are throwing down church rules and pride and going the lowly way with Jesus. Glory.

September 21

Held meeting at tent afternoon and at night. I preached two sermons. Two received the baptism and three professions.

September 22

Held meeting at tent afternoon and at night. I preached two sermons. One profession and two baptized with the Holy Ghost.

September 23

Held meetings at tent afternoon and at night. Three professions. I preached at night. Wonderful meetings. Glory, glory. Brother Mitchell came back here today from Ohio.

September 24

Held cottage meeting, anointed three for healing. Meeting at tent afternoon and at night. Two baptized with the Holy Ghost. I preached at night.

September 25

Was woked last night about an hour after I had gone to bed to pray for a gentlemen who wanted salvation. Held cottage meeting A.M. and at tent afternoon and at night. I preached two sermons. Four baptized with the Holy Ghost and four professions. The fire is still spreading for miles and miles in every direction.

September 26

Meeting at tent and afternoon and at night. Glorious success. I preached at night. A show put up on the opposite side of the street but we held the crowd and they tore down their tent and retired apparently very much embarrassed. Ten professions and four baptized.

September 27

Meeting at tent nearly all day with but very little intermission. I preached two sermons. Powerful meetings and big crowds. People from twenty miles in the country. Wonderful meetings. Four baptized with the Holy Ghost and four professions. Wonders and signs are being done. Glory.

September 29

Meeting afternoon and at night. I preached two sermons. Two professions and one received the Baptism.

October 1

Meeting yesterday and today at tent as usual, One profession and one baptism. I preached two sermons. Weather cold but the people about fill the tent every night.

October 3

Meetings going right on at tent. Tonight was indeed a wonderful meeting. I can hardly describe it. First was a prayer after singing then received the offering, then received nine into the church with great freedom and joy. Then we prayed a concert prayer for an old man a sinner, he was saved, then shouts, praises, well words are short. At the proper time I made the announcements and preached on the near and soon coming of our Lord, the altar was filled. Five professions, one baptized with the Holy Ghost and one brother fell under the power and a sweep of glory came down in our midst and about 12 or 14 were under the power at the same time. 8 or 9 were down at once and several conversations were held in unknown tongues, prophesying the soon coming of the Lord. Three years was definitely given for some sign. We did not get in until about one.

October 4

Meeting at tent 10 A.M. Baptized 20 at the pool afternoon. I preached at night and administered the sacrament and feet washing. The tent was packed and jammed and many, many outside. I sure had great responsibilities but the Lord gave me great victory and wisdom.

October 6

Had no meeting yesterday, took the tent down and repaired it. Held meeting again tonight at tent. Five professions and one baptized. Nights cool but a good crowd. I preached.

October 7

I preached at tent at night.

October 8

Rained, but we had meeting at tent afternoon and at night. I preached two sermons. One profession, several at altar.

October 11

Held three meetings at tent. I preached three sermons. Good meetings all day,

October 12

Held meetings at tent. I preached at night.

October 13

Held meetings at tent. I preached at night.

October 14

Held meetings at tent. Closed out tonight after a ten weeks successful battle. 225 professions and 163 received the baptism of the Holy Ghost. 78 baptized in water. 106 accession to the church. Quite a number healed. We moved the meeting to the church for Saturday night. We had a glorious meeting tonight. About 75 in the altar. At one moment the power fell upon some of us and nearly everybody in the tent were on their feet in an instant. Two professions and one baptized with the Holy Ghost. A large number testified to saving, sanctifying power and filling. One scene was very striking when about fifteen men walked out just in front of me who had been delivered from drunkeness by the power of God. While they all raised their hands heavenward, I also lifted my hands up and in a short prayer thanked God for them and asked God to keep them true. Glory. Well, I cannot describe the meeting but it was a wonderful meeting from start to finish. How they all love God and me and how I love all of them God only knows.

October 18

I am very tired and much worn with the toils today and last night but I have the pleasure of knowing I have done my duty. Had a glorious meeting last night. Much power manifested. Several at altar. The meeting this afternoon, divine healing service, was glorious and victorious. After I preached I think 13 came forward for healing. The power fell as we anointed and prayed for them and some said they were instantly healed. I believe it was the finest service I ever held on that line. The house crowded. After this service a few of us went down to South Cleveland and held a little service and three professions. Then back up to the church again at night. Good meeting but I was so much worn I could not press the battle so as to do as much as was needed, but some at the altar. Glory. I preached three sermons last night, and today. Six came into the church.

October 21

I preached short sermon at night at church.

October 26

Had meeting Saturday night and yesterday was indeed a full day. I married a couple at 9:20, attended Sunday school at 9:30 and taught a class, preached at eleven, went to a home at 1:30 and anointed and prayed for a little was sick, at 1:40 baptized three, at 2:30 I preached again on divine healing and anointed seven and prayed for nine for healing. Meeting again at night. Preached four sermons. Received four into the church.

November 2

I went with others a week ago today to Union Grove, held a few meetings with the saints, came home Saturday and was here over Sunday. Preached seven sermons. Yesterday afternoon I preached or rather told the reason why I could not belong to lodges or secret orders. Last night we received nine into the church. Had a glorious service last night. One profession and several under the power.

November 10

I went to Chattanooga on Monday, November 2, and remained till Saturday. Preached eight sermons. I was here at home for Saturday night and Sunday. Sunday the meeting hardly broke after Sunday school commenced at 9:30 a.m. until about ten o'clock at night. No preaching in the first service after Sunday school. We knelt to pray and before we ever arose from our knees the power fell, people talking and praying in tongues and while yet on my knees I made the altar call and part of that was in tongues. The altar was filled and some fell under the power and was wrought on very much by the Spirit. Very many manifestations. During the service a message was brought to me to come and pray for a woman who was, as they said about to die, as soon as I felt like I could leave the service I took Brother Clark and went to see what was wanted. On arrival I found her suffering intensely and she had had no sleep for two nights. We knelt to pray, I anointed her and began to pray but instead of praying with intellegible words it was a paroxysm of groans and cries. Brother Clark was able to pray some. Deathly silence was in the room aside from our prayers and groans. Before we ceased and had taken our hands off of her she affirmed that the pains were gone and that she was at perfect rest. We returned to the church house where I had previously announced that I would preach on divine healing. It was 2:30 P.M. and the house was crowded. I preached in the power and I could feel my flesh twitch and move on my bones. I referred to the gift of healing, how I desired it but never had obtained it. I spoke of the need of it in the Church, that suffering humanity might be relieved. I made an altar call for all who desired the gift to come to the altar and pray definitely for this gift. I suppose forty or fifty gathered around me so I barely had standing room. A glorious scene followed. At about the close of the prayer a brother came to me and asked for healing for his baby. A chair was placed for him, he sat down with it and we gathered around him to anoint it and pray. The others did the praying but I anointed it with oil and I could do but little else but cry and groan under agonizing cries while our hands were upon it. From this then there followed, I suppose, fifteen or twenty, one and two at a time who came for healing. I could do but little else than anoint and lay my hands on the patients and cry while the other brethren prayed. Some testified to instant relief; while others made no statements at all. But the power was there greatly. One handkerchief was laid in the chair, anointed and prayed over and sent to one who was sick. I will add that she was at the meeting at night. This work continued until dark and the people were gathering for night service. Some of us had eaten no dinner so we slipped out a few minutes and took some refreshment. When I returned the house was packed and I had barely room to stand while I preached. The climax of the day was reached at night when a brother suddenly shouted out at the top of his voice and the power fell so extensively that all most instantly the whole congregation arose to a standing position and I think 200 people were shouting, leaping, clapping their hands and talking and praising God in tongues all at once. The demonstrations were wonderful. The altar was full of seekers. Two sermons.

November 26, Eleven P. M.

On the tenth of the month I left home for Chattanooga. Had a wonderful meeting there that night. Preached two sermons there. Then on the 12th I went to Memphis, Tennessee, 310 miles to a Pentecostal convention. While there I preached ten sermons. Organized the Church there, helped to ordain one, Brother Goins of Florence, Alabama. This brings into the work very soon several churches, also bids fair to get a number of churches into the same body in South Carolina and one or more in China. Several received the baptism with the Holy Ghost, some sanctified and some converted. The fire fell the second service and one man rose right up while I was preaching and received the Holy Ghost and the remarkable part of that meeting was that the last part of the text was preached by the Holy Ghost by His own demonstrations by a number of people under the Spirit performing their part instead of my words from my mouth. Glorious meetings. I came to Chattanooga again on the 24th, then on home yesterday. Had meeting at the church here last night. Had a wonderful time again. During my sermon I broke down and went to crying and the Holy Ghost caught up Homer, my own son, and he went to preaching in Tongues until he and I and others fell under deep groans and weeping and praying. This continued for some length of time when was really demonstrating the last part of my text after while I was able to finish my sermon and close the meeting. Today now has been a wonderful day. Thanksgiving Day. Commenced meeting at 10:00 A. M. Had singing, preaching and testimonies until noon, then just outside the house we spread a great dinner, then came in, sang, took up the offering and received 15 into the Church and continued the testimonies and then received two more into the church and then at night again received eight more, making 45 in all. To describe these services would not be possible. Wonderful, but that does not tell it. Songs, shouts, speaking in tongues, giving right hand of fellowship, testimonies, tears of thanksgiving, preaching. Well, I can't tell it. I conducted all the services. Preached two short sermons. Praise the Lord.

December 19

I just arrived home night before last after an absence of about three weeks holding a meeting at Sobel, Tennessee, about forty miles northwest of Nashville. Six professions and nine received the baptism with the Holy Ghost. While there I preached 23 sermons. Brother White and Sister Clyde Cotton were helpers with me there. The Lord gave us great liberty and victory. Came to Chattanooga Thursday evening where I preached one sermon. We had some hardships to undergo at the meeting near Sobel, but only count them as light afflictions. I am home again now as far as I know until after holidays and the annual assembly.

December 19

Nearly 12 at night. Just home from church. The first night I came home I heard of some trouble in the church and I came upstairs but not to sleep until just a little nap just before day. I feel tonight a great meeting is the result of the night of prayer. God gave us wonderful victory. One sanctified and baptized with the Holy Ghost and spoke in tongues a good deal. One or two converted. Great victory among the saints. I don't know how to describe the meeting. I preached one sermon.

December 20

Taught a class in Sunday school. Preached afternoon and at night. Altar was crowded with seekers. Two sanctified and one or two professions. House full. Two sermons. God victory in the meetings.

December 23

Preached at the church at night.

December 24

Preached a little sermon of welcome at night for the children's Christmas meeting.

December 25

Held Christmas meeting morning and at night. I preached two sermons. One received the Holy Ghost and several at the altar and some got wonderfully blest. Baptized one in water.

December 26

Preached the funeral of a little child. Preached at night. Big congregations.

December 27

Taught a class in Sunday school. Held meeting afternoon and at night. Preached two sermons, 12 or 15 at altar.

December 28

Commenced a ten days Bible school at the church house. Preached at night. Only a few out on account of rain but wonderful demonstrations of the Spirit. Conversations were held in tongues. Several of us under the power in agonizing prayer, talking in tongues, etc.

December 29

Conducted the Bible school and preached at night. Nothing special took place only God wonderfully helped ne to preach.

December 30

Taught in the Bible school and held testimony service at night and were on our knees at midnight and prayed the old year out and the new one in. 340 sermons this year.

1909

January 1, 1909

Preached a funeral at 8:00 A. M. Held the Bible school all day and preached at night. One saved from sin and one baptized with the Holy Ghost.

January 2

Held a church business meeting and council to consider the case of J. H. Simpson who has been causing us trouble by division and offences and contentions for several months. After considerable persuasion on our part I finally could bear it no longer. I fell on my knees and prayed and cried and my wife cried and prayed and others did the same after which I got up and went to him, and took his hand and with many tears and heart rending cries I bid him good by and told him we would meet at the Judgment and I wanted to part with no malice or hatred but love and pity. After this scene the Church took action and excluded him on the charge brought against him Romans 16:17. On top of this action God gave us a wonderful meeting at night. Tongues and interpretations, much demonstrations and power. House was crowded. Among others my son Homer gave a message in tongues which was interpreted to mean, "Jesus is coming soon. Get ready. Those who are not ready are going to hell," etc. The power of intercessory prayer fell on me and I fell off my seat and commenced groaning and praying in tongues and strong crying and tears.

January 3

Taught a Sunday school class. Held meeting afternoon and at night. One received the baptism with the Holy Ghost. House crowded. Wonderful meetings. A large ball of fire was seen pass across the front of the church house outside. Another sign was seen in the heavens. Brother Woodworth from Virginia was with us and preached. I cannot describe the power and demonstrations in the night meeting before the preacher arrived.

January 4

Taught the Bible school all day. Meeting at night. The Spirit gave the interpretation of two or three short messages for the first, clear. One saved from sin. Great power and demonstrations. Bible school was wonderful too. Homer is wonderfully used by the Holy Ghost, too. Preached.

January 5

Taught the Bible school all day. Preached at night. Two professions and one baptized with Holy Ghost.

January 6

Taught Bible school all day. Meeting at night. Four professions, one baptized with Holy Ghost.

January 7

Assembly opened today. I act as clerk and chairman. Harmonious action all day.

January 8

I led the meeting last night and tonight. No one preached tonight but a wonderful meeting. Three baptized with the Holy Ghost, one profession. Some healed. Wonderful, glory.

January 9

Church meeting and Assembly. I was selected as general superintendent of all the ministers and churches by the Assembly and moderator for the Assembly for another year. Glorious meeting at night. One saved.

January 10

Taught a Sunday school class. Delivered address and ordained two bishops and five deacons and the house was packed and people stood for hours. As I made altar call 20 or more came in. The days fruits was four converted and four baptized with the Holy Ghost . Wonderful. The ordination service was wonderful powerful. Glory to Jesus.

January 13

Held ministerial council. Meetings at night. Some healed and some converted.

January 15

Visiting sick, writing and having meeting at night. Preached two sermons.

January 18

I was unanimously selected pastor for another year by the church at Cleveland Saturday night. Yesterday I taught Sunday school class and preached afternoon and night. Two sermons. The Lord gave me wonderful messages. House crowded. Altar packed. I preached with great victory. Cried during altar service. Numbers of old men seeking the baptism of the Holy Ghost. I got up the night before and built a fire and was greatly exercised in prayer for hours. The devil is raging against us. Men are trying to overthrow the work. J. B. Simpson, who has been excluded from the church for causing divisions and offences contrary to the doctrine is doing much damage and harm. The Lord will reward him according to his works. I feel so sorry for him and his precious family. May God overrule it all for good. Went to look after the poor and supply them today, to pray for sick at night and to a prayer meeting at a cottage.

January 20

Held meeting at church at night. Good work done.

January 23

Held meeting at church at night. House crowded. Brother Hackett preached.

January 24

Taught a Sunday school class. Preached afternoon and at night. Two sermons. Altar crowded afternoon. At night a very peculiar incident occurred. During the testimony meeting Mrs. Julia Simpson arose and after a very few words of testimony she began a tirade against the church and especially against me. I sat quiet and listened until she was about to sit down and I called for a song, when she suddenly returned and said she wanted to say some more and I said, say on until you get through. When she was through and after the song I quietly arose and gave the message God had given me before with joy and victory, not alluding one moment to the words of Mrs. Simpson, although some might have thought I was referring to what she said but I did not mean it that way for the message was given me before I knew anything her intentions even to talk. The house was crowded with people but I believe the Lord will work it all out for good. I have no spirit of revenge in my heart but I do feel so sorry for Mr. and Mrs. Simpson and their children. I don't know what will become of them. I am going to pray for them and be as kind to them as I can.

January 27

I conducted the meeting at night. Preached a short sermon. Several in altar. Good meeting. Several spoke in tongues. Last night went out in the country and held a prayer service.

January 28

Seven of us went out in the country had a prayer service with a blind girl. We felt that the Spirit taught us some good lessons in battling with demons. We afterward prayed in another room and I was very much exercised in prayer, intercession and groaning. Also after we started I got down in the road again under the same agonizing crys but not quite so severe. We held a church business meeting at night. I acted as moderator. Business transacted with love and harmony.

February 1

Weather has been very cold for a few days. Held meeting Saturday night, taught a Sunday school class yesterday, held meeting yesterday afternoon and last night. Not so large attendance as usual on account of cold. I preached three sermons. J. H. Simpson is still giving trouble and doing much harm. God have mercy on him and pity him. He has written me some very sharp, cutting letters, making threats, etc., and demands $66.00 the amount he and his wife and father put in the house when it was built.

February 3

Meeting at night. Preached one sermon.

February 6

Meeting at night. Preached one sermon.

February 7

Held Sunday school, taught a class. Meeting afternoon and at night. Preached two sermons. The Lord gave us wonderful meetings. Tongues and the interpretations. Homer is being used wonderfully with others. Several in altar. One baptized with the Holy Ghost. Glory, glory, glory.

February 11

Two days ago I went to the mountains to help Brothers Mitchell and Bryant give out a lot of presents to the poor children and to preach to all who came. I suppose there were at least 700 people there. When I got to the station it was raining and no one to meet me so I had a two hours walk in the rain and mud and carried a sack of Testaments across my shoulder. Yesterday was bright and nice though the wind was cool. About 500 children were made glad because of the gifts of toys, nuts, candy, etc. The older people were given Bibles, Testaments and books. I came home last night and preached here. Two sermons.

February 15

This is Monday morning. Held meeting Saturday night. Taught a Sunday school class, held meeting yesterday afternoon and last night. The Lord wonderfully helped me in preaching. The church house was crowded. Preached three sermons. Rainy this morning.

February 16

Last night after supper, we, with Brother Bryant who had just come home, were singing. We heard Homer, my 16-year-old son, up stairs in agonizing prayer. We soon left off singing and went up stairs. Homer was caught away under the power and control of the Spirit. He had been agonizing in prayer when he suddenly arose on his knees and quoted the text, "If you love me, keep my commandments and I'll pray the Father and He will give you another Comforter," etc. in a tongue, which was interpreted by Brother Bryant. From this text he preached a sermon in a foreign language, then he made his altar call, and it appeared that numbers came forward and began to get saved. Then he went through great extacies [sic] of joy over the salvation of souls. Pen cannot describe the scene. The language was clear and distinct. Others in the town are very frequently caught away in the Spirit in a similar way. While the devil is raging, yet God is blessedly working. Sick are being healed, devils cast out, etc., etc.

February 17

Held prayer meeting at church at night.

February 19

I am fasting now for two or three days, waiting on the Lord for His best.

February 20

Meeting at night. Several messages given in tongues and the Holy Spirit gave the interpretations through me. Wonderful meeting, 15 or more came into altar. One profession and one baptized with the Holy Ghost. House full of people.

February 21

Taught a class in Sunday school. Held meeting afternoon and at night. The Holy Ghost gave more messages in tongues and the interpretations through me. Several in altar at night, one saved. Preached two sermons.

February 25

This is Thursday. I was called to Chattanooga Monday evening. The women gathered in at Brother Lemons to talk and hear me talk about Jesus and spiritual things. We had prayer service. The next day at a meeting I anointed five or six for healing and at night we met again for services and the power of God fell upon us so we could not close until near midnight. I gave several interpretations after messages were given in tongues. Wonderful meeting. I came home yesterday and went to our meeting last night. Weather bad and but few out but He gave us a wonderful meeting again. I am wondering what the Lord is going to do for us. Preached four sermons.

February 27

Meeting at night. I preached one sermon.

February 28

Taught Sunday school class. Preached afternoon, held meeting at night. House crowded.

March 8

I led the meeting last Wednesday night. Had a wonderful meeting Saturday night. Several messages given in tongues and the Holy Spirit used me to give the interpretations. The Spirit fell on the congregation and they shouted, praised God, stood up and well it is indescribable. Several in altar. I taught a Sunday school class yesterday morning. Held meeting in afternoon. Just had a sermon but it seemed to be very impressive. Had another wonderful meeting again last night. Testamonies, shouts, praises, messages in tongues with the interpretations, sermon and altar service. During the sermon messages were given at intervals in tongues and I gave the interpretations and continued right on with the discourse without the least bit of confusion. It was indeed wonderful. The Spirit indicated that workers were to go out from this place, north, east, south and west and said, "separate unto me those whom I want for the work whereunto I have called them." Only Brother Castret was personated, saying "I will be with you and make you a success." I preached three sermons. The Book of Acts is being reproduced.

March 10

Held meeting at night. Several messages in tongues and the Lord used me to interpret. The Holy Ghost gave Brother Tom McLain a special message of encouragement. Wonderful meeting.

March 11

Brother R. F. Winsett is teaching a singing school here at the church and giving my children training at home.

March 16

This is Tuesday. The meeting Saturday night was not well attended on account of the bad weather. But I preached a short sermon. Sunday morning I taught Sunday school class. Afternoon the house was full. I preached, using a map of the world I had prepared last week. Sunday night I preached again to a crowded house. Afternoon while I was preaching some messages were given in tongues and I gave the interpretations. These fit in just right. At night some message were given in tongues and I gave the interpretations. One was to Brother Falvius Lee. In giving the interpretation I knelt down right before him and as the message was given he fell off his chair and was very much affected. Sister Clyde Cotton gave the message in tongues. I must say, too, that last Friday evening the Holy Ghost, through Sister Clyde, gave me a special message which lasted about three hours. Brother Bryant came in during the time and gave part of the interpretations. I understood a good deal of it. He was showing and telling me something of my future work. Told me of several countries I was to carry the gospel to besides a lot of work in the United States and America. Also gave blessings and encouragement to my wife and children. Last night I preached at a private house on the opposite side of town. I expect to go to Chattanooga this evening.

March 21

I came from Chattanooga yesterday where I preached three sermons. In one meeting I suppose I have ten or fifteen interpretations. A wonderful meeting. The power was wonderful. I preached three sermons here last night, this afternoon and tonight. Some healed too. One received the baptism and two professions. Big crowds. Taught Sunday school class this A.M.

March 28

Preached at a funeral service last week. Preached at church last night. Taught a Sunday school class A.M. Preached afternoon.

March 29

About 10 o'clock Brother Mitchell offered to give me $15.00 to go with him to Cincinnati. With a very short time for consideration I decided to go, so I packed my suitcase and was off at 4:30 p.m.

March 30

Arrived in Cincinnati about 8 o'clock this morning. In a few hours Brother Mitchel took train and went on home. I remained and attended a Pentecostal mission afternoon, and another one at night. Both in the city. I was not very favorably impressed with either one of them although there seemed to be some good people in them.

March 31

I left Cincinnati, Ohio for Cambridge City, Ind. I walked out from there and took dinner with Mary's sister Martha and visited Omer Taylor and his father and uncle, and in the evening went over to see Murray. He took me to a Friends meeting at Dublin at night.

April 1

I boarded interurban car at Dublin and went to Indianapolis, met Will Pruitt and from there to the home of Will Sawyer. In the evening I phoned up to Westfield and talked with Let and mother and heard Aunt Esther's voice. I went at night to the Pentecostal mission in the city and gave them a short address. I was with them a while before they knew me.

April 2

Went from Indianapolis to Westfield. Brother Cyrus Carey met me at station. When I arrived at mother's Uncle Noah, Aunt Esther and some others were there. Mother and all were glad to see me and I was indeed glad to see them for I had been away nearly six years.

April 3

Visited with Mother. Kizzie and Lizzie came there to see me. Had a good home like time.

April 4

I went to Chester to Sunday school and meeting. They invited me to preach which I did as the Lord directed. The Lord gave a very impressive message and all seemed to be helped by it.

April 5

Abbie took me to see Aunt Asenith and sister Ella and Harry. Had a very good day. Talked over phone with Wesley Hiatt, Carl and Alice. Yes, I must say that Sunday Mother and others with myself took dinner with Cyrus and Abbie and Aunt Esther. Elwood T. came after me and I went to his home and stayed a little while. Went back to mother's at night.

April 6
Was with Mother I believe all day.

April 7
Went to midweek meeting at Chester. Was at Uncle Noah's a little while last evening, saw Zeruah and Jim, Robert and Julia, Morton and Mary. Mortons came to Mother's a little while at night. Wesley Bond took me to the train in the evening and I went to Indianapolis to hold meetings at the Pentecostal mission for a few days. Stayed with Will Sawyer. Preached two sermons at Chester. Went to Indianapolis and preached six sermons there.

April 14
I talked a few words with Mother and Let last evening over the phone and told them goodby. I took the Interurban car at Indianapolis bound for Louisville, Ky. Bought my ticket there for Florence, Alabama. Stopped at Nashville, Tennessee over night. While at Indianapolis God gave me favor with the people, and I was at the homes of William Alexander, Brother Osborn and D. M. Bye. One sister healed, Brother Sawyer received the baptism of the Holy Ghost a day or two after I left his home. So I don't feel that my work there was an entire failure.

April 15
I arrived at Florence, Alabama where I began meeting at once with Brother John B. Goins. Continued there 11 days. Sister Clyde Cotton came two days after I arrived and helped me through the meeting. About twelve or more special miraculous cases of healing. Two professions, four received the Holy Ghost, some restored, four received the gifts of healing. Completed the organization of the church and ordained three deacons. The Lord gave us some wonderful meetings. While at Mother's the Lord gave me $2.25. At Indianapolis He gave me $1.00 and a ladies gold watch. A sister handed me a package saying she wanted me to relieve her of the package, not understanding I took it, put it in my pocket and after I got to my boarding place I opened it and found it was a nice gold watch. The lady was an entire stranger to me that gave me the watch. At Florence He gave me $15 and some stationery.

April 26
Held meeting last night until nearly twelve and then boarded the train for home, stopped at Chattanooga a little while to see

Brother Lemons. Arrived home about 5 P.M. While at Florence, Alabama I preached 20 sermons.

April 28

I started for Tampa, Florida. Home long enough to counsel my dear wife and children and some of the church and exhort them to continue steadfast in the faith. While on the train I was taken very sick with bloody flux. Brother T. L. McLain was with me. When we arrived in Atlanta I was so bad I could hardly sit up and it was past nine at night. We finally got to the home of Sister Sexton where they prayed for me and I was healed. We came on that night and arrived at Tampa, Florida at 6:00 p.m. the following day, April 29. Commenced in tent the meeting the same night. Held three meetings a day ever since except one day it rained.

May 5

I am feeling very well but we have not been able to break through much yet. The devil seems to be arrayed heavily against us. Some at altar and probably a drunkard converted but I have had no real liberty yet in preaching and we have not yet been able to reach victory in prayer. Have preached ten sermons up to date.

May 10

This is Monday morning. Have held meetings in the tent every day and night since above date here in Tampa. The dear Lord is giving us blessed victory. The saints are getting freedom that they have been deprived of because of being held down by their leaders. Yesterday was wonderful. But little intermission between services. I did not get to rest until after midnight. Preached three times. The tent was about full last night. Many very serious. Some in altar. Once received the Holy Ghost yesterday. A gentleman down under the power when we left last night. Brother McLain is a good helper. Is on the floor here by my side under the power of intercession now, almost like the agonies of death. He has just now broke out in tongues, in a plain language, now singing in tongues. I can hardly describe the meeting yesterday . Glory to Jesus. God is now burdening my heart for the means so I can get the company together as soon as possible that God is preparing, so we can stay together. Am receiving more invitations for work. Have preached nine more sermons.

May 13

This Thursday before meeting. Have preached seven more sermons. Am still here at Tampa. The work is progressing slowly on account of so much prejudice, but those who come are evidently being considerably impressed. The volley of questions that were poured into me yesterday nearly all day was wonderful. Afternoon during the discourse they asked anything that came to them with honest purpose to get things clear. It never bothered me in the least, only added to the fire. At the close of the discourse we knelt to pray. I prayed in tears and some one took up the prayer and I fell over under the power of travailing prayer and agonizing cries. I lay there under the power agonizing and talking in tongues, etc., until about dark. Probably an hour and a half or two hours. At the night meeting as it opened I was seized again with weeping but when the time came for preaching the Lord had me ready. The Lord put me through with plenty of truth and toward the close with a flood of tears. The altar call was made and they began to come in, when a man rose up in the congregation and asked for the privilege to ask some questions. I told him kindly that we would hear him privately but not now as we had to deal with these souls at the altar, but he insisted that he ask the questions publicly. But he was finally silenced and I called for the singing to proceed and he left the tent. I perceived it was a scene of the devil to hurt the meeting which it did apparently for a little bit. But God is with us and helping and one man was restored and evidently sanctified and was lying under the power when we had to leave him at midnight. Glory.

May 17

This is Monday. I am resting after a hard days work yesterday. I preached three times yesterday besides the other work and at midnight last night I was too tired to sleep. We set the Lord's church in order yesterday at Tampa, Florida with about 20 members. A great crowd out last night. Friday afternoon: The power fell upon several of us and while we were down they told me a man ran into the tent saying he was Jesus, one or two of the sisters began to talk to him in tongues and he was about to hit one of them with his fist when a man jumped in and prevented it. They continued to talk to him in tongues till he left. A woman came in and as she appeared to be looking on the scene with scorn a sister broke out to talking to her in tongues and she seized a club and was about to strike the sister when a man, who appeared to be her husband, caught her and took her away. The demonstrations and power were wonderful. The Lord has sure given me a favor here with lots of the people. Numbers have been convinced. A lady came to me last night and said she came to scoff but was caught and begged me to pray for her. The crowds have increased wonderfully. We closed the meeting at the tent last night to get ready for the camp meeting at Pleasant Grove. I am to preach in the mission tonight and tomorrow night here in the city, then go to the camp ground ready for the camp meeting Thursday. I feel that if the meeting here could have continued for a month or more that great good could be accomplished. Preached 9 more sermons.

May 22

We are now at the Pleasant Grove camp ground. Came yesterday. We have a furnished house specially arranged for the preachers. We appreciate it so much, out to itself where we can be alone with God. The meeting commenced yesterday morning in the first service with good earnest. While I was preaching the power fell and what shrieks and screams and agonizing cries are seldom heard, which lasted for several minutes and then I made the altar call and the people piled in. Two received the baptism and some reported converted. The afternoon meeting went right through without any preaching. I can hardly describe it. Last night the only preaching I done was to step up on the altar and read a short message given in tongues, the interpretation of which I had written. I followed the reading with a few words of exhortation and made the altar call, and when I looked down to see about changing my position I could get no where. So I stood there while altar work continued with loud cries, shrieks and much prayer until some fell then I was able to sit down on the altar in the midst of the seekers where I remained until about midnight giving instructions and interpretations. Wonderful meetings. The Lord has promised us great things here if we will be humble and obedient. Preached four more sermons.

May 24

The Lord gave us wonderful meetings yesterday and last night. Altar crowded with seekers. I can hardly describe the manifestations. Several are being healed nearly every day. Brother McLain and myself feel very tired in body. We were up till about two last night and then had to pray for some early this morning and then into meeting and still lots of work to do. Seven more sermons.

May 27

Yesterday was a wonderful day in the camp. In the beginning of the service in the morning one or two messages were given in tongues and I gave the interpretation. Afterward I was seized with two or three paroxisms of weeping, when finally I fell on my back under the power and after screaming for a while as though my heart would break, I became more quiet when a brother spoke a few words in tongues and they said I gave the interpretation which was, "Get quiet and hear me speak." Immediately following this a sister began to speak in tongues and the interpretations followed, then tongues in a few words and then the few words interpreted alternately until the sentence was finished. This lasted I was told for half an hour. When she ceased some one else spoke a few minutes and the interpretations followed, then another and another and another. Some one said I was down in that condition for two hours. That was all the preaching that was done. The altar was filled with seekers crying out to God when I rose up. Afternoon Brother Evans read a text from the Bible and said a few words and sit down and I took it up and preached a little while when a brother rose up and made some confessions and was willing to step out wholly for Jesus, and as he sat down I started to sing "Where He Leads me I will follow," etc. and soon a man tumbled into the altar all broken up, a lady fell in as though she had been shot and they kept piling in until the altar was filled. The meeting never closed until about midnight. Can't describe all of it. Men, women and children screaming, shouting, praying, leaping, dancing and falling prostrate on the straw. Wonderful. Preached 6 more sermons.

May 28

I must write a few words about the meeting yesterday. Yesterday morning I went as usual and started the meeting and as I waited on the Lord the work began by testimonies, tongues and interpretations, and I just sit there and looked on. People soon began to be prostrated under the power. Never did make any altar call but they were piled around at the altar and all about in the front of the tabernacle. Then one by one they came to me for prayer for some disease. We would kneel each time and deliverance came. Afternoon I preached on the Church under the power of the Spirit and finally gave opportunity for people to join. 64 presented themselves with shouts, praises, tears, sobs, etc. Wonderful will not tell it. The greatest time of Church joining I ever saw yet. The Holy Ghost in messages through others gave the assurance that this was going to spread and that the real Christian people every where would see and flow together. We repaired to the creek nearby where I baptized one who had to go away. The real baptismal service will take place D. V. Saturday afternoon. Last night I went and sat down and the fire began to fall, and one received the Holy Ghost and people fell into the altar and in the aisles and at their seats and the work went on until about midnight with no preaching. Four or more baptized with Holy Ghost. Night before the Lord woke me and for about two hours probably between one and three I was exercised in prayer and tears agonizing for the work. I am paid well for the loss of sleep.

May 29

The meetings yesterday and last night were wonderful again. Yesterday morning I lay under the power on my back I suppose for an hour giving interpretations. A number were laying around under the slaying power. At 3:00 p. m. I was requested to preach on the Church again and a number of questions were asked and answered. I guess about 35 joined the Church. A number of ministers from other churches. It is wonderful how the Lord added the people to His Church. A number were put forward for examination for the ministry. Last night while sitting in my place at the beginning of the meeting waiting on the Lord about a message or directions some way about the meeting. While they were singing a sister Wood came and spoke to me in tongues and God gave me the understanding of the message which was being interpreted, "Tell the people the mystery of my work and what I will do." I supposed He meant for me to preach so I arose at the proper time and stated what the Spirit said, and said I did not know just what to begin to say but trusted the Lord would direct and show us His will. At that moment two sisters rose up back in the congregation side by side and one began to speak in tongues and the Spirit through me gave the interpretation promptly, then the other one spoke in tongues and the interpretation was given and this manner was continued for some little time, then the two sisters went to several different persons in the tabernacle and delivered messages in tongues, sometimes in concert and I gave the interpretation of every message. At last the sister took me by the hand and we began to walk toward the platform and she was talking in tongues. As we three walked together the interpretation was "These are they that follow the Lamb whithersoever he goeth and they shall walk with me in white." As I sat down in the stand she lay her land on my head and save me a message that was not interpreted openly but I was made to understand it. She then turned to the audience and delivered a short message to them and gave the interpretation of what she said but did not quite finish and I rose at once and completed the interpretation which was, "And this is the mystery I wanted to show you and if you want to see me come to the altar." The altar was at once filled with seekers praying and crying out to God, I felt as if I never wanted to return to the common feeling and ways of life again. I really dreaded to speak naturally again. Preached one more sermon.

June 1

I am in Jacksonville, Florida, this morning. Came here yesterday from Durant. This is Tuesday. Last Saturday at the Camp meeting I spent about eight hours examining candidates for the ministry. In the evening I baptized 42 persons. The meeting Saturday night lasted nearly all night. Sunday at the first service we received forty or fifty into the Church. Then I preached, showing my chart, on the condition of the world, etc., and the offering for missions was about fifty dollars. While I preached some fell into the altar. Afternoon I gave the charge to the ministers and ordained six bishops and six deacons and set apart seven evangelists and six for Christian workers. Big day. Preached at night and closed the meeting about one o'clock at night. They gave me near one hundred dollars for month's work and about the same to Brother McLain. We are now on our way to Atlanta to commence the camp meeting tonight. Preached three more sermons. About 25 received the Holy Ghost and several converted and reclaimed.

June 11

Have been here in Atlanta now for ten days. Have only preached three times up to date. Have sure had a time of suffering here. The devil has prejudiced the people against me here from some cause. Others have been doing preaching and a lot of people can hardly bear me but I go right on as though nothing was the matter. The Holy Spirit makes me understand that it is not me they are against but Him in me. I've sure shed a lot of tears and suffered much in agonizing prayers, not for myself, for I have not pitied myself, but for others. One man has already confessed to me but I told the Lord to not let folks confess to me but to confess to Him for it was not me they had wronged but Him. I believe everything will come out right. I am getting just what I need. I believe God will give me a great victory over the devil yet. Glory. Halcy and Homer are here in the city and Homer has been with me most of the time since I came.

June 14

I am still in Atlanta. Don't seem like I am doing much good. The camp meeting services are now placed in my hands. I want to definitely give them over to the Holy Ghost. I want Him to have complete control. Preached last night, large crowd.

June 16

The power began to fall the first service. The people began to get free. Monday afternoon a little girl received the Holy Ghost and the night service followed the afternoon service immediately. Freedom and liberty prevailed. No preaching. Yesterday the services run very smoothly. Quite a few demonstrations. Some cried, others laughed and shouted. Messages given in tongues and interpreted. Last night was a sweet service. No regular order and yet perfect order. I sat on the platform and the singing was led by the Holy Ghost, testimonies also. One would lead a song and some one else in another part of the congregation would take up the next verse and the whole congregation would join until it would swell into volume so beautiful. This form continued as several songs were sung. The time came for me to give the message after which the altar was filled. Seven I think received the baptism in the last two days and nine during the two weeks before. I have preached four more sermons.

June 24

Meetings have been going on every day and night. Some times continuing from 6:00 A. M till 11:00 P. M. without closing. Many signs and wonders have been done by myself and Homer and Sister Clyde and others by the power of the Spirit. A brother had been seeking long but had failed to get through. I was led in the Spirit to go to him on my knees, stretch his hands out and nail them to the cross, then to fall over with him in my arms and go through the death struggle for him, then after I had been as though dead for a little bit I arose and appeared to pierce his side and cut off his head and then put him in the grave and cover him with dirt and he lay there a while quiet and then I made as if I moved the dirt from off of him and he was resurrected and I at that moment the power struck him and he went on till he received the baptism. It is wonderful what is taking place here. Yesterday afternoon after I had been preaching a little while the power fell and I fell into agonizing cries and when I opened my eyes again the altar was crowded with seekers. More than once the altar calls have been made in tongues by some one and I would give the interpretations. One night a sister stepped up on the altar by my side while I was preaching and gave messages in tongues and I gave the interpretations and into the altar they came. Fear is falling on the people. People are getting saved, sanctified and filled with the Spirit. Preached 13 sermons since last writing. I baptized 13 in water today.

June 28

Closed the camp meeting last night but had a baptizing and healing service this morning. Baptized 12. Made lots of friends. Preached four sermons. They say over 40 received the Holy Ghost. Several converted and some sanctified. This has been a hard battle but I feel that God has given us the victory. Have had some special experiences with deceivers and some of the saints being deceived and causing trouble in the meetings. The Holy Ghost has been equal to every emergency. Have received nearly or quite $60.00. Will leave the city D. V. tomorrow at three o'clock. Rainy this afternoon.

July 6

Homer, Halcy, Sister Clyde and myself left Atlanta June 29, arrived at Rome in the evening. Had three services there. One received the Holy Ghost and one sanctified. The folks begged us to stay longer but we felt it necessary to come on home which we did and arrived here July 1. Meeting at the church that night and one converted, no preaching. The next night the power fell and much good accomplished. Saturday night was good, one converted, others blessed. Sunday I taught the Sunday school class and held the meetings afternoon and at night. A blessed time, specially afternoon. Last night we ordained two brethren from Chattanooga. Prayed for the sick last night and today. Wonderful experiences. Preached eight sermons since last writing.

July 10

Been having meeting at church at night this week except one night at my home. The rain has prevented us pitching the tent yet but several are coming in for the meeting. Preached funeral yesterday.

July 13

Taught Sunday school class Sunday morning. Preached afternoon. Meeting at night. Yesterday I went out in the country, preached funeral of Sister Lee. Meeting again last night. Today I preached funeral sermon of a man who shot himself, Brother Goins and others came for the meeting.

July 16

Have received word that mother is very sick and will probably not recover. We put up the tent yesterday and commenced the meeting last night. It is in the center of town opposite the jail. A Mr. Beard came and demanded us to stop the work of pitching the tent with threats but we went right on. Last night just before service he came in to the tent and asked me to read a paper he had which I was about to do, but as soon as my eyes fell on the heading, "To the Holy Rollers" I positively refused to read the rest so I don't know what it was. But it created quite a sensation. God gave us a blessed service. We dedicated the place to God and as I offered the prayer the glory struck us and filled the tabernacle. I wept, others praised, others spoke in tongues. I preached part of the time with great joy and part of the time in tears. Several came to the altar. Quite a number asked for special prayer.

July 17

Meeting going on at tent. Great time tonight. Big crowd, quite a number at altar, one profession and two sanctified.

July 18

Went out in the country and preached a funeral, A. M. Held meetings at tent afternoon and at night. Great crowds. Three baptized and spoke in tongues, three sanctified.

July 20

Preached two sermons, one funeral and at tent at night. One profession five sanctified and four received the Holy Ghost. Having great meetings at our home every forenoon.

July 22

I was arrested last evening, charged with violating a city ordinance. Had the trial this afternoon in the court room. Big crowd, and a great time. The people seem to be determined to make us stop our meetings. I had the privilege of preaching some truth to the officers, lawyers, doctors as well as a lot of other folks on the witness stand. I took my Bible and proved that we were only doing according to its teachings. I got up from the witness chair and stood while I did it. I preached last night at tent, this afternoon in the court room and tonight at the tent. Three sermons. The verdict will not be rendered until Saturday.

July 23

Meetings going right on with power. Two professions. Four sanctified, four baptized with the Holy Ghost. Iris received the baptism. This puts all my family into the experience except little Milton who is yet too young.

July 24

The decision of the trial was a fine of five dollars and the cost. They threw off the fine but we appealed to a higher court and turned the cost on the city and gave bond. We had a wonderful meeting and very large crowd. Four professions, two received the baptism with the Holy Ghost.

July 25

Taught Sunday school class. Meetings at tent afternoon and night. I preached at night, and at a certain point in the discourse Homer gave a message in tongues and I gave the interpretation and another and another and all at once as the power fell most of the congregation rose right up almost as one man. The altar was about filled with seekers. Three baptized with the Holy Ghost, one sanctified. I was told there were at least 4,000 people at tent last night. Lots of people are very much affected. The devil is roaring.

August 1

Meeting going right on at tent. People still getting salvation and the baptism with the Holy Ghost. I preached tonight. I received a telegram this evening that mother was deceased. I wanted very much to go several days ago and wanted to go to the funeral, but on account of the meeting going on and the responsibilities here I could not get off. I feel like I have sacrificed going to see mother and bury her for the gospel's sake. God gives me grace and the comforter abides. Mother is the only mother I'll ever have and is loved much, but she had good care without me and the gospel is precious and souls are valuable beyond any price. I conversed with Mother about her future welfare when I was to see her last April and she said, "All is well." Mother was 82 years, seven months, two days old.

August 4

This morning at our house God gave us a wonderful meeting. After considerable praying and agonizing for lost souls, the victory seemed to have been won and Sister Clyde run to the organ and commenced playing in the power and some of us began to sing in the Spirit, and finally about a dozen I suppose were leaping, dancing and all keeping perfect time. Pen cannot describe the wonderful glory demonstrations and grandeur of the scene. A looker-on probably could describe it better than I can. It was indeed wonderful to me as I and Brother Flavius Lee sang in other tongues in perfect harmony and time with the music while the others kept the time as perfectly with their feet in what might be spoken of as dancing. At the close Brother McLain gave a message in tongues, interpreted that "this was only a foretaste of what He would do for us if we would perfectly yield up to Him and let Him have perfect control. Wonderful beyond expression. Glorious.

August 5

Gracious meetings today. We formed in line at our house in evening, (over thirty) and marched to tent, singing as we went, stopped at two places and Brother White, preached to the people who gathered around. I preached at tent. Some trouble in the audience about scattering pepper or something and broke up the meeting.

August 6

We marched to tent again at night, about 80 when we entered the tent. Had a good service. I preached. Several in altar. Some trouble again with pepper and hot drops. After the close of the meeting I had turned out the lights, and there was quite a crowd outside and a few of us were waiting when somebody began to cut the ropes and Brother Bryant ran out and told them to stop it but they handled him roughly and took him roughly by force from my side and then Mr. Beard came to me, having ordered the men to cut on, and asked me sharply what I had in my hand. I showed him and told him, "my Bible." When I showed him my Bible he seemed to mellow a little and talked a little more like a gentleman, and about that time the tent fell. One pole right on the organ, the other broke down through the paling fence and just missed Homer a few feet. Homer ran out and mounted the fence and stood up there and preached a sermon. Sister Gamble also preached them a sermon. Lots of people there by that time. Then I started a song and we all sang and praised the Lord a little while. The mob was still working about piling up the tent. Mr. Beard asked me a time or two if I would take it away if they would stop, saying it had to be moved from the ground. I answered him that I did not know what I would do, that the ground belonged to us and we had a right there. They started to pile it out in the street and carried one pole out and for some cause all at once they dispersed. Beard and Hardwick were the leaders of the mob. We gathered in the altar and prayed for the mob, that if they could ever be saved to spare them and give them a chance to repent. If there was no chance for their salvation, that they might as well be taken away so as not to hinder the Lord's work. We finally about 1:30 took the organ into a shop and came on home leaving a watch there to see if anything else took place. They also gave me quite a hint that they thought I would not be permitted to remain in the city long. Praise God, we all endured the thing fine and rejoiced right through it. I am writing at 3:30 at night. I think I told Mr. Beard if they wanted it off the ground they could have the job, but for some cause they quit the work and left as stated above.

August 7

We marched to place where tent was, stopped in altar aisle and sang and prayed, then marched and sang to public square, then north and back to church. There the Lord gave us a blessed service. No preaching. Altar full of seekers. 18 joined the church in the face of all the persecutions that are raging. After the meeting closed the sheriff came in and served an injunction on us about late hours and loud noises, and against our erecting the tent in the city limits. I don't know yet just what effect it will have on us only they can put us in jail for every offence. But we will give it a test in the courts.

August 8

Taught Sunday school, class. Preached two sermons afternoon and at night. Fine meetings all day. Big crowds.

August 10

The injunction was served on us last evening in regular order. We went on and held meeting last night any way at the Church. Several at the altar. I preached. We have discontinued the meeting at the church until Thursday night. Have meeting at our house every day. The Holy Ghost fell on us again and gave quite a refreshing shower. We are waiting in the balances about what we will do about further meetings here.

August 16

Taught Sunday school class yesterday, baptized 19 afternoon. Preached three sermons. Had communion service at night and washing of feet for the men. I led the service and did the preaching.

August 20

Brother Bryant prevailed on me to take the tent and go with him to Athens, Tennessee, but when we got there the brethren could not get any place to pitch it so we (Brother McLain and I) brought it back yesterday, leaving Brother Bryant and others there to continue the meeting there in the hall. We had a great meeting there the night we were there. Three baptized with the Holy Ghost. On last Tuesday night we had a special meeting for the women to wash each other's feet. Glorious time.

August 22

Preached three sermons last night today and tonight. Taught Sunday school class. Two professions of religion.

August 25

Went to Athens day before yesterday to set the church in order. A large crowd and about the time I commenced to preach some wicked men opened a can of chemical of some kind and the odor so filled the air that the people could not start it and so broke the meeting up. A dozen or more women and girls succomed to the effects of the stuff and it was with much difficulty that life was restored. We worked with some till two or three o'clock in the morning. We got the tent seated partly yesterday and had the first meeting in it last night. Good crowd. I preached. The tent is now located in South Cleveland.

August 28

I got Brother Goins to take charge of the tent meeting here and Brother McLain and I have been to Blue Springs for two days. Preached four sermons. Will probably go to Athens again tomorrow.

August 30

Went to Athens yesterday. Wife went with me. Organized the Church there and Sunday school. Preached twice there and came home and preached at tent at night. Three sermons. One of the church houses up in the mountains was dynamited last week. We are sure living in perilous times. Threats of violence are being made most every day. Had a great meeting in tent last night. Twenty or more in the altar. Quite a lot of others affected. Two professions and one sanctified. Big crowd.

September 2

Went to Blue Springs last night and the night before. While preaching last night a man drew a rock to hurl at me but something prevented. The Lord helped me to give the truth amid great laughter on the part of the audience last night. The way I presented the truth caused the laughter and it was very impressive. I preached tonight at tent, 18 or 20 in altar, one received the Holy Ghost. The meetings at tent have not been going to suit me while I have been away, so I am here now a while I think. Preached three sermons.

September 6

Been holding meetings at tent every night. Had a great meeting specially last night. One profession. Great crowd. Taught my Sunday school class yesterday. Preached 4 sermons.

September 9

Having our trial today. Only about half through, probably not that far along. I preached at tent at night under very difficult circumstances on account of being bothered in the court all day. But the dear Lord did help and bless me,

September 10

Concluded the trial. The jury rendered the verdict, "guilty" and fined us two dollars apiece and the cost. Our council appealed the case to the Supreme Court without cost to us. Preached at tent at night.

September 12

Preached two sermons, one last night at tent and one today. Taught Sunday school class, and baptized 13 with water and held a big meeting at tent at night. A wonderful meeting, great crowd. Closed the tent meeting. 14 joined the church. Some came back who went out with Simpson last winter.

September 14

Held a farewell service for Brother and Sister Hockett at night at church house. They go to California tomorrow.

September 15

Brother Sam Perry and family stopped with us last night and today. Went on to Alabama this evening. Held prayer meeting at church at night.

September 19

I taught a Sunday school class. Preached two sermons.

September 25

I am here with Brother Patterson at Sobel, Tennessee. Started from home the 23rd, arrived here yesterday. Brother T. L. McLain is with me. Expect to organize the Lord's Church here this afternoon, D.V.

September 8

Organized the church at the time appointed. I am preaching now every day. Three sermons up to date. Having meetings just in the day time.

October 2

Have had meetings every day. Preached four sermons. Baptized four yesterday in the Cumberland River. Ordained a bishop and a deacon.

October 2

Preached two sermons. This is the last day here. We start to Arcadia, Florida, D. V., tomorrow.

October 6

We are now in Arcadia, Fla. Arrived here last night at about nine o'clock after traveling about one thousand miles. We were met at the train and given a very hearty welcome by Brothers Myers and Thomas. Will commence the meeting tonight, D. V.

October 8

Preached 5 sermons up to date. Several seekers in the altar the first service. The power fell this afternoon for the first that amounted to much and two received the Holy Ghost. This was only after hours of prayer before noon in an orange grove by

Brother McLain and myself. We became willing to die to get the power to fall. Great crowd tonight. The power fell in spots nearly all over the house. The altar filled and the aisles partly filled with seekers. No one got through but we feel like there was much good accomplished. Several seekers exercised with violent jerks. I feel so humble but God is with me.

October 9

Preached three sermons today. Four more received the baptism with the Holy Ghost. Great crowds and more seekers than could get into the altar or any ways near. Numbers are being convinced.

October 10

Preached three sermons. Great crowds all day and at night. The Spirit sure helped me preach wonderful to myself as well as to others. Organized the Church with 44 members with others still to come in. I am very tired tonight. Six received the baptism of the Holy Ghost. The services were wonderful in power and no demonstration.

October 11

Preached two sermons. Three more baptized with the Holy Ghost. Altar full of seekers and some in aisle. 16 more joined the Church.

October 12

Preached two sermons. Baptized two in the Peace river. Ordained two bishops, two deacons and presented two with evangelist's Certificates. I delivered the charge to them before ordaining them, and examined them before that. Had a great crowd to preach to at night, and lots of seekers but no one got through.

October 14

We left Arcadia yesterday morning and came to Pleasant Grove Camp Ground where we commence the camp meeting tonight. I feel very small to conduct such a tremendous meeting as this bids fair to be, but I can do all things through Christ that strengtheneth me. Later: The meeting opened tonight with fair attendance. Good interest. One, a Methodist preacher received the Holy Ghost the first service. Preached one sermon. A number of seekers in altar.

October 15

Preached three sermons. The work is going steadily on and the crowd and interest increasing. How wonderful the Lord helps me to preach. Such scenes and demonstrations. Dozens shouting and praising God with uplifted hands while others greatly exercised with agonizing cries and groans, and still others falling into the altar and a great commotion and yet all in perfect order directed by the Holy Ghost. No one got through but lots of seekers.

October 18

Preached six more sermons. I feel very much worn after these days of toil. Four or five have received the baptism with the Holy Ghost. Great crowd yesterday. Numbers of seekers in the altar at every service. The demonstrations and services are wonderful. Several messages and interpretations given last night. Some have fallen in aisle, some in altar, some off their seats and yet I feel that there is some little hindrance which prevents full power of God from falling. A judge of a court received the baptism. A doctor is seeking. Many others of different ranks.

October 20

Preached six more sermons. Two more received the baptism. The saints seem to be wonderfully edified. Brother McLain is fasting and praying while I preach, and it is indeed wonderful to me what the Holy Ghost puts through me.

October 21

Yesterday there was a tendency toward a wrangle brought about by the father of a young man who had been disfellowshipped and each time God gave me great grace to go above it and knock the influence out that it seemed to hurt but a little. Eight more have received the baptism and two converted. Preached four more sermons. I am glad to hear that wife and children are getting along fairly well, the Lord is blessing them and using them.

October 25

The camp meeting closed last night. About 24 baptized with the Holy Ghost. Some saved and sanctified. About 30 accessions to the Church. Several baptized with water. Preached six more sermons. Brother Perry helped me out with the preaching as I had to leave the services a few times on account of being sick. Taking everything into consideration, we had a wonderful meeting. We are out here in the country today and tomorrow, resting and writing, eating oranges, etc. Ordained one bishop and three deacons and set apart one evangelist last night.

October 27

Came from Durant to Lithia last evening where I dedicated a church house today and set in order a Church with about 35 members. Preached three sermons.

October 30

Went from Lithia to Wimauma on train and about six miles across the country to Antioch where we held three services, then came back to railroad and came on train from Willow to Parish, Florida where we commenced a meeting tonight with a good attendance. Preached four more sermons.

October 31

Held three services today. Good attendance. Preached three sermons.

November 2

Meetings afternoon and night. Preached three sermons.

November 4

Preached three more sermons. Night before last was spent in prayer and sleeplessness. Good attendance, some in altar but not much results seen yet but God is helping me give the truth.

November 6, 11:30 P. M.

Meetings yesterday and today as usual. Preached three sermons. Worked hard for a week and nothing apparently done but tonight as I preached the Lord used me to have the congregation real serious, then laughing, then serious, then laughing and so on until finally the power fell and four or five or more fell and went a time followed I cannot describe. Two received the baptism, one converted, one sanctified and a lot of people convinced. I wish I could describe the scene but I can't. I about gave my life as I have often done before. Oh the screams and shrieks, groans, shouts, tears, tongues, and effect on the congregation is not known fully. Praise God for victory.

November 7

Preached three sermons. 11:00 o'clock at night. Worked hard all day, several in altar at every service. One man converted, sanctified and baptized at night. The way it worked was so convincing. Many hungry now.

November 10

Preached two more sermons. Three more baptized with the Holy Ghost. I am going through the greatest trial of my life. Have just received yesterday the intelligence from the Church at home of which I was pastor, that they had expelled me from the pulpit on account of me disagreeing with Brother Goins, who was preaching in my absence, on some teaching he was giving and asked him to correct the mistake or be relieved from acting in my place. Certain letters will explain the situation. I had been hearing of the teaching Brother Goins was giving and that it was not satisfactorily received by the Church, so to know the truth of the matter and to prevent being responsible as pastor for wrong teaching being given from my pulpit, I wrote Brother Goins the following letter, through the purest motive, and as I considered it for the welfare of the Church. Letters in front part of book.

November 11

Preached three more sermons. Lots of people at altar last night and tonight. Four more received the Holy Ghost.

November 13, 11:00 P. M.

Just in from meeting. Preached four more sermons. Nine more received the baptism. Lots of seekers.

November 14

Preached two sermons. Set the Church in order at night with 12 members. The devil raged today and yet the Lord gave the victory. One man has threatened to stick his knife in me as I get on the train, but I have to fears. Close with good victory.

November 17

Left Parish yesterday, took train to Bradentown, there took a steamboat and came to Saint Petersburg across the Tampa Bay, about a three hours trip, then took train to Largo. Brother McLain and myself spent a few hours on the beach of the Gulf of Mexico today. Went across Clearwater Bay in a sail boat. Had a nice time. Commenced the meeting tonight. Preached 1 sermon. Received two letters tonight, one from Brother Bryant and Brother Lawson, and one from Brother Lemons, insisting that we come home at once on account of the trouble Brother Goins is causing. Oh, it makes me heart sick to think of the sad hearts at Cleveland, and the souls here that may be lost by our having to leave here, besides the disappointment to the saints here. I am weighing the matter to try to decide right, but I suppose we will have to go.

November 26

I arrived home from Largo, Florida November 19. Have been under a pressure in regard to the trouble here in the Church with Brother Goins ever since I came home. Days and nearly whole nights in agonizing prayers, groans and much weeping. Spent yesterday in Thanksgiving services at the Church and God took above the difficulties and gave us a good meeting. I preached the Thanksgiving sermon. I am enduring much suffering and waiting long to try to get fixed up with Brother Goins but it is all in vain so far. Matters are rather growing worse.

December 1

This is now Wednesday. Last Saturday morning Brother Goins came to my house and in the presence of four other men railed and ranted, accused, etc., both in the form of a prayer and a discourse, against Brother Bryant and myself, and as Brother Bryant was about to speak I had to call said Goins to order and demand order in my own house. It can be truly said with Paul, "In peril among false brethren." We finally agreed to separate and call a meeting for Monday night separate and settle the trouble. Then on Sunday night Brother Goins preached in a ranting, boastful, accusing spirit making some of the awfulest expressions I ever heard in a pulpit. Monday night came and the members were there, and the Church decided for Goins to make his statements and then me make mine and then for every member who wished to stand with Goins to do so. When the statements were closed, the moderator put the question and a few arose with Goins, then Goins seeing he was beaten in violation of the rules held up his Bible and urged all those who were going with God and the Bible, stressing the Bible. A few more rose up. When they were counted there were only 43 and some of them were not members. Goins stood up and made a little talk, stating he was now out of the Church deliberately of his own accord surrendered his credentials throwing them down on the pulpit. At the proper time I took them and put them in my pocket and brought them home and saw them go up in the flames. As the meeting closed quite a number called out for their names to be taken off the book. The meeting was dismissed at once and then the people who were for Goins became enraged and the saints had to endure much accusation. It was thought that the only thing that kept down violence was the presence of the city officers. Some threats of burning the house and some of dynamite. People were raging around me but we saints kept sweet in our souls. We thought the trouble was settled, but yesterday it seemed to have broken out afresh again and really conditions from outside appearances are very much unsettled. I have asked Brother Goins four or five times for my book containing the memorandum of the church work which I have kept for years, which I had entrusted to him to keep the memorandum for me in my absence, and he has refused me every time and treats me with contempt. Last night he promised to send it to me this morning, but it is now 11:20 a.m. and no book yet. These are indeed perilous times for us here. Can't tell just what the next hour is going to bring. I must say that Brother Lemons was the hero in the meeting Monday night because of the heroic stand he took for the truth and right.

December 2

We met at the church house last night for prayer meeting. The other crowd were not there and the Lord gave us a blessed service. Every saint felt free and received a great blessing. Shouts and tongues and a general uplift among those who had been bound down so long. Wife finally secured the book and brought it home.

December 6

This is Monday morning. Brothers Bryant, McLain and myself went last Thursday to visit dear old Brother Felker and wife about ten miles out in the country. We held meeting at Church house Saturday night, yesterday afternoon and last night, We are having quite a battle but we believe God. I preached three sermons. On Tuesday morning November 23, just before day, a peculiar phenomenon was seen above our house by two witnesses. It appeared like the headlight of a locomotive motion up and down above the house, hidden from view, then appearing again. This lasted for several seconds, probably minutes. Then it vanished away. That day was a day of weeping and agonizing prayers with me and some of the brethren, though we knew nothing about the light above the house for several days afterward. I know the dear Lord loves me and He is ever with me to help me or I would not be able to endure what I have been suffering for over three weeks.

December 10

Have been holding prayer meetings at Church this week. I preached one sermon. Weather cold.

December 12

Taught Sunday school class, conducted funeral service. Held meeting at church afternoon. So rainy at night there was no meeting. Preached three sermons last night and today.

December 15

Night before last Mrs. Tomlinson and I went to Brother Million's to spend an hour with them and their sick little boy. While there we knelt to pray and while in prayer, wife saw a vision of angels, one on each side of me holding my arms as if to lend strength protection. I with Brother T. L. McLain start for Arcadia, Florida this morning for a camp meeting. Brother W. S. McMannen from Fenhollaway, Florida comes to fill my place here while I am gone.

December 17

We arrived in Arcadia, Florida today about 11:00 A.M. Were detained in Jacksonville, Florida on account of missing one train caused by our train from Chattanooga being late. Held meeting tonight Good interest. Good crowd.

December 21

Have been having meetings here every day and night. F. M. Britten uses half the time preaching, I the other half. The work is not moving as we would like, some hindrances some way but I believe some good is being done. Some have been reclaimed. Several seekers. The best liberty today and tonight that has been. Preached five sermons.

December 22

Held a service in the jail with the prisoners. I preached to them. Most all were much affected. Two or three or them prayed and cried right out.

December 28

Closed the meeting at Arcadia Sunday night, December 26. The Lord gave us a good day on Christmas. I held all the services that day. The camp meeting was not what I desired. The preaching of F. M. Britton had a tendency to hinder and drive people away from the meeting. While he said a lot of good things, yet the liberty was taken away and largely made the meetings cold. It was reported that he came there expecting and boasting that he intended to tear up the Lord's Church, but he was unsuccessful. It was revealed to a brother that he was a Haman and I a Mordecai, and while he (Britton) denied in and accused the brother to be of the devil, yet from general observation one could see that there must have been some truth in the revelation for he was evidently hanged (in a spiritual sense) on the very gallows that he had prepared for me. This of course hindered the meeting and there was only two baptized with the Holy Ghost and one reclaimed. The church seems to be solid yet and others want to join as soon as opportunity is given. I expect to go back there soon. We left Arcadia yesterday and came to Tampa and took a steamer and came to Saint Petersburg and on the train to Largo where we stayed last night and came on out here to Midway church today. Will be here only a few days. Preached 5 more sermons at Arcadia. I received a letter from home saying "more trouble." The Goins-Simpson crowd came in to the meeting and demanded the use of the house half the time. On being refused Homer Simpson made for Brother Bryant and Sister Scoggins stepped between them, and I don't know it all but Brother McMannen tried to preach and could not for the disorder caused by those parties, so they closed the meeting and the janitor began to put out the lights when Homer Simpson forbid him, and as he was going on with it,

Aikman grabbed him and Lemons, (Janitor not even a Christian) give him a good shaking up when the two Simpsons and Goins piled on Lemons, and he was too much for all of them and Homer Simpson took up a chair and struck Lemons with it and Lemons wrenched it out of his hands and run the whole bunch off. They arrested Lemons, also Aikman, Jake Simpson, Homer Simpson, Goins and Brother Scoggins were arrested. The trials were set for today. It seems awful to me for such to be going on in that sacred place. I expect to go back soon and will learn more about the results. We are praying for the church to be kept steady and humble. God bless them all. I will say a little more. During the confusion that was going on that prevented Brother McMannen from preaching, Brother Bryant called all to prayer. As he did so Jake Simpson said out loud that he had better pray for it would be his last prayer. That was sure a bold threat, but Brother Bryant was still unharmed last account.

December 31

Am still here near Clearwater, Florida. Have preached four sermons. This is the last day of the year. As I look back over the past I wonder if I have done my best. I am unable to say only in this way, it looks like I have under the circumstances in which I was placed. I have traveled more extensively. Have held more meetings in cities. My borders have been very much enlarged. I have calls now for meetings, the which if I should answer each one and do the work that is needed at each place would consume most of the new year. Preached 314 sermons this year.

1910

January 5, 1910

I preached five sermons New Years Day and the next day, Sunday. We left Clearwater Monday morning. Arrived home last night about midnight and I found the Simpsons-Goins crowd had forced an entrance in the church house and was holding meetings any time they wanted to regardless of entreaties not to do so. I could not sleep any last night, but Brother McLain and I went and awakened Brother Bryant and heard all about the trouble, then the next thing was to set about to find some way to prevent this imposition and the trouble they were causing. At last we decided to enjoin them legally so that plan is on the way. We only await results. I have not had my clothes off for two nights. Am very tired and sleepy tonight. Went to Athens and back today. Dear Brother Brawner sent my family a barrel of oranges from Florida while I was gone. In the cases cited to trial they kinder compromised some way. Goins, Simpson and their crowd broke into the church house on Sunday, January 2, 1910, by removing a glass from window and took a lock off of the door and held a meeting, they went in at night also.

January 18

We successfully enjoined the Goins-Simpson element so we had no trouble in holding the Assembly. Quite a number of people here from different places. They selected me again for general overseer for another year. Also appointed a publishing committee to start and publish a paper.

January 30

Preached two sermons, They selected me pastor today for this year after two or three weeks of prayer, consultation, etc. The great question was whether I could be satisfied that the Lord wanted me to take the work here rather than in the field evangelizing when there were so many calls and open doors. They also insist on me editing the paper and I suppose I will accept that also. The only thing that I regret is that I can't make more of myself so I could fill all the calls and act as pastor here too. I would love to give more lives than one to Jesus if it were possible.

February 6

Have spent my time the past week in making preparation for the starting of the paper. Preached three sermons last night, today and tonight. Awful pressure of the evil spirits in the meeting but God took me above them and gave me the victory. The Goins element is so hard for the saints to get above and they always come and some times put in their testimonies, which bring an awful feeling over the meeting, but God takes me above it. Praise God. They are working in the court to try to take the church house away from us.

February 10

This is Thursday night after coming home from a cottage prayer meeting. I led the prayer meeting last night at the church house. Last Tuesday we were summoned to the court house to be present the depositions of J. H. Simpson, J. B. Goins, P. A. Wingo and Ralph Aikman were taken to appear against us some way in court. The whole day was spent. They testified all they could against the manifestations of the Spirit. Their testimonies were taken in shorthand and are to be placed on record against us and the Church of God. Their object probably is to try to take from us the church house. They accused us of being fanatics because we practice under the power of God and by prayer, casting out demons, speaking in tongues, interpretations, divine healing, etc. The Church of God is assailed in the article by one, F. M. Brittian, which is preserved in front of this book. We are going steadily on, having no evil thing to say of those who are so up in arms against us. I received a long letter today from Goins, wanting to make peace and at the same time accusing us. I see no surrender as long as an army is up in arms and will not put up the sword and raise the flag of truce or peace. On last Tuesday night a few of us met at Brother Henry Tucker's home for prayer. Before prayer the brethren were talking when all at once unexpected to me I began speaking in tongues. And talked at intervals for a few minutes. Afterward I learned that a stream of light, like fire was seen by two or three persons, flash down and up very near me. I remember my whole body was electrified by the Spirit but my eyes were closed. I had been engaged in prayer several times previous to this and had felt led to pray that the fire might be seen again as at Pentecost. Praise God it is coming and I believe it will be seen more and more.

February 14

Taught Sunday school class yesterday and preached two sermons. The sermons were listened to attentively and with apparent good results. Last night I stood out in the aisle near the rear of the house and preached to the young men. I then walked to the pulpit and probably a dozen young men came forward for prayer. Goins still continues to give us trouble. I called for volunteer prayers and he broke in and prayed a long formal prayer against me. After the service closed some of the sisters were under a burden of prayer for souls and as we knelt for prayer Goins broke in again in a long condemning prayer and ruined that service. The cry of our hearts is, "O God, remove him out of the way of souls being saved."

February 19

Last Monday morning the court decided to give us the church house one week and Goins and Simpson clan the next week, etc., come today at 12:00 P.M. We held prayer meeting last Wednesday night. Last night in the night I was awakened and my work for today was outlined which I carried out I believe fully. First I was to see an attorney for legal advice, after I learned what I did. In the evening I went to see Mr. Simpson to see if we could not agree for me to have the house Saturday night and Sunday A. M. and them Sunday P. M. He was willing so I got our attorneys to talk it over and it is possible it will be arranged that way. I also got their answer to our bill of injunction from the clerk and master to copy to preserve which shows some awful remarks, answers and accusations, etc. I also had a talk with Iris about her disobedience to us and gave her fatherly counsel and advice. This was done while she cried. I did not scold her, I talked kind. I went to church and preached about an hour with victory from second Psalm to a full house and in the midst of it some of the Goins crowd ridiculed me in a way, though I could see it, it did not effect the discourse. The Lord gave me grace above it. God keep me humble.

February 21

The Goins, Simpson crowd went square back on dividing the time for the house differently, so they will have it next Sunday and the following week. I taught Sunday school class yesterday and the following week. I taught Sunday school class yesterday and preached afternoon and at night to full house each time. Our Sunday school and meetings are broken into and I don't know what we will do, but we are going on, walking softly before the Lord. Preached four more sermons. I married a couple a few days ago.

March 1

We had the meeting at our house last Saturday night, also Sunday school and meeting Sunday afternoon. Between fifty and sixty in Sunday school, and probably above that number in the meeting afternoon. Had blessed services each time. The Spirit was with us very sensibly. I preached. We are reading the first issue of our paper today. Have 125 subscribers.

March 2

Went to prayer meeting tonight at Brother Dilbeck's home. While there I was seized with a tremendous pain. The power fell on the saints to pray for my deliverance, and while in agonizing prayer streaks of fire was seen descend and break over the earnest praying saints like sparks or stars. Victory came and the pain ceased. To God be all the glory. Amen.

March 6

Held meeting in the church last night and today. The Lord honored us with His presence this afternoon and tonight. Some at altar and some came forward for prayer. House about full at all the services. I preached three sermons. Some hindrances yet on account of the actions of some of the Goins, Simpson faction. We are gradually overcoming it I believe. A big blaze of red light appeared over our house again a few nights ago and made such a bright light that the house made a shadow as the light gradually passed off westward and faded away.

March 14

Taught Sunday school class. Preached three sermons Saturday night, yesterday afternoon at my house and last night in South Cleveland.

March 18

Been having meeting every night this week in South Cleveland. Preached five sermons.

March 19

Preached the funeral of Anna Champion. A blessed service under the power of the Spirit. Preached at the church at night. Blessed service. Several in altar. One profession and others blessed. Preached two sermons. Yes I must say this morning Brother McLain came and we were requested to pray for some parties at a distance and the spirit of prayer and intercession fell on me and lasted for nearly an hour. Groaned and agonized and prayed in tongues and cried all under the power of the Spirit.

March 20

This has been a good day in the service of the Lord. I taught
Sunday school class A. M. Had a fine Sunday school. Preached
afternoon and night. The Lord put some burning messages
through me with the power. Seekers in altar each service. Praise
Him. Went and prayed for the healing of Sister Logan after
meeting at night. Preached two sermons.

March 26

Have been holding meetings every night this week in South
Cleveland. Last night was the most wonderful. I did not preach.
While they were singing the first songs I gave my book to some
one and began to feel the Spirit of the Lord moving in me. I soon
kneeled down and was taken off in the Spirit for some little
time. They finally had some prayers, after which were a few
testimonies. I then sit up and was about to arise and read a few
verses of Scripture when a sister gave a message in tongues.
As she commenced I was suddenly jerked from my seat down
on my knees by the power of the Lord as if some one had taken
hold on me and suddenly thrust me down. The same message
was repeated by the sister in tongues at the close of which the
interpretation was given through me, a second and a third
message was given and the interpretation followed each. Then
the power came on me heavier and I was lifted to my feet and
was whirled about, stamped the floor and taken through many
different exercises of my body, gestures and signs. All the while
speaking in tongues as He gave utterance. A message was given
in tongues and the interpretation followed, exhorting people who
wished to seek the Lord to kneel at once and call on God who was
near. A number fell down and the power shook up some of them
considerably and some received great blessings, but none received
the baptism. I can't describe the workings of the Spirit but it was
wonderful. Preached two sermons this week.

March 21

Taught Sunday school class yesterday. Had the Sunday school at
our house. Meeting yesterday afternoon in the out edge of town out
of doors at Brother Scoggins. Last night in South Cleveland. My work
yesterday was very tiresome physically and I really felt after it was
done that I was an unprofitable servant. People said I did better than
usual but I did not feel that way. The Spirit uses me in some peculiar
ways. Last night while I was preaching right on my speech was
taken by the Holy Ghost and spoke a few words in tongues, quick as
a flash Homer gave the interpretation and I went right on with the
discourse. Preached two sermons. Anointed two today.

April 3

Held meeting every night last week at cottages and last night at church and today taught Sunday school class and a Bible class after Sunday school and preached afternoon and had a wonderful meeting at night. Preached four sermons.

April 7

Meeting every night this week except Tuesday night we had a Bible lesson. Tonight one profession and others got greatly blessed.

April 11

One profession at the meeting last Friday night.

April

Meeting Saturday night. Taught Sunday school class yesterday, held it at our house. Meeting yesterday P. M. and last night. Out door meeting yesterday. Great meetings. Preached three sermons. Bought a lot in South Cleveland Saturday on which to build a tabernacle for meeting and Sunday school in that part of town.

April 15

At a meeting last Tuesday night one received the baptism with the Holy Ghost. I am working with the paper every day.

April 17

Taught a Sunday school class. Held meeting afternoon and at night. Several at altar. One profession. Preached two sermons. House crowded at night. Mama and Milton gone to Charleston a few days.

April 25

Taught Sunday school class yesterday A. M. In the afternoon I preached at Brother Scoggin's house. The weather today is very peculiar. Has been snowing from early morning. Several inches of snow has fallen and it is still falling at one P. M. Plums, peaches and apples are as big as small marbles and the forest trees nearly in full leaf. To sit here in the house by the fire and look out of the window it looks like the dead of winter except the green leaves on the trees. It remains yet to see whether the fruit will all be killed or not.

May 1

The Lord gave us a blessed victorious service last night and a fine Sunday school and two grand meetings today. The power fell wonderfully and several in altar and a lot of people got greatly blest. Can't describe the services. God was wonderfully with us. Preached two sermons.

May 17

May the second, Brother McLain and myself went to Pulaski City, Va., on the train, was met there by J. J. Lowman and his brother who conveyed us about ten miles in the country where we held meetings every night until May 12. Had tarrying meetings in day time. Three received the baptism with the Holy Ghost and several convinced and were seeking. About 19 seekers in altar the night we closed. We held the meeting in a Methodist church house and some of the members were very much opposed to us being there and they forced in a preacher on Sunday who denounced us, accounting us of the devil and he mimicked the tongues and shook himself in mockery of the power of God that many times shakes our bodies. They undertook to bluff us out by talking mob violence, threats, etc., but we went right on till we got through and when some of their own people received the baptism and began to witness their mouths were sure stopped and they were put to shame. I preached twelve sermons while there and the people loved us so good they could hardly bear for us to leave but we had to tear ourselves away from them and arrived home about 9 P. M., the 13th of May. The work at home had piled up and I am rushed day and night. Saturday I had to look after getting the tabernacle ready for dedication on Sunday. Preached Saturday night at church. Sunday morning taught Sunday school class and afternoon held the dedication service at the tabernacle. The Lord met us there. Our Sunday did fine singing and after I preached the sermon I gave opportunity for people to come forward and lay their offerings on the open Bible and while the singing was going on it was interesting to see the people one after another rise up and come and lay their offerings on the Bible. This continued for some little time with no begging nor excitement; by about four o'clock we had all the amount asked for either given in cash or pledged and while all the large congregation stood I offered the dedicatory prayer. Then the Lord set His seal on it as He took charge. People sang, shook hands, loved each other, shed great tears of joy, talked in tongues under the power of the Spirit, and above it all was heard great shouts of joy and victory. The Lord wonderfully blest His people and manifested His presence until hard hearts seemed melted like wax. Held regular service at the church at night. Preached three sermons. Busy with the paper Monday and Monday night until late. Preached funeral today with other work that has kept me very busy. I have dozens of letters piled up yet to read and answer and accounts to make and the time passing so rapidly by.

May 22, Midnight

Another day's work for Jesus. Taught Sunday school class at my house A. M. Organized Sunday school at tabernacle P. M. Held meeting at tabernacle at night. Blessed service. The Lord gave me wisdom and blessing in dealing with the people. Quite a lot of young men and some women and girls came forward for prayer. Preached two sermons. One a Sunday school sermon. We are gradually building up in spite of the opposition and trouble we have had.

May 24

Preached funeral of another baby.

May 30

Taught Sunday school class yesterday at Church also at the tabernacle. Held meeting at church Saturday night. Funeral service yesterday morning, another baby. Meeting at tabernacle last night. Preached three sermons.

June 9

I taught Sunday school class A. M, and P. M. and preached in tabernacle at night last Sunday. Heavy rain all day but we had Sunday school. Over twenty in attendance. Last Monday I ordered from Sears, Roebuck, Chicago, eleven band instruments for a brass band at a cost of $124. Two ministers, F, N. Roberts and John X. Smith came in today. Our meeting commences next Sunday, D. V.

June 14

Had a wonderful meeting at the church Saturday night. Lasted until about midnight. Nobody preached but the Spirit had control. Sunday A. M. and P. M. I taught Sunday school class. One at church the other at tabernacle. Our Sunday schools are on the increase again, 75 and 134 respectively. I am directing the meetings, others are doing the preaching. Brother Smith leaves this morning for Arkansas. Received the band instruments.

June 15

Had a formal opening of box of instruments and dedicated them to God. The Lord melted us down with His love and presence. I preached funeral of Will McDonald's baby, A very impressive melting service. Meetings every day and night at tabernacle.

June 20

Taught Sunday school classes yesterday at Church A.M., at tabernacle P. M. Preached two sermons. Been seven or more professions of religion and some baptized with the Holy Ghost. Some reclaimed and wonderfully blest. Had some wonderful blessed meetings. The Lord is blessedly working on hearts.

June 22

Wife had a very bad spell this morning but the Lord blessedly relieved her in answer to prayer. I conducted a funeral service. Held meeting at tabernacle. Several at altar. Brother White and his daughters came this evening. They travel and sing and preach. Preached seven sermons.

June 28

Have been holding the meeting at tabernacle of a night and Sunday afternoon. Taught Sunday school class at church Sunday A. M. at Tabernacle. The schools are increasing nicely, having gone up to over 90 at Church and over 140 at Tabernacle. Last Sunday night was wonderful. I preached under the power of the Spirit and in the midst I threw off my coat almost like lightning and finished my discourse with no coat on. Estimated 1,000 people there. The altar service continued till about midnight. Several under power stretched out on the shavings in the old fashioned way. Several, professions, renewals, some baptized with Holy Ghost and spoke in tongues as evidence. A wonderful meeting. Preached five sermons. Wife was taken suddenly ill last night after I went to meeting when I got home she was apparently about gone, but we rallied our forces in prayer and deliverance came. But though the severe suffering subsided it left her very weak and sore. Not able to be up today. We are giving our depositions at court house in the injunction case about the church trials. Yesterday brought us quite a surprise. I had been invited to preach in a grove just out side of town at Brother Scoggins'. Quite a crowd gathered and were served with lemonade. Had a song service after prayer a table was loaded down with food stuff, etc. by nearly all who were there and presented to me. It about broke my heart. We had been faring very scant for quite a while. It was a melting service all the way through and the power of God was present to bless folks. We have lots of company during the meeting. I am writing near midnight. I have to keep late hours because of so much work to do.

July 7

Wife has been getting better, able to attend to her domestic duties and Sunday school work. Held meetings at Tabernacle until Monday night, July 4. I taught a Sunday school class at Church A.M. Sunday and preached. Taught Sunday school class at tabernacle P. M. and preached at night. Monday July 4 was a wonderful day at tabernacle. Opened the meeting at 10:30 a.m. and never closed till about ten at night. Homer A. Tomlinson, my son, delivered the Fourth of July oration under the power of the spirit. It was wonderful. No arrangements or program had been made but everybody was to obey the Lord. At about 1:30 dinner was spread and everybody ate and drank for the glory of God for a little while. At 2:30 I opened the service for the sacrament and feet washing, preached the sermon and administered the bread and wine and started the feet washing. As we broke the bread a peculiar solemnity took hold of all present. It was blessed to see the saints kneel at the altar in companies of 10 or 12 at each altar, women at one and men at the other, The deacons passed the bread and wine to each kneeling company. There were probably 125 or more engaged in this and the feet washing that followed. A full description of this wonderful service cannot be given. Wonderful in the extreme. Singing, playing organs, shouting, talking in tongues, singing under the power of the Spirit. Once while Halcy, my daughter, played under the power, Homer sang with her under the power, and Iris was greatly exercised by the power in what was spoken of as dancing. It was wonderful how the power fell. The meeting went right on and as the people came in for the night meeting the power was so great that several were drawn right to the altar some fell in the congregation, as fast as those at altar would get blest and leave others would fall in and take their places, never did know the full results, but quite a number were saved from sins, sanctified, reclaimed and from seven to twelve received the baptism with the Holy Ghost. The signs and wonders that were done can hardly be described. Devils were cast out, the sick healed, messages in tongues, interpretations. Such love and unity among such a crowd of saints is scarcely ever seen. Folks here from Chattanooga, Athens, Ducktown, Rome and probably other places. I preached four sermons. Brother Bryant with a company of eight or nine left yesterday for Ducktown. Sister Bower will probably go the 11th to Bahama Islands. Brother White and his company will probably go the same day in his mission from town to town. Brother Mitchell is here with us a few days again. Rain, rain this week. We got a few of our players together last night to practice on the band instruments for the first time. Our work here that was so injured by Goins and Simpson is about regained again. Sunday schools number, one about 90, the other about 140. On account of the trouble the one school run down to about 35, but now we have two schools and the large number at both as stated above. Praise God. He gets all the glory as far as I am concerned.

July 11

Held meeting in Church Saturday night. Taught Sunday school class yesterday A. M. Sunday school class P. M. at tabernacle. Preached two sermons yesterday. Sister Bower leaves today for Bahama Islands. Brother Mitchell leaves for Harriman, Tennessee. God is still helping us for His glory.

July 17

Wife was very ill yesterday and we prayed and fought back the powers of death and demons for about twelve hours until we finally gained the victory. It was the awfulest battle with death and wicked spirits I ever experienced. But praise God for victory. She is still weak but feels very well, she is not up. I taught Sunday school class and preached at Church. A. M. Taught Sunday school class and preached at tabernacle P. M. Two or three professions and one filled at night. Quite a wonderful meeting. Two sermons.

July 24

Nearly midnight. Held meeting at tabernacle all week at night. I taught Sunday school class at church. A. M. and preached. Taught Sunday school class at Tabernacle P. M. and preached at night. Several at altar. Preached three sermons. Mary's mother came from Kansas yesterday morning.

July 25

Preached at Tabernacle at night.

July 31

Taught Sunday school class A. M. and P. M. at church and tabernacle. Preached three sermons.

August 12

On August 4 I came to Alabama City to engage in a tent meeting with Brother Lemons. Brother Falvius Lee came with me. I returned home August 8 to attend court as a witness. I returned to Alabama City again August 11 where I am now. I preached three times here last Sunday. All together since last writing have preached five sermons. I leave Homer in charge of the paper with mama and Halcy to help him. I wrote an article for the paper as I came down on the train.

August 15

I am very tired and worn this morning but all is well in my soul. Yesterday was a great day. I preached three sermons and hundreds of people heard gospel. Several at altar and one (a Campbelite preacher) received the baptism with the Holy Ghost. Some professions. Preached five more sermons. While I was preaching in the afternoon service, the power fell on me and I was down on the ground in front of the platform, and all at once I jumped on the platform and ran around like a little boy and jumped down again and I was told this morning that as I jumped down off the platform the power struck some back in the congregation like a current of electricity. This teaches me again the importance of yielding up completely to the Holy Ghost even if I do act like a child at play. Glory.

August 18

Finds me still at Alabama City, Ala. Have preached three more sermons. The people are still coming. Some few professions and some hungry for the baptism. I have written seven or eight letters today, answers to some received. I go tomorrow D. V. for Charleston, Mississippi where I am to engage in a ten or twelve days meeting. Brother Lemons will remain here yet an indefinite time. I feel anxious to have Brother McLain with me but he did not feel willing to come at the time I came, but went to Spring Place, Ga. I think he will be with me pretty soon. I have a call to organize seven or eight churches in Alabama. I feel very much pressed in spirit to get my company together soon and I am contemplating the purchase of a car to have for a house and in which to travel while in America. A firm in Chicago offers me a car all fitted up ready for use for $2,000. I am now asking God to give me large sums for His work. I have a letter from Homer that I will preserve in forepart of this book.

August 22

I arrived here in the country out from Charleston, Miss. Saturday, 20th of August. Had meeting yesterday and last night. Indications are very encouraging for a good meeting. Preached three sermons.

August 24

Have been having meetings day and night. Rain has hindered some. Held a funeral service yesterday. Preached four sermons. The Lord is helping me to preach but nothing much done yet. Some seekers but none got through.

August 27

Been having meeting day and night. Some professions, some sanctified, some healed. Quite a powerful melting service today. Have preached seven more sermons.

August 29

This is Monday morning. The Lord gave us a good day yesterday. Preached two sermons in one service. The people are accepting the truth. Four sermons.

August 33

Baptized six yesterday in water. Altar filled with seekers last night. Had the Lord's supper and feet washing today. The Lord wonderfully blest. Quite a number had never seen feet washing.

Those who engaged had never witnessed the ceremony before, but the Lord made them happy. When I preach tonight it will make six more sermons. I close the meeting tonight. Start for the camp meeting at Memphis, Tenn., tomorrow, D. V.

September 3

Am now at the camp meeting at Memphis at Jackson Mound Park with Brother Adams, Brother Yokum of Los Angeles, California. Came today. The Lord has given us same good services. I have led two or three services. There are quite a number of campers on the ground but the congregations are not large yet. I have met a number of people and formed a number of pleasant acquaintances. It seems like everybody loves me and I love them. I go home tonight, D. V.

September 7

I arrived home on the morning of the third early. Taught Sunday school classes at church and tabernacle. Preached at church A. M. Yesterday I preached funeral of a little child. I am very busy getting ready to go again.

September 12

I am now at Gintown, Alabama. Came here three days ago. The working of the Holy Spirit commenced at once. Six have received the baptism already and many, many in altar. As I preached yesterday many fell under the power of intercessory prayer and what was gained will yet be revealed. This is Monday morning and I am so exhausted this morning I am hardly able to be up. People came to meeting yesterday over twenty miles. I have so many calls for meeting I hardly know what to do or where to go. God help me. Preached four sermons.

September 15

Thursday morning. The meeting is still in progress. God is working wonders. Sinners get the jerks until they can't hold themselves still. The power has fallen back in the congregation. People lay under the power for hours. Some groan and moan, some froth at the mouth. Many are jerked violently. Some dance, some shout, some cry, some have many motions of the body. One girl wrote on her arm with her finger the name of one who was down seeking salvation and she did not know the name, then reached up as though she was writing the same name on the Lamb's book of life. The girl, whose name she wrote, fell over a sinner and got saved, sanctified and baptized with the Holy Ghost before she ever got up. Brother McLain was taken through some of the most wonderful demonstrations one night I ever saw. They really beggar description. Two services there was so much power falling I did not need to preach. Last night I preached while some were receiving the baptism. One minister convinced last night, and asked for prayers. Five received last night. This makes 19 in all in six days. Preached four more sermons.

September 17

Saturday afternoon. Wonderful meetings and great signs and wonders. 25 received baptism. The preaching yesterday was wonderfully demonstrated by some while I gave the message. I am unable to express it. About the middle of my sermon the Holy Spirit took it up and for about fifteen minutes it was wonderful. What wonderful revelations God gave me of the last half of the first chapter of Col. We are getting ready for setting the church in order. Preached five more sermons.

September 19

Monday morning. 10 more received the baptism. Set two churches in order at once yesterday. One for Gintown, one for Coalburg, the saints of which were here from eight or ten miles away. I preached yesterday and gave instructions on the church for about two hours. And the large congregation was very attentive and much interested. Preached three more sermons.

September 20

I had quite a time last night. I and Brother McLain and Brother Haynes and Sister Clyde Cotton marched into the tent to music and on arriving at the altar I turned and read a few verses from Saint John 2, and then repeated the ceremony and announced Brother Haynes and Sister Clyde husband and wife. After the congratulations, I made a little talk and we received five into the Church. Ten called the candidates for ordination with their wives to take their places in front of the altar. I delivered to them the charge. As they knelt at the altar I ordained one bishop and four deacons and proclaimed them officers in the Church of God. After this I gave instructions about the Lord's supper and administered that to about forty or more. Then I gave instructions about feet washing and then we engaged in that. Then came the goodby and it was nearly eleven o'clock. I am fresh this morning and feel good. Going on train in a few minutes to Coalburg to baptize about ten miles. This will say goodby to Gintown. 35 received the Comforter in the ten days besides all the other good work done. Four more sermons.

September 22

My birthday. I am at Kimberly, Ala. Arrived here last evening. The baptizing at Coalburg was blest of God. 17 baptized. It was a beautiful sight to see seven little girls all in a row march down in the water together and how the Lord did bless as I baptized them one by one. Took the train and went into Birmingham that night. I busied myself yesterday in writing for the paper. We are here for only two days. Preached one sermon.

September 24

I am still at Kimberly, but we take our leave this morning. Had some good meetings. We closed last night. Organized the Church, ordained a deacon, administered the Lord's supper and feet washing. One received the baptism yesterday. Preached five sermons.

September 26

We came to Fulton Springs Saturday and commenced meeting at night. Preached two sermons. The tent will be pitched today and the meeting commence in earnest. The work is getting on nicely at home.

October 1

I arrived home today at about 12:30. A storm blew the tent down at Fulton Springs. We mended it and pitched it again and some good work done. Preached three more sermons. Left the meeting yesterday in the hands of Brother Kennedy and Brother McLain came home with me. We stopped in Chattanooga last night and prayed for Brother Lemons who is sick this morning. Bro. Lemons has been sick for about six weeks. God gave us great burdens in prayer for him. I don't feel like we can give him up for the work, but if he does not reach victory soon he cannot stay with us long. I believe God will spare him. All well at home. I find Brother Mitchell here again. So glad to see him. He is putting up his goods again here in Cleveland. I'm glad to get home and find all well and happy.

October 6

Last Sunday was a great day for us at Cleveland. I taught Sunday school class at church house, went from there to pool and baptized seven. Came home and went to tabernacle P. M, Taught Sunday school class there. Over 100 in each school. I preached after Sunday school. At night the meeting opened in a good quiet way and gradually increased in interest until suddenly the tide swelled so that I suppose more than 100 were either weeping, wringing their hands, talking in tongues, preaching exhorting, running up and down the aisles, dancing, shouting or down seeking God. A wonderful time indeed. The large audience stood and looked on with bewilderment and amazement. The Spirit outpouring seemed to come in torrents. Waves of glory thrilled the saints and scared the sinners. I led the meeting last night at Tabernacle. Went out to see old Brother Felker today. He is very old and he wanted me to advise him about the use of his money in the Lord's work.

October 10

Taught Sunday school and preached at church and tabernacle. Great meeting at night. Preached four sermons. I expect to start for Florida tomorrow to conduct camp meeting.

October 15

I am now at the Pleasant Grove Camp Ground in the preachers cottage. This is my third time here. The meeting commenced Thursday night with good interest and has been gathering ever since. It is already wonderful how God is favoring us with His presence. Have preached five times. Just barely got started today when the power fell and I'll not attempt to describe the signs and wonders done by the power of the Spirit. The Lord is using me in demonstrating the sermons under the power of the Spirit. Wonderful. Brother McLain, F. J. Lee, Roy Miller, Esther Cecil, Efford Haynes and wife are here with me.

October 18

It is now nearly time for night meeting. We have been having severe tests but we are going on. Storm last night. Some of the trees were torn up considerably. Tents blown down. Rains about every day and night. No sunshine at all. Many sick to be prayed for. It is a time of deepening into God by the saints. Some getting the baptism, some reclaimed. Not many attend but the campers. I have preached about nine sermons since last writing. Nearly every time I preach, the Spirit gives a glad witness to the truth and not infrequently demonstrates the truth by signs and wonders in some way through some of His children. Although the rain continues the meetings last from 6:00 A. M. to from ten to twelve at night and sometimes later. Decisions are being made for eternity.

October 21

Preached nine sermons. The work is going right on. People healed. Quite a number in altar but few are getting through. The saints are getting great help judging by their testimonies. Today as I had hardly got full in my discourse a man arose and said he had a message to deliver, said he was warned of being in danger of being overcome by a "bull" and warned them against me, inferring I was a dangerous man. I managed to keep the congregation in check although not all the time quiet, but as he sat down I remarked that we should love Jesus and that we had no ill feeling toward the man and we would pray for him so we all knelt in prayer for him. We arose and I continued my discourse with great liberty and convincing power. The man looks so pitiful. I feel so sorry for him. He has a blessed daughter and she seems to be so embarrassed about the way her father acted and talked. He claims the baptism with the Holy Ghost. His name is Evans. There was only love in my soul and not a ripple of retaliation struck me while he was shaking his fist at me and calling me a bull. Praise God. I baptized 12 yesterday in water. Some real old men and women. This afternoon we had the Lord's supper and expected to wash feet but there were so many to eat we had to defer the feet washing until next week. The Lord gave us a very sacred service. Numbers wept and sobbed. The death of Jesus seemed so real as I preached and as we engaged. People crowded the altar tonight. Large crowd. I am now writing at midnight.

October 24

This is Monday morning. Very cool last night. Bright and warm this morning. Preached four more sermons. Yesterday I preached on the Church and the Lord made me a wonder to myself. Many who had been fearful and opposers were convinced and 24 joined. Some came in who had been holding back over a year. It was wonderful to see the love and unity. Some very strong characters saw the truth and beauty and threw away their creeds, churches and notions and came in to assist us in the reformation.

October 25

Preached three times. We had announced meeting for all night last night. We gathered at the tabernacle for service. We felt a good spirit at the first but I fell upon my face and remained that way for some time while some where testifying. I arose and sat on my seat and still others were testifying when a zigzag light as I was told came in just above my head, another light like as of fire was seen in another part of the tabernacle just the heads of the people. Still another was seen in like manner. These lights, which seemed to be in streaks or sheets, six or eight inches in width, played about until many people saw them plainly. The power fell upon the people, some talking in tongues, dancing, falling, shouting, wringing their hands, jumping and jerking when finally as if by magic all were standing packed around me when a sister took the Bible and began to read the 18th of Revelation in other tongues. I soon caught the inspiration and after she read in tongues I read what she repeated alternately until we reached the end of the chapter, when she stopped short although I don't think she was looking at the verses. Following this were signs and wonders, showing how His people were going to be gathered together, then the Spirit gave songs, joy and great victory, and revealed to us Isaiah 51:11. The fire was seen in the tabernacle next morning before the service closed for it continued all night. Fire was also seen at two cottages at other times.

October 28

The last night of the camp meeting we ordained a deacon and a bishop, started arrangements for a Pentecostal school and college and about $1,000 subscribed to start it. The meeting closed with a sweet feeling and fellowship, handshake, embraces, tears, shouts, etc., and an altar service, all was over and the camp in quietness about midnight. We came to Parish yesterday and we are now in the very room where the burden was laid upon us to pray for the brass band and we have the instruments with us now and are practicing in the same room where God gave us such victory about it one year ago. We are here for only a few days this time. Only three more sermons.

October 31

Preached three sermons yesterday. The weather is so cold we don't seem to be doing much, but a great burden fell upon me yesterday and I cried and agonized for quite a while here in the room.

November 2

Weather warmer. Preached three sermons. Last night after I preached great numbers piled into the altar. Higher classes as well as others. Two have received the baptism. Great burdens of prayer on us.

November 7

The meeting at Parish resulted in six receiving the baptism besides others greatly blest, some sanctified, etc. We left the dear ones at Parish, although they begged us to stay longer, November 3, and came to Arcadia, Fla. The camp opened with good interest. The meeting yesterday was wonderful. Great things done besides two received the baptism. After I preached for an hour on the value of a human soul, the altar was filled. Strong men came in weeping, may eyes were flooded with tears. I'm sure vows were made that will bring great and good results if not broken. We commenced the meeting Friday night and this is only Monday. Quite a shower of blessings fell last night. Preached seven more sermons.

November 9, Wednesday, 2:00 P. M.

Preached eight sermons. Two more have received the baptism. Meeting still goes on.

November 14

Monday morning. Have had some wonderful meetings since last writing. Large crowds yesterday. Automobiles as well as lots of other vehicles. I preached three times yesterday. I can't describe the meetings, wonderful messages by myself in preaching, demonstrations, etc. Saturday night I preached in tongues. I invited the people to come to the altar and they came. Last night it was too cold for much altar work but a few came in, but God showered down some wonderful blessings in the early part of the meeting. Tongues and demonstrations. Preached nine more sermons. Held meeting on the street in town Saturday P. M.

Had a good service and gave out a lot of literature, I must give an incident that took place yesterday while I was preaching. I meant to illustrate the being joined and compacted together of Eph. 4:16, and as I took hold of a brother and pressed him close to me the power of God struck him and he was wafted about in a marvelous manner showing what will occur in power and signs when God's people really get to the oneness. It was wonderful. I stood and gave the message and interpreted what the signs were to the amazed congregation. Again while I was telling how people had to leave off a lot of opinions and become child like the same brother Guthrie illustrated under the power how people should become like a child. Wonderful demonstrations of His power again last night. Lord's supper and feet washing tonight, D. V.

November 16

Had one of the finest communion services I ever saw. Closed the meeting last night. One received the baptism, some joined the church. Closed with a good feeling and the church in good condition. Brothers McLain and Flavius are going home this morning. We are packing up to go to Alva, Fla., for a week. Preached four more sermons.

November 17, 10:00 P. M.

We came to Fort Myers yesterday and held a meeting on the street at night. Good service. Friends gave us entertainment. Came here to Alva on a gasoline boat this morning up the Calloosahatchie River. Held meeting tonight. Had a fine service for the first. One received the baptism. Several at the altar. A number seem interested. Preached two sermons. On street last night.

November 19

This is Saturday night after meeting. People are getting interested. Several at altar. Preached four more sermons.

November 22

Preached four more sermons. Altar crowded Sunday night. Had meeting all day, dinner on ground. Preached three times. Yesterday afternoon the Spirit gave me two messages, telling me again about my work and indicating He was making me level-headed so I could do the work here as well as elsewhere in the right way. The people here seem to be amazed with the preaching. I was reminded of how the Holy Ghost witnessed in every city to Paul about what would befell him, so the Holy Ghost witnesses in many places I go that it is my mission to gather His people into one, and how He will be with me and work with me. I love Him. These messages were given by two that knew nothing about my call or any other messages ever given me. Praise Him. I must go on.

November 23

Organized the church here this afternoon, An old gentleman took quite a stand against me but I loved him right on and although he interrupted me often and finally broke in in quite a heated discourse against me and my teaching and really seemed mad, yet I went right ahead and when I got ready and made the proposition for people to come, here they came right contrary to the advice given them by the old brother. The power fell in the altar tonight. One went all the way through, others very much blest. Preached two more sermons. Cool nights.

November 25

I now write at 2:00 A. M. Just got in from the last meeting. Had a wonderful time all day. Had the Lord's supper, feet washing, baptizing at the river, dinner at the meeting. Baptized five and six received the Holy Ghost at night service, great demonstrations. Three more came into the church. I preached five sermons besides all the other work, praying for sick, altar work, singing, answering questions, etc., etc. We are to leave on boat at 7:00 A. M., so but little sleep. I ordained a deacon.

November 28

Came to Fort Myers and stayed all night and left early the next morning and came to Garner where we were met by friends with teams and came fifteen miles to Crewsville. Had meeting the same night and the power fell in a wonderful way at the first prayer. Yesterday was Sunday, had three services. Preached three sermons.

December 2, Friday morning

Preached six more sermons. The weather is cold and no fire in the school house where we hold the meetings, but the Lord is blessing and two have received the baptism. Quite a number are camping but we don't feel that we are doing as much good as if the weather was warmer. God is burdening me with the importance of systematic work. I was out lying on the cold ground last night before service on my face under a heavy burden and agony about the work when something seemed to touch me and my crying ceased and tears dried up almost at once. I feel that God has something special to reveal or put me into very soon. As the hart pants after the waterbrook, so panteth my soul after thee, oh God, is true in my case. I see so much to do and so few to do it. God help me. I and my boys were invited to stay at the finest and best home in the community. We accepted the invitation and came here Tuesday night. We had been going out four miles every night before. Mr. and Mrs. Collier are very kind to us though they are not even really saved, but I believe the Lord is talking to them and we are praying for them.

December 5, Monday morning

Preached seven sermons. The Lord has given us good services but not many saved. The missionary discourse I delivered yesterday was not without effect on the hearers. Three have offered their services and others much impressed I'm sure. This is last day at Crewsville.

December 8

The Lord gave us a great meeting at Crewsville the last day and night. The Lord's supper and feet washing service was very sacred and the presence of the Lord was there. At night we formally accepted Brother and Sister Hadsock and Marion Whidden into the band and pinned the badges on them. Quite an impression was made on the people in the farewell service. Then some came into the church. The meeting closed about eleven o'clock at night. Came to Wauchula on Tuesday, the 6th and commenced the meeting the same night. The weather is cold and rather disagreeable for meeting but we are going on carefully and prayerfully. I am somewhat perplexed about what to do. So many urgent calls for meetings. One in Mississippi is giving me special concern just now. To go there will deprive me of the privilege of home on Christmas and making preparations for the Assembly. I don't know just what to do. God help me. Have preached eight more sermons.

December 10

Services every day. I now write at 10:20 at night after meeting. Sure had a time tonight. Large audience. Hard to preach because of confusion. But I went through with victory. Some fellow put a continuous fire cracker in the house, and the officers hunted him up and got him, and I preached right on above all the confusion and made an altar call and the altar was filled with seekers. Well, it was quite a cross to me but the Lord gave grace. I hardly know how I did get along, but if I made a bobble I don't know it. The Lord helped me to give out the truth right while the cracker was going on. The large audience behaved remarkably well in the confusion. As I preached this afternoon everybody was melted to tears. Preached three times today. Preached six sermons more. Wife wrote me, I got it today, that the court had decided the church case in our favor so we get the house and no cost to pay. Praise God. Victory. I love Jesus.

December 11

After meeting at night. This has been a big day. Large crowds, specially tonight, good order. Preached three sermons. One baptized with the Holy Ghost. Wonderful display of the Holy Ghost among the saints. The audience are listening and watching and I feel that the truth is having a good effect. God helps me to give out the truth.

December 14

The meetings have continued Monday. I felt much exhausted but went through just the same. Last night I preached from 1 Tim. 6:3-5, and I don't think I ever wound up an audience so in my life. The Spirit held them spellbound for an hour. And such wisdom and logic I believe never before fell from my lips, but He gets the glory. It was all with kindness and love but close and cutting. People of learning were there. Preached four more sermons. I write this A. M. Meetings this P. M. and night. I have forgotten whether I made a note before of how the Lord has given us a camera and Brother Haynes is a fine artist and photographer.

December 15

I write at night after meeting near eleven o'clock. Preached four more sermons. The Spirit worked with the saints tonight blessedly. The Lord helped me to tie up and convince the people but they seem to be so fastened by the devil in some way that they can't get loose yet. They sit spellbound for an hour at a time and drink down the truth. Hope the break will come soon. We are praying earnestly. The church at home has sent for me to come home at once but I can't go now until after Sunday.

December 18

I write at twelve o'clock at night after the close of the meeting. Preached eight more sermons. This has been a great day. Preached three sermons to large congregations. Some converted, some sanctified and three got the baptism. Wonderful demonstrations in the morning service. The power fell while I was preaching and demonstrations fit in so blessedly. Set the Church in order and we are leaving them in good condition and all the saints greatly blest. Board the train tomorrow morning for Lulu, Florida,

December 27

The night before I left Wauchula I dreamed a dream that put me to wondering and I began to question in my mind whether I would go on to Lulu or come home so at breakfast a letter was handed me from Brother A. J. Lawson calling me home at once. So immediately I decided to come on home which, I did. Brother Cecil had gone to Clearwater, Brother and Sister Haynes remained at Wauchula, Brother Roy Miller, Brother Hadsock and wife came on with me as far as Palatka and went to Lulu and I came on home, arriving home the next day, Tuesday, December 20, 1910. I had dreamed of a lion having got out of his cage and I was called to the scene and was able to win his confidence by kindness and love until he consented to go back in the cage at my command, which he did and caused no more trouble. When I returned home I found our folks troubled about Mr. Simpson, who has given us so much trouble in the past, making his boasts of what he was going to do again. He was at our meeting last Sunday and God gave me a message on love to start with and I believe the lion will be caged without much trouble if I can only remain full of love. I bought new carpet and lamp flews [*sic*] and shades for the lamps and we fixed up the church house so it looks nice again. Brother Felker sent us his notes which gives us $400, now we hope to pay off the church debt soon and have the house free of debt. I am spending my time writing, preparing copy for paper, letters, preparing for Assembly, etc. Had a nice time Christmas day, it being on Sunday. I taught Sunday school class both at church house and tabernacle. Also conducted the review at both places with great liberty. My precious wife was sick when I came home, but we prayed for her and she began to improve at once and is well now. Praise God. Some have come already for the Assembly. I commence meeting at church tomorrow night to continue through Assembly. Preached one sermon at church Sunday.

December 31

The old year is about gone. The Lord has seen fit to spare me through another year. Held meeting. Held meeting at church house four nights this week. The last night of the old year about 150 stayed until the new year came in at midnight. We had a wonderful meeting. The tide rose higher and higher until just at twelve o'clock all arose to their feet and with loud voices and uplifted hands gave glory to God. Then as if moved almost by some unseen power all were on their knees as the new year was come in. Consecrations and vows were made. Great meeting, preaching, testimonies, shouts, laughter, tears, groans, prayers, demonstrations in many ways. Goodby old year, welcome to the new. I preached three more sermons, making in all this year 304 sermons. This will close up this book. Commence a new one with the new year, 1911. So closes 1910 at midnight between 1910 and 1911.

This gives a partial record of the work of A. J Tomlinson since January 1, 1907 to 1911.

1911

January 12, 1911

This is my first writing this year for reasons. First I had no book as I wanted to commence in a new book with the new year. Second, I had no time. Third, I have been sick. At the beginning of the year I was occupied daily with the 6th Annual Assembly as I was General Overseer and acting as clerk also. The Assembly went off fine, being well attended. I got sick at the last, although I went through with the business. Mary was baptized on the 7th of January. Brother Lemons pushed the floating ice away and baptized five. On Sunday the 8th I ordained a brother Scott of Chattanooga as bishop. On Monday night I conducted a business meeting at the church. Selected F. J. Lee as pastor and some other business. Ordered tent of M. D. and H. L. Smith, Dalton, Ga., to be shipped at once to Miami Florida. J. B. Mitchell bought it for $25. I expect to start south as soon as Mary is able for me to leave and I am able to go. Mary has been very sick for a few days.

January 24

Praise the Lord I am well again. Last Sunday was a great day for us at the church. At the morning service after Sunday school I had charge of the meeting and when I had preached up to it I disclosed the fact to the church that Brother Felker had given us the notes he held against the property which was $350, except he wanted $35.00 interest. After appropriate remarks, prayer, tears, praises and thanksgiving I laid a dollar on the pulpit and said I'll give this toward the $35.00. Others followed until when I counted amid tears and praises I had $23.00. I ventured another fifty cents while they sang and I cried and when I counted again I had $36.50. We all cried and praised God. Finally dismissed at nearly one o'clock. I had charge of the afternoon service. The house was packed and when I preached up to the right place I told of the experience of the morning service and announced that we just needed $235 to pay us entirely out of debt. I then announced that I had $1.50 and $25 given as the last of the amount if we could raise the rest. I then asked if any one wished to add another $25.00 to the amount and one arose. We dropped on our knees and thanked God and cried and asked God to bless that one. I then took out a ten dollar gold piece and held it up and stated how that was given me for my personal needs, but that I would sacrifice it and be one of ten that would make one hundred dollars. One after another stood until we got the hundred dollars and we praised God and cried and shouted and sang and then we only lacked eight some odd dollars, so I said it would only take fifteen persons at five dollars to make $75, and as we prayed and cried and shouted one after another rose until that was reached. Then I said there was only a few more dollars wanted to pay out the rest. They began to come forward and lay their money on the pulpit and amid blinding tears I counted until we had enough and I leaped up on the altar on my knees and shouted and praised God telling them to stop, stop, for we had enough but they still kept on coming until there was over five dollars more than I thought I needed. Then amid blinding tears and praises we made the announcements and closed the meeting, Never saw such a revival in my life in raising money. It was the crowning victory on that line of my life. Nobody knew I was going to do what I did. It was a surprise to the people but God did it. When I commenced it nobody thought I would succeed, but God had given me the assurance and faith beforehand. I stated the case and cried and praised God and He did the rest. I did not beg the people to give. I had been sick for two weeks and had not been able to get out before, but God gave me the strength. Praise His dear name. I expect to start for Florida and the Bahama Islands day after tomorrow.

January 30

Left home on the 26th and arrived at Miami, Florida at about 2:00 A. M. January 28. Came on to Cocoanut Grove the same day in the afternoon in a carriage. The folks had the tent already pitched and ready for meeting. We are here right on the sea shore. I preached Saturday night three times yesterday. Big crowd out last night. Four sermons. J. W. Buckalew has joined our band as musical instructor. We organized and commenced this morning. We now have ten in our band. Each one an instrument and have a folding organ besides. The names are as follows, viz. Myself, Efford Haynes, Mrs. Haynes, W. R. Hadsock, Mrs. Hadsock, E. H. Cecil, Roy Miller, Marion Whidden, Luly Williams and J. W. Buckalew. The Lord graciously blest us this morning as we met at the tent to definitely organize the band. When I left home all was well at home. The tent here is arranged here so as I preach I face the ocean and in the day time I can look out over the deep blue sea and think of the heathen beyond. The cry of my heart is, 0

God, help me bear the responsibilities that naturally fall upon me as a leader of the World Wide Mission Band and give me souls and means to supply our needs.

February 1

Just after the afternoon service. Three or four have been definitely healed since we came here. We are practicing on the band music every day before noon and holding meeting at tent afternoon. This afternoon was a special time of weeping and crying over lost souls after I read and explained Isaiah 64. Preached five sermons.

February 5

Preached 7 more sermons. This is Sunday morning. One by the name of Cossey is here doing much injury opposing me but we are going right on and asking God to give us victory above all opposition. Roy and myself took a little boat last evening and went away out in the bay to a larger boat got in it and prayed for nearly an hour. The Lord met with us there and blest our souls and took us into quite a spell of intercessory prayer. The opposition is strong here but we hope to conquer.

February 6

Preached two sermons yesterday. Baptized four in the Biscayne Bay. Quite a crowd at the baptizing. We seem to feel a little victory stealing into the meeting. The weather is fine for tent meeting. So pleasant.

February 9, A. M.

6 more sermons. The battle here is hard but the band practice is going on nicely and the Lord gave great manifestations of His presence yesterday at the meeting. We have not been able to get any one to the altar yet for repentance. It seems to me that but little is being accomplished, but we are all trying to perfectly obey the Lord.

February 13

Eight more sermons. Closed the meeting last night. Great day yesterday. Organized the Church, had the Lord's supper and feet washing. Ordained one bishop, two deacons and granted an evangelist's certificate. One converted last night and one baptized.

February 16

This is early in the morning. We left Cocoanut Grove and Miami last night at seven o'clock on the steamer Miami for Nassau, Bahama Islands. We are on the steamer plowing the waves of the deep blue sea this morning steaming toward Nassau. I have not seen our band any but Brother Cecil this morning, but we are alright. Am going farther and farther away from my precious wife and children. God bless them. One more sermon.

February 18

We arrived in Nassau Thursday February 16. A.M. Brother Evans met us at the landing. We had but little trouble getting through the custom house except we had to pay one pound as duty on the tent. Had a street meeting the same night and every night since. Some at altar tonight. There is need for much work here and on the out islands. Blacks and whites all come to meeting together.

February 19

Near midnight. Our first Sunday in Nassau. Held eight services by dividing out some. I preached six sermons. We held street services where some knelt for prayer and professed religion in the middle of the street. One received the baptism. Successful day.

February 24

We pitched our tent in a beautiful place on the sea shore and have commenced the meetings. Holding meetings at other places in town every night. Large crowds on streets and at tent. Several in altar last night. God is moving. Our family worship lasted this morning for two hours or more. Had a band practice in tent also. Several of us in agonizing prayers and soul travail, Several of us stayed in tent last night, Some opposition and threats but we are going right on by the help of the Lord. Preached three sermons.

February 26

Sunday night after service. Preached three more sermons. Held nine services today in Nassau. I was only in four of them. We are making good impressions on the people apparently. The work is moving on nicely.

March 4

Three services a day all the week. I have been preaching both at the market in the open air and at the tent. Have been marching down the street beating the drum, then beating it lightly at the street services while the organ was played and during singing, then after the close of the street service would march to the tent and beat the drum and collect the crowd. The audience at the tent are getting very attentive and much subdued under the power of the gospel. Preached six sermons.

March 6

This Monday morning. Held services yesterday at tent and the Sponge exchange and market shed and on the streets. Six

services. I preached at tent last night to a large congregations
probably not less than a thousand people. I dismissed the
congregation and quite a number retired and seekers began
to drop in the altar. Others kept dropping in as the power fell
and several were seized with violent jerking, some fell and were
very much exercised under the power of the Spirit. Some were
converted, some sanctified but I don't know that any really got
through to the baptism. We finally closed the service about
eleven o'clock. Some left under the power. Many people were very
serious. We prayed at home then until near one o'clock. Three
more sermons.

March 7

Tuesday morning. Two of our band are leaving us this morning,
Esthil Cecil and Marion Whidden. The battle here is on and it is
hard to give them up right now when they are needed so much
but God will not forsake me. I preached last night I suppose to
about 2,000 people. Some converted and one baptized with the
Holy Ghost. The cry of my heart is, 0 Lord, make me able for the
emergency here. I tried for half an hour I think last night after I
dismissed to get the people to leave the tent. Considering the pack
and press of people and the kind of people we have to deal with
here we had excellent order. God is giving great victory right over
discouragements and oppositions. Praise Him. Things at home are
going very well.

March 9

Three more sermons. This is now nearly midnight. I feel a little
dilapidated. The devil is working so hard against us. Last night
a man came bolting into the tent while I was preaching making
some kind of threats and shaking his fist at me. The police
took him in a very few minutes. Tonight I had just finished my
discourse with good effect on my congregation when a man came
bolting in and right on up to me drunk. I got our folks to sing and
I talked to him a little and when the song was over I stood on the
altar and held him around the neck and prayed a prayer for the
congregation and the man too until many tears were shed. This
too while the man tried to pull away from me but I held him fast
and prayed the harder. It knocked us out of altar service, but God
helped us to get a victory any way. I have been in tough places
and had hard times before, but I never struck such a place as
this before. I feel somewhat perplexed as to just what to do, but
God will direct and help me. The Word is tieing the folks up until
they are beginning to see where they are, they seem amazed at
the doctrine, but so far unable to act. 0 God, my heart goes up
to Thee in prayer for help. This is a rough night at sea. I hear the

roaring of the waves as the surf beats on the shore probably a mile away as I write in my room.

March 11

As I write this afternoon I feel great responsibilities upon me. Souls are perishing and I feel that I am such a small factor in proportion to the great need that I almost vanish from my own sight. The enemy is sure against us having an altar service here in the tent. Last night as I was making the altar call a large man, looking self-important with cane in hand, came forward and asked permission to speak a few words. I detected in him an enemy to the cause and would not grant him the privilege, but ignored him and told him if he wanted to preach to get congregation of his own, and went on with my propositions. This of course hurt the service, yet we all felt it was another victory won. The Lord sure helped me to preach the Word, and many listened with apparent interest.

March 14

This is early in the morning. I was very tired when I came in last night. Sunday night was quite a service. It was thought I preached to more than 2,000 people. Big crowd last night too. Two received the baptism yesterday. Power on some at the altar last night and Sunday night also. Some times the large crowds are hard to handle. I have to stand where I can look over the entire congregation besides preaching for an hour. Preached four more sermons.

March 15

We closed the meeting at tent last night. I don't think I ever saw such an unruly crowd in my life. During the prayer at the close it was impossible to make them show any reverence to God. Of course, there was quite a number who reverenced God but the majority were wild and unruly. Just about the time I dismissed two women got into a fight and how they scratched and tore their clothes was a plenty. Some men, I suppose, undertook to separate them and they got into it and there was quite a rabble but I succeeded in getting the crowd away after working several minutes. We decided it was best to hold services now for a while in private homes. Some are getting through to the baptism. We are now looking to the Lord for directions about going to out islands. God help us to understand Thy voice and make no mistakes.

March 22

On Friday evening, March 17, at 3:30 a party of nine of us, myself, T. W. Buckalew, B. Prom, Roy Miller, C. M. Padgett, E. Haynes, Mrs. Haynes, Lulu Williams and Flora E. Bower, embarked on the schooner boat H. T. C., a sailboat of 15 tons capacity, the Ragged

Island mail boat under Captain Horace Wilson, bound for Ragged Island. Friday night we had a very rough sea. The little bark plunged and pitched and at times even the jib pole and whole front plowed beneath the waves, but always came out uninjured. Sister Haynes and Brother Prom were both sick when we started and during the heavy sea all had a touch of sea sickness except Brother and Sister Haynes. Myself and two or three of the boys stayed out on deck all night and the water splashed over us many times. I was sick but a very little and it did not hurt me to amount to anything. Some of the others were very sick and suffered very severely. On Saturday evening we arrived at Farmers Cay and the captain thought best to anchor in the harbor until morning on account of the heavy wind and sea. So we all went ashore and the people met us and gave us a glad welcome. Sunday morning, March 19, 1911, at 9:30. Just got aboard the schooner after spending the night on Farmers Cay where there are 172 persons. They live in stone and plaster houses with thatched roofs. All colored people. They received us gladly and gave us a special welcome. We held service in their little church house last night. Had a splendid island service nearly all of the little island were present. At the close of the discourse (sermon) delivered by myself, many hands went up for prayer. They gave us a little collection and we gave them tracts and papers. They entertained the sisters and Brother Haynes in their homes and we boys slept in the little church house. This morning we were given a nice breakfast of native grits, bread, tea and fish. We all feel much refreshed. As I write the little settlement fades from view as we journey on toward the south bound for Ragged Island. Beautiful day and nice sea. We surely will not forget our pleasant visit at Farmers Cay. Before leaving Brother Haynes photographed a view of the quaint little houses and a small group of the natives.

March 20

About four o'clock last evening we were put into a harbor and anchored on account of a lack of wind and the sailors rowed us ashore on Brigantine Cay where we stayed till night. Carl Padgett and I went away off to the middle of the island and spent our time in prayer. The Lord blest us in prayer very much. Out on at island where was no inhabitants reminded me of John on Patmos. I almost wanted to say for days just to wait on God and pray. The wind rose so the sailors hoisted the sails about eight o'clock so we sailed all night. We are now on the deep blue sea as I write at 7:40 A. M. Monday morning. Tuesday was a slow day on account of the lack of wind. We finally arrived at the harbor of Ragged Island and cast anchor about eight o'clock in the evening. We stayed on board the vessel all night and this morning was brought to shore in a smaller vessel and landed about ten o'clock. It was a beautiful sight to see the natives coming down the hill from the town to meet us. About 100 people met us at the landing and gave us a glad welcome. News of our arrival had been brought to the island by some of the sailors who came to shore last night. As soon as we could after landing we opened the little organ and played and sang and read the 95th and 96th Psalms for a greeting to them. Then we prayed and after I made a few appropriate remarks we sang and dismissed the people with a few more words of prayer. A white lady gave us a kind invitation to her home and we came, and she served us with tea after which we bathed and brushed ourselves up while some went out to pray. I too went out into a thicket and prayed and thanked God. Since I commenced to write a brother came in saying a place was open for meeting tonight. All are feeling good and blest of the Lord. About 400 inhabitants here. We are now it the home of Madam F. C. Wilson, who has given us rooms during our stay.

March 24

I have had opportunity to look about a little. The people live in small stone and plaster houses. Streets are narrow with stone walls on either side. The natives, men and women and children go barefooted principally. The old women with short dresses and rings in their ears and on their fingers and beads around their necks look very odd indeed. Many of the men have jewelry in their ears. They raise sisel [sic] for ropes and manufacture ropes in their way and make mats and baskets and hats. They have a way of getting salt so they have large salt pits. The men fish and turtle. They have no horses, mules or cattle. The people are very kind to us and bring in food of different kinds. Grits, meal, bread and other things. We hold the services at night in a little chapel owned by some kind of Baptists. Then there is a Church of England house and a Plymouth Brethren Hall. The first night after I preached three of the Plymouth brethren withstood me sharply and accused me of preaching damnable doctrine, but I gave them the rope until I saw them hang themselves beautifully and we had prayer and closed the service with victory in spite of the trial on their part for controversy. Last night the service went off smoothly. A very pleasant outdoor service was held last evening. The brass band rendered excellent service and a good impression was made. Some of our company are not feeling well but we have victory in our souls. We are now 211 miles southeast from Nassau, about sixty miles from Cuba. Very dry and warm. Preached four sermons. My heart cries out to God for souls. It is nearly time now to go to the evening outdoor service.

March 26

High noon. Just returned to my room from a formal native Sunday service. Very cold and formal but they showed us profound respect. We are to have the service tonight, When we came here we found the island dry and suffering for want of rain. We felt such a sympathy for the people. Once while in prayer I felt an intensity in my heart and prayed for rain, others prayed for rain and the rain came and refreshed the parched island. Last evening, we held a short street service, photographed the natives at the meeting. The wind blew so strong and showery so we came to our rooms, but quite a number of natives followed us and later others came until quite a crowd had gathered and I took advantage of the time and preached to them. Before leaving Nassau Brother Evans insisted on us bringing with us cooking utensils and a supply of food. In praying about it I told the Lord I felt queer about doing that and told him I felt like trusting Him. We brought enough to do us on the boat and it is wonderful how the natives have brought us supplies until we here fared almost sumptuously. Bread, grits, fish, sugar, cakes, beans, peas, eggs, chicken, peanuts, cocoanuts, watermelon and other things. Last night before retiring our band spent nearly two hours in weeping and thanking God and prayer. We felt so thankful for the supplies that our Father sent in by the natives. It is very interesting to see the men and women as well as the children come to meeting barefooted and many of them with much jewelry hanging to their ears and rings on their fingers. We are doing our best for them. Giving them tracts, gospels, beside the singing, preaching and praying. The wind is strong now and unless it abates we will not be able to get off tomorrow. The will of the Lord be done.

March 27

10:00 P. M. We failed to get off today, so held services again this afternoon and tonight. Held services last evening and last night. The power struck several but none have gone through. Six have been converted. The captain and his mate. Numbers are accepting the truth and seeking. Preached two more sermons. We expect to sail tomorrow if the sea is favorable.

March 30

Now on Long Island. We were up early on the morning of the 28th. Most of the folks on Ragged Island were out to see us off. They carried our luggage to the landing only about 100 yards. As we arrived there we opened the organ and sang and read Acts 20:28-38 and 2 Cor. 13:11 and had prayer. After prayer we formed a line and all the natives passed by and we took them by the hand and a many a "God bless you" was said. We then stepped on the little boat that was to carry us out to the schooner H. J. C. As we started off we sang, "God be with you till we meet again." At last the last handkerchief waves were given and we were gone. Goodby Ragged Island maybe forever, but we felt a sweet assurance that we had been faithful and the gospel had been preached to them as a witness. We breakfasted on the schooner as we entered the Broad Atlantic. Some of our party were sick again but not so many as before. We sailed all day and all night and early in the morning of the 29th of March we sighted Long Island. It was about ten o'clock before we effected a landing and then only Brother Buckalew and myself with the captain and his brother. Brother Buckalew and myself went on to Clarence town a distance of four miles to arrange for the rest and conveyance and the crew unloaded our luggage and the remainder of our party on the shore by means of a little row boat. It was interesting as they battled with the waves with the little skiff. We had to walk and carry our things for a mile on the sandy and rocky shore before reaching the highway that led across the island to the town. Brother Buckalew and I returned with a horse cart and extra horse for Mrs. Haynes to ride. Some of the natives had already volunteered their service and we met them as they were carrying our grips, drums, etc., on their heads and one man with two large baskets full on a horse's back. We had rented a little four room house for $1.25 a week where we arrived at in the evening all safe in time to have supper before dark. Sister Bower and Lulu had come on ahead and already the natives had loaned them some rough cooking vessels and they were cooking out of doors, Prom having found some wood and water. We took our instruments, band and organ, and went down on the street and held a nice service at seven o'clock. 200 or more people gathered to hear as we played, sang, prayed and preached. A gentleman volunteered to take up a collection for us because they were so well pleased. The captain and his crew had been so faithful to us on our voyage that we parted with them very reluctantly. I kissed the captain and rewarded him for his services and waved them off having delivered to him some letters to mail, for here on Long Island I will have no opportunity to send nor receive mail for quite a while. When we told the natives what we were here for, quite a number rejoiced and said, "Happy, happy," and bowed and twinkled their eyes. They commenced bringing in food last evening and again this morning before I arose from sleep. We slept on the floor on our blankets and the Lord refreshed us very much. Mrs. Haynes is still sick, but all the balance are feeling fine. We are shut away from the outside world completely, but it is all for Jesus. No religious work here except Catholics and the natives do not like them, but seem so glad we have come. We are now in a village of about 600 inhabitants without the gospel. This town is not so closely compact as was Ragged Island, but they live in little stone and plaster houses with thatched roofs. There are a few wood buildings. We are located where we can look out the broad Atlantic Ocean. There are eight other towns on this island. Some larger and some perhaps smaller. Much work to do. Folks at home can't hear from us, neither can we hear from them.

March 31

Held a good open air service last night. The natives are bringing in food to us. It is wonderful how He is supplying our needs. Brothers Buckalew and Padgett started this morning to visit a place about twelve miles distant and some settlements between here and there. Roy and I have been visiting and praying for the sick. The natives show us much kindness and appreciation of our visit with them on the Island. The little huts where we have been show penury and want. No chairs. No beds except some kind of scaffolds that they have fixed up.

April 1

We were very kindly invited to hold our service in a hall last night and it was filled to overflowing. The Lord gave us a very pleasant service again. The natives seem to appreciate us even more than they did at Ragged Island. They bring us food of all kinds they have. Chicken, eggs sweet potatoes, crabs, onions, beans, peas, watermelon, popays [sic], grits, sugar, etc. I have learned to eat crabs and lobster. I was very much in wonder when I first came on the island as when I would salute or greet them and ask "how are you" they would answer "so and so." I don't know what they mean by it. An old native told me this morning that the people were well pleased with our message of love and that nothing of the kind had ever been brought to them before. They listen very attentive and show the utmost respect to us and the gospel. They grind their own grits on hand mills and it is not infrequent that we see "two women grinding at the mill," The days are very hot but the nights are more pleasant.

April 3

This is Monday morning just after breakfast. Sunday is over with its blessings. The gospel been gradually loving its effect on the people from the very beginning. Yesterday afternoon about fifty or more knelt for prayer and a spirit of weeping came on quite a number of them. No apparent results were reached, however, except a good interest manifest. Last night the house was crowded and I preached with nothing more than ordinary unction and no extra liberty, and at the close I did not know how to make an altar call as there was no room, so I just said, all that want to kneel for prayer just find a place to pray the best you can. They began to kneel and we began to pray when presently one fell over and began to scream and this created quite a little stir, soon another fell and another and another and on and on until the floor was filled with seekers down under the power. Some would try to move or help them and they too would fall under the power and such a time as this island had never seen before. Such crying with loud voices, begging for mercy, demonstrations and bodily exercises as even I never saw before, that is, so many at one time. The shreaks and groans and cries of despair that rendered the air at times almost seemed like we were plunged into a cesspool of hell. The physical operations were so great and so many engaged that the table was moved about until two men took hold of it with a thought of moving it and just as they did so, a wave of power fell and it was with difficulty that they held it up and able to stand themselves. The wave finally subsided and the men moved the table out of the house. Others still kept falling. Along in the course of the service a man came in almost breathless and wished to speak with me. I listened as he told how he and his wife and daughter, 18 years of age, had gone home and the daughter had fallen at home just like the folks at the meeting. He wanted to know what to do with her, if he should bring her to the hall. I told him not to be uneasy that she could remain at home just as well. I saw he was anxious so I volunteered to go home with him to comfort him. When I arrived I found the young woman lying on the floor crying and screaming and they had her hands tied together with a rope and her feet tied together. I stayed a few minutes and returned to the hall. About midnight the father came to the hall all elated and glad and said his daughter had gotten up and so happy. We left the hall a little after midnight and one was still down but quiet as if in a trance. Some saw visions, some were converted, some sanctified and filled with the Holy Ghost. I don't know all that was done but to say the least, it was a wonderful meeting and much good accomplished. Folks are coming in this morning happy and glad which is much different from the way they have been. The scene could not be fully described. Men, women and children were weeping besides those who were down under the power. Brothers Buckalew and Padgett came in this morning from their journey and report good times and lacked nothing while away. Don't know yet how long we will remain here. No chance to hear from home and no chance to send word home. Sacrifice for Jesus. Preached four sermons since last record.

April 4

We made a photograph of first natives we saw after we landed
on Long Island. The power fell on a number in the meeting last
night. One young woman came to the meeting and remained on
the outside because there was such a crowd she could not get in.
When the service was dismissed she went home and about the
time she reached her home she was struck down under the power
of God and it so engaged her parents that they would not let her
in but thrust her trunk out at the door and drove her away. A
relative took her in for the night. She is here now lying under
the power in an adjoining room. She says she is so hungry for
God. She wants to go through with Him at any cost. The enemy
was stirred last night because I spoke so clear about a clean life,
mentioning adultery, or having more than one wife, and other
things. God is working on many hearts also.

April 7

Had meeting every night and some receiving the baptism at every
service. Baptized five in Great harbor. God [sic] a picture of it. We
are still practicing with our instruments and learning to march,
form a circle and commence playing, so we can commence a
street meeting in that way, The folks here are still supplying us
with food. It is wonderful how God is taking care of us. It gives us
great joy to see the shining faces of those who are receiving the
baptism. How they are coming out.

April 11

Three sermons. Last Sunday morning as I preached, the hearts
of the people were melted as I showed the Church of God, its
importance, etc. At the close of the discourse, at a proposition as
to how many wanted to join the Church of God (Bible Church) I
suppose 60 or 70 rose up. We had quite a time shaking hands.
Sunday night after Brother Buckalew preached he got one to
come to the altar and called on me to pray a closing prayer as if
he intended to dismiss, and I felt very dry and weak as if I could
hardly pray. I commenced, however, and the Lord took hold of
me and soon people were bathed in tears, sobs and groans were
heard and when I looked up the altar was full of seekers. The
meeting did not close for a while. Some fell, others wept and I
don't know the results of the meeting. Thus closed the meeting
at Clarencetown, Long Island. I suppose about 15 received
the baptism 14 baptized in water. I have not learned the exact
number that came into the Church. Sister Bower has the names.
Yesterday morning early five of us started for Deadman's Cay on

foot, a distance of fourteen miles. We left Brother Haynes and the three women to return to Nassau on the first boat on the account of the ill health of Mrs. Haynes. About fifteen or more of the natives came with us to escort us on the journey. Two pack horses were loaded with our grips and some of the sisters took our drums and other small luggage on their heads. Soon a native came along with a horse and insisted on me riding so I rode most of the way, though reluctantly because all the others had to walk. As we journeyed the sisters sang beautiful songs as if they wished to cheer us on the way. Occasionally some would have to turn back and as we left them at saying the final farewell they cried like babies. About eight or ten came all the way with us and some returned the same day while others stayed over night. The Lord had some rooms for us and the people received us very kindly and gave us lunch, lemonade, popcorn, grapefruit tea and bread. About seven o'clock we went out on a hill and rock pile and began to play our band and soon I had about 150 people to preach to. I stepped up on a rock and delivered the message. At the close they gave us a little collection and we gave out a lot of tracts. Came to our rooms very much jaded and feeling the need of food. We kneeled down and prayed and thanked God and we felt sure our heavenly Father had some way to give us some refreshments. We had scarcely got up from prayer when a native came and invited us to "tea". We ate and thanked God, and laid down to rest with only our blankets and pillows, but we all feel refreshed this morning and ready for service. This morning an old lady came to the door and presented us with seven nice ripe tomatoes, three big onions and a very large sweet potato and a piece of a yam. This is the beginning here.

April 12

Yesterday was heavy labor. Had a long band practice and afternoon we took our instruments and marched about three miles to a shade in the road and we played and sang till a congregation gathered and we gave them the gospel and tracts. We came back and at night we went back to the same ledge of rocks where we were last night and played and sang till a large crowd came and we gave them the gospel again. I never saw such a place for a meeting, but God was with us. It was an interesting sight to see the large crowd as they sat and stood close together on that ledge of rocks in the beautiful moonlight. Some followed us home and this morning some came in for prayer early. They are bringing us food and supplying every need. A dear brother came from Clarencetown yesterday and as he took his departure again this morning he cried and words he spoke of how much the Lord had blest Him by our visit to Clarencetown, etc. was enough to pay us for seasickness, hardships, sacrifices, etc. for all the trip. I am getting some of the most valuable experiences of my life. I am seeing more and more the value of the band and instruments. Some who came with us from Clarencetown are still here and rendering excellent service by their testimonies and singing. Nearly everybody in this country go barefooted, men, women and children. I write now after meeting at night. We held a service in the shade of a tree about three miles distant this afternoon and our last service on the rock pile tonight. I preached from a part of Christ's sermon on the Mount. And what an impression it made on me as I saw the large company sitting around me on the rock like I imagine they were when Jesus was preaching that wonderful sermon. As I closed the discourse and talked about going away tomorrow a number began to weep. I've had lot of different experiences, but this one was one that has made a deep impression on me. They just sit down and cried right out like their hearts would break. There we were on that ledge of rocks in the moon light and that crowd around us and a number weeping and me so impressed with Jesus' sermon on the Mount and the crowd around Him, I could not suppress the tears. Well, I never saw such a meeting in my life. I am unable to express my feelings and the impression it made on me. Surely I'll never regret my visit to Long Island. At the close we sang, God be with you till we meet again, while not a few were in tears. Our stay here has been short (we expect to go on tomorrow) and we have seen no definite results from our labor, yet we have reason to believe some good has been accomplished. Some came to our room for prayer and many heard the everlasting gospel. God supplied our needs in a wonderful way. We were almost compelled to eat four meals yesterday, the people supplied us so bountifully. We will hardly ever forget this place, though we may forget the individuals.

April 14

Yesterday morning we bid Deadman's Cay adieu and took boat for the Bight on Long Island, When we took the boat some of the people who had been so blest at Clarencetown with others were on the shore to say goodby. They cried like babies. It seemed they could hardly stand it for us to leave them with the thought that they would never see us again after God had made us such a blessing to them. They stood on the shore and wept as long as we could see them in the distance. When we arrived at the Bight the boatman landed us and we walked up the hill and began to play the band. We were invited into a house where we rested a few minutes and had prayer with those who came in and gave out literature, gave some instructions about experimental salvation and bid them farewell and took the boat and came on to Miller and where we landed the boatman carried us out on his back. We carried our luggage to a near house and then walked a mile or more where they received us gladly and while we arrived late in the evening they arranged for us a meeting and quite a crowd gathered and the Lord gave us a good meeting and good food and good beds. This morning we bid them farewell and came in the little boat to Simses. We had just landed when a gentleman came and met us and gave us a cordial welcome, he having heard some way we were coming. He escorted us to his brother's home (Mr. Sims) where we were received very pleasantly. This was "good Friday" and there was two services to be held at eleven o'clock, so we watched for the time of dismission and when they closed we marched to the drum to the school house yard and there held a service about two P. M. Quite a crowd present. At the close we were invited to the home of Mr. Sims where tea was prepared for us. After tea, we retired to the boat and got our grips and were shown to a pleasant house with thatched roof and some furniture. We came in and peace filled our hearts. We had prayer and dedicated it to God during our stay. We were invited out to tea again and then went to the school house ground where we held a very pleasant service. We are winning the favor of the people already. Preached two sermons. This is now 10:30 at night after the service. Beds ready for us on the floor.

April 15. 3:40 P. M.

Just got back to our home at Simses. We went this morning to Millington on a sail boat several miles up the coast where we held three services and the last one was very impressive as at the close of the discourse, which I preached in tears, I turned the drum down and make an altar of it and invited the people forward for prayers. They commenced coming as we sang and, well, we prayed and cried and it was very impressive. They gave us a good dinner of bread, tea and grits and we bid them goodby. We left them literature, gospels and song books. Three sermons.

April 17

We have held six services at Simms's since we came and every one very impressive. All out of doors in the sunshine in the day time and moonlight at night. The last service held tonight was very impressive. At the close of the discourse nearly all said they wanted the baptism with the Holy Ghost and kneeled down on the ground several deep around the drum. Tears and sobs were seen and heard and the spirit was at work. We finally sang "God be with you" and shook hands with them amid tears and sobs and said goodnight. About fifty said they meant to continue seeking until they received the baptism and spoke in tongues according to the Bible. Three men have volunteered to take their sailboat and carry us to Exuma, the next island tomorrow, a distance of forty miles. Dear Brother Simms has been very kind to us and others too. We expect to say goodby to Long Island tomorrow morning. One more sermon.

April 18

This is now 10:10 at night. We left Long Island today about eleven o'clock in the schooner Doubtless. Three men, Maxwell Pinder, Maxwell Gray and Theophilus T. Knowles offered their schooner and services free to take us to Exuma Island. The schooner went aground off the coast of Exuma before reaching the place of landing, so they landed us and our luggage in a little oar boat. The folks at Simmses prepared us lunch and we ate it on a rock on the shore where we landed. Then we had to walk two or three miles before reaching the village and along the shore and then through the bushes, thorns, over rocks and at last we reached a road. Just before entering the village we discovered a well and turned aside and were refreshed with the water. As we entered the village (Salt Pond) the people ran down to meet us and although we were strangers they did not know we were coming they gave us a glad welcome and escorted us to a little stone house and as we arrived on the porch we opened our instruments and played a few strains and sung a few songs and Brother Buckalew read and preached to them. This service closed about 6:30 P. M. At 8:15 the crowd were back again for service and I preached to a very attentive audience. At the close we gave out tracts and gospels. The experience we had in getting from the boat to the village was very interesting. We had to carry our luggage, band instruments and fight our way through the thorns and briars. The thorns tore our clothes and flesh until some times the blood would run out. We are to have a service tomorrow morning at five o'clock. We are tired but full of victory and grace.

April 20

We held the early morning service at Saltpong (Williamstown) and bid them goodby, some of the natives accompanied us carrying our luggage. We walked about seven miles to Forbshill, where we were received gladly and while we thought of pushing on to the next place but they pressed us and constrained us to stay over night, so we had a very pleasant service in their little chapel at night. This morning we walked about two miles to the strait between Little Exuma and Great Exuma where we took a little boat and crossed over to Great Exuma and landed an hour or two at Heartswell where we had a service and gave out tracts. Then we came to Rolletown in the same little boat and arrived there about one o'clock. They gave us refreshments and we held a very pleasant service in their chapel, besides a prayer service we held in a home where we were entertained. Before reaching this place the boatman landed the boys and they walked on the shore while he walked in the water and tugged the little boat through a narrow shallow channel. At the close of the service at their chapel we gave out tracts and said goodby, but they all followed us to the shore and sang beautifully as we marched. We stepped aboard and give them the last farewell wave and was off to sea again. Toward night the wind dropped and left the sea in a calm and the boat was to skull the rest of the way. We were so hindered on this passage that we did not reach Georgetown until after dark. The village was all astir when we reached it about eight o' clock at night, oweing to a messenger who had walked in and informed the people of our coming, and the cornets the boys were blowing. They gave us kind greetings, carried our luggage and led the way to a house God had waiting for us. Quite a crowd gathered in and around the house and we sang a song, read a Scripture greeting, had prayers and I gave them a short message, explanations, etc. Soon chairs, table, food and water was brought in and we sat down and enjoyed the refreshments. I write now at about ten P. M. at Georgetown, Great Exuma Island. We will await the morrow and see what develops. One sermon.

April 22

This is now Saturday, 10:20 A. M. Just came aboard the little sailboat bound for Nassau. We held three good open air services yesterday. The people at Georgetown are not as appreciative as at other places we have been. There is more drinking. They think they can drink and go to heaven, too. We gave them the truth but in our short stay there is no indication of anybody receiving it. We marched and played the instruments for the first time on our way to the street service last evening. Five of us can play real well for our practice. The vessel we are on is named Francis and eight tons. I preached last night with some liberty. The people were on either side of the street for about fifty yards and I had the middle of the street. It was easy to walk and run occasionally illustrating. I feel now that we are about done for the present on the Bahamas. We feel drawn back to America.

April 25

This is Tuesday. We arrived in Nassau about midnight, Sunday night. I found 16 letters for me. Among them was letters from home stating the hard trials wife and children were having. It nearly broke my heart to think I was so busy working for Jesus, going through hardships and making sacrifices and then my

precious family at home suffering so. In my heart was found
no rebellion but a quiet submissiveness to His will who says all
things work together for good to them that love the Lord. A letter
from my daughter Halcy shows how they are standing the test
at home. Also one from Homer. These letters which show the
martyr spirit and true heroism has given me reason for being
very proud of my precious family. These letters are in front of
this book. This special test has come upon us no doubt for our
good and our position in glory will be above that we would have
occupied had not this great trial come our way. God gives me
grace. We arranged to start for America this morning and get our
luggage aboard, and the sea was so rough that the captain would
not venture out. The storm commenced the night we arrived at
Nassau, we were in some of it, but it got more severe and has
continued until now and we may be delayed several days. This
adds to our trial for I can't get word home and they don't know
whether I have their letters or not. God is giving grace but we can
pray and trust God to bring all things out right. Another letter
received on the New York steamer this morning from the hand of
my dear wife gives me a little consolation although it is a week old
today. This letter is also preserved in front of book. Since writing
above I have decided to copy the letters here: "Friday afternoon,
Cleveland, Tenn., April 7, 1911. Dearest Papa: I wonder how you
are this evening. I do wish you were at home. We need you oh so
bad. Mama is sick again, been pretty sick for about two weeks,
but papa, she had the worst spell today she has had at all. Even
Brother Bryant give her up, but I didn't, papa, even though she
got so she couldn't hardly talk and was cold, I couldn't think
the Lord would forsake us and you out working for Him. She is
resting better this afternoon for which we are very thankful. She
called for you all the time. Said if you were only here, believed
she would be better. But said tell you not to come home and leave
your work on her account. But papa, we do need you so much.
Of course, dear, we haven't said much about it, but mama hasn't
been well since you left, you know all about it. Now, dear papa,
we don't want to worry you, for we are so anxious for you to do all
you can for the Lord, but I just wanted to tell you so you all could
pray for us. No doubt, this very day you are praying especially for
us. I feel as though you are. And dear, we certainly are praying
for you, for I know you have lots of hard places such as we know
not of. We are all suffering together, aren't we, dear papa? And I
do want you to especially pray for Homer, he certainly is having a
hard time—pray mightily for him. I know he is the dearest boy in
the world and awfully close to God or he would be overcome. Dear,
don't let this letter discourage you for we expect to be faithful.
Though He slays us, still will we trust Him. We girls are all right.

The only thing is being so hindered in our school work. This is such a busy time for me now. But God knows all about it. Surely we'll get through some how. God bless you, dear papa. Pray much for us and do as God directs and we will pray for you. I want to get this off on this mail so must close. We are in hopes mama will be alright again in a few days. But I get awfully discouraged some times, papa, she hasn't been all right in so long. Bye, bye. With much love, Your daughter, Halcy.

Cleveland, Tenn., April 10, 1911 Dear Papa: Will write you a few more lines if I can. I am a dreadful feeling human and am now entertaining sarcastically that terrible and inhuman malady, i-t-c-h. Oh, that the overflowing fountain of the healing oil of God might apply its soothing essence to the mortifying skin of my body. The terrible terror of this infernal disease is so uncontrollably distracting as to turn the soporific bed to a sleepless pile of cotton. Last night as I lay upon my bed sleepy, but sleepless, and the fragrant beams of the moon cast their glossy luster on the window sash, it was no easy job to cast away the thought of the terrible epidemic that was depriving me of going to meeting, depriving me of going to school, making me walk like some poor fellow and low down sot that had the _____ causing me to feel that every one who approached me did so reluctantly. Mama is sick; she has the sympathy of great numbers. I am worse than sick; I feel that I have the disdain of hundreds. Oh miserable creature that I am, who shall deliver me from the mortifying skin of this body! I have to run the tabernacle meetings for a month. What more irksome and direful representative of the Church of God could have been chosen? After having endured various humiliations and adversities all day Sunday, last night when preparing for bed, suddenly as the ribbon lightning, unexpectedly as the day of Pompeii's destruction, firm as the declaration against Babylon, came a vivid message from heaven, "I will bruise Satan under your feet shortly." Now papa, if ever you prayed for a perishing soul, pray for mine, that it perish not with my body. I am still living for God day by day. My entire time is in the service of God. I scarcely know what an idle moment is. What reward am I receiving for it? What compensation do I now realize? "If in this world only we have hope in Christ, we are of all men most miserable." I believe it was the Lord that spoke those words to me last night, papa, so I believe I will try to be encouraged. I am not altogether discouraged, but I am bordering on despair, it seems to me. Mama is much better, I am glad to say. (I can't half write.) She is able to sit up some and can eat a little but not much. Pray much for her. Brother Bryant said he was praying for you continually almost. Said his orphanage work was prospering. He is now in a deal for some property. He said if Sister

Bower wanted to he would be glad for her to come and be matron in the home. Humbly (and feeling a little better), Homer Tomlinson.

April 11, Dear Papa: Mama seems to be awful bad. She last night for the first time consented for us to send for you. It seems almost like the proper thing for you to come. Of course, though, you use your own judgment in the matter. Her spells seem to be getting worse and worse and very much more frequent, Brother Bryant seems to think it is gall stones passing her stomach or rather through her liver. She called pitiably for you last night when she was in the very throes of death it seemed. Homer

Cleveland, Tennessee, April 17, 1911, My dear husband: I was so glad to get your good letters. Got one Friday, the other one Saturday. Was so glad the work is still going on, but dear papa, you can't tell how bad you are needed at home till school is out any way. We are all sure having a test. I am writing this in bed, can hardly stay up long enough for them to make my bed. I have to be waited on; Homer is having awful, awful case and time with the old _____. Has not been to school for over a week, can't go this week, can't even split the kindling on account of his hands. Iris has the roseola. Can't go to school or do much. Milton getting naughty because I am not able to look after him. Halcy needs every moment for herself, but has to go to school the best she can and wait on us too. Papa, we sure need you. Can't you come on and let the rest run the meetings until after school is out? We have all tried to live closer to the Lord this time than ever before, and why we have these tests I can't tell. Jesus knows. I felt real well this A. M., got up, could not stay up only about half an hour, and suffered so bad for a while. If I lay right still and keep real warm I rest very well, but so nervous I can't sleep much. Homer, the precious boy, is doing the best he can with the paper work, but if he gets better he needs all his time for his studies, and if you could come—take charge until after school is out and help wait on me and help the poor children out that much. I am not able to write you the news, will tell you when you come. Write what you can do as soon as you get this. You will find the other letters we have written. By, by, dear. Trust to see you soon. Your afflicted Mary."

All of the above going on and me shut in here at Nassau, Bahamas because the sea is too rough to venture and no way to send any message home to relieve them. But we all have a spirit of submission to the will of God. The storm is still on and I don't know when we will be able to cross the sea to America. I met some men on the street today from Ragged Island where we were a month ago and they said the work was still moving on nicely. This is encouraging to us, proving our visit there was not in vain. Several had been baptized in water since we were there and still others expecting to be baptized soon.

April 26. 2:00 P. M.

Received about an hour ago the following cablegram from home, addressed to Brother Hackett. "Notify Tomlinson wife dangerously ill." I returned, "Coming soon." Here I am shut in by the storm on the sea and my precious family needing me so bad. I rest in Him and pray, God knows what is best. I am serving Him with all my heart and my family is true, too, and why this is allowed by the hand of providence is unknown to me but by His grace I am able to say, "Thy will be done." The storm is still on and but little indications of abatement and I can only pray and ask God to comfort and bless the precious ones at home. As much as I want to help them I cannot. I know there are kind friends and neighbors to care for them and they will do all in their power for them, but that is not husband and papa. I confess I tremble and have some fears that that over persuasion by somebody may weaken them and cause remedies or physicians to be resorted to. So I say, O God, don't let their faith fail in this trying hour.

April 29

We left Nassau, Bahamas about 10:30 April 27, 1911, on the Frances E, a gasoline and sailboat. The storm had abated some but sea very rough. Some of our party soon got sick, others kept up all the way. The vessel rode the waves and landed us safe in Miami in about twenty hours. The quickest run they have ever made. We had much delay at Miami in getting through the custom house examinations, etc., as there were some foreigners on board. I wired home and the answer came soon—how is mama? Answer immediately. Start home at six P. M." A. J. Tomlinson. Answer—"Mama resting easy today. Glad you are coming," Homer. I was much relieved and I feel my family were somewhat comforted to know husband and papa was on American soil again. J. W. Buckalew and myself left Miami at six last evening, arrived here about ten today (Jacksonville where I now write.) Brother and Sister Haynes go to Maitland, Sister Bower to Tampa, Lulu to her home at Crewsville, Roy and Carl remain at Miami, Prom to Cocoanut Grove. Thus we will be separated for a few weeks. I leave here at 8:25 tonight for home. I am very anxious indeed to get home. I left my tent and fixtures at Miami.

May 11

I arrived home on the 30th of April. I found my wife very weak and low although slightly improved from what she had been. Children had proven true and faithful in the test. The sheriff came to see about calling a doctor but wife politely told him she was trusting in God and wanted no physician. Praise God for such a wife and children. Wife has been gradually improving ever since I arrived home. The work is piling up but I am coming out from under it. Children are finishing up their term of school. They are getting better too. I preached a funeral since coming home and delivered a sermon lecture at the church the night of the 7th of May to a full house. On the 9th of May, 1911, we organized The Faith Orphanage and Children's Home Association. I expect to be home a little while yet, although I am wanted to conduct a camp meeting in Florida and to hold meetings elsewhere.

May 15

I went to Sunday school and meeting yesterday and preached last night at church. On Saturday, the 13th, I commenced to write a book. It had been on my mind for a month or more and at last I consented to write it while on my knees in prayer. I quietly arose and went to work and wrote the introduction. The name "The Doctrine Explained."

May 22

Preached a funeral sermon a week or so ago. Last Friday morning just after midnight, dear wife was attacked again and while we prayed and did everything we could she suffered until ten o'clock the same day, about ten or more hours. Such suffering as I never saw before and never want to see again. She was not able to stay in bed and had not been able to be up for several days. She was very weak. She became so outrageously affected that at times she became almost unmanageable, jerked away from us and looked wild and daring like a maniac, but we held on until finally the victory was reached and yet it looked to us like death. There she was lying on the floor with me holding up her feet, Homer and Milton at her head, Halcy on her right as she lay and Iris on her left. We were alone in the room with the door closed. Several neighbors and friends in the house, but we were alone. I'll hardly ever forget that scene. How God came down and comforted and blest us. We finally picked her up and laid her on the bed, for by this time she was helpless and seemed to be sinking away. Brothers Lee, McLain, and Bryant and the children kneeled around her and prayed. After this she requested that we send for all the church, neighbors and friends as God had told her to take them by the hand and give them a message and a blessing. With no effort scarcely the notice traveled rapidly and the people began to come. She began giving the message and blessing and the presence of God was there to bless. Her strength came and the radiance of heaven came into her face and all who came and heard the message and she took by the hand were wonderfully touched by the Spirit, both saint and sinner. I never saw the like before. She preached for five hours, stopping only long enough to take a few spoons-full of water occasionally for she could not be raised up. Probably 200 people were thus present and really received and felt the blessing. The next day was the same. Power fell in the room many times during the day. Yesterday (Sunday) was much the same and some today. She has eaten comparitively nothing for days and days. She is very weak only as the Spirit comes on her, then she shines, shouts and gives the message and blessing. Don't know what the results will be, but it has worked wonders already. The Simpsons are affected as well as many, many others. She says she may not be able to arise any more and yet she may be spared, but she is entirely subject and submissive to His will. At this writing she appears like she will recover yet we have no assurance yet, but we are saying His will be done.

June 6

My companion is still with us and has so much improved that she has her dress on and sits in a rocking chair. Her strength and appetite are gradually coming back and we are very much encouraged about her complete recovery. I went to Chattanooga early Sunday morning to hold the dedication service of their tabernacle. Before time for the service I was waiting at Brother Thompson's home and while there his daughter and a friend both about twenty years of age took poison and tried to end their lives. We found it out and with some difficulty we at last made them see they would go to hell if they died in that way and we finally succeeded in getting them to want to get over it and kept them moving until a physician came and relieved them of the effect of the poison. They both promised to live better in the future. I delivered the discourse at about eleven o'clock and at exactly 12:00 A.M. the tabernacle was given over to God formally while the congregation were standing. The power fell and the demonstrations showed that God had really taken charge for the place was filled with His glory, Five were baptized in the river afternoon and at night we had the sacrament and feet washing. Came home early Monday morning. Preached four sermons. I am very closely engaged in the interest of the paper. All my time is taken.

June 19

Put up tent the 8th and I commenced to take charge of the services so I preached four sermons and had to give it up on account of a rising on my back which has given me much pain for a week, but I have worked every day in the office.

June 26

Preached two sermons yesterday at church house, Yesterday afternoon the Lord manifested His presence as I preached. The people were instructed and edified. At night the power fell in a wonderful way. People were thrown down and jerked about and lying under the power. A man's wife fell under the power and he got mad and tried to take her out of the altar but she lay like lead on the floor and he could not lift her and she got saved. Others were converted. Well, it was almost like Pentecost, Glory. Homer led the meeting at the tabernacle and they had a shower down there,

July 2, Midnight

We have been having meeting every night the past week at the tent and prayer meetings twice a day at F. J Lee's. The meetings have been gathering in power and love and this afternoon the Lord wonderfully blest as I preached and then we went to pool and I baptized seven or eight. Tonight the power rained down in torrents and swept some into Pentecost, others into other experiences and quite a number were refreshed. Halcy played the organ under the power and well, it was Pentecost again. Preached seven sermons. Wife is still improving,

July 4

Thank God. Another day for Jesus. Quite a number met at F. J. Lee's at nine this morning, had a fine service until 10:20, went to the tent and the services were grand and glorious as we worshiped and praised and testified until an opportune time when I called an altar service and it was filled with seekers. Some were saved and the power fell on others. Dismissed for dinner at twelve. At a little after one we commenced again and I preached and talked and finally got the folks stirred up and laid my Bible on the altar open and called for an offering and they commenced to come and kept on until $10.00 was freely given to pay for the rent of the tent and nearly four dollars for oil. Then I preached some more and when I got to it rightly I poured out the wine as in Luke's gospel and started four glasses. This over we commenced washing feet as in John 13 and about 150 or 200 took part amid shouts and songs. This over and we broke the bread and took the wine again, then we sung a hymn and then meant to go out of the tent but it was raining so we formed small groups all about over the tent and prayed. Then closed. The night meeting was good. Have preached 4 sermons.

July 17

A number of things have taken place since my last writing. Have preached about six sermons. Monday evening July 10, a young woman (Lillie Mae Fletcher) who had come into the orphans home uninvited and who had been occasionally having fits took a spell and has had two or three hundred convulsions probably during the week and causing considerable of excitement and trouble. She came into the home from Chattanooga, June 4. We are very much perplexed about the matter. Last night about one or two o'clock a house which had been vacated only two days burned. It was only about one hundred feet from our house. This caused some excitement in our part of town. I am engaged to go to Virginia tomorrow and the perplexities are causing me to feel that I may not get to go. Responsibilities are upon me that I should not have to bear but God will give grace and direct.

August 1

I just came home last evening from Virginia where I have been for 12 days. I organized three churches, ordained one bishop, preached at seven different places, four received the baptism and I preached 16 sermons.

August 26

I returned four days ago from Mississippi where I held meeting 16 days. 4 baptized with the Holy Ghost. A number converted and sanctified. The power fell so at times that men fell off their seats down on the floor. The whole house full were melted under the mighty power of God. The last day was wonderful. While I was preaching the glory and power fell so some fell flat on floor, some rejoiced and glory filled the place, I felt like going up and did leap over the table, not without touching it. Baptized 4 in water. Preached 31 sermons. I was to have gone to Boaz, Alabama two days ago but work here pressed me so I could not get off and then I was to have gone today and still could not get off, so I got Brother McLain to go for me. Preached at church tonight.

August 30

Preached at church and tabernacle Sunday and at night. Two sermons. I received a long letter yesterday from W. S. McMannon of Florida, strongly criticizing my article in August 15 issue of the paper. Others are commending it.

September 12

Arrived home today from Boaz, Alabama and Alabama City,
Alabama, where I have been for ten days. Preached 19 sermons.
Did not have the success in soul saving and people going through
to Pentecost as usual, but God was with me mightily in giving out
the messages and many were convinced. Boaz was a new field,
a city of educated and refined people, but God made me able to
meet them and not a few were blest.

September 15

Preached funeral of Kins Newberry's baby.

September 17

Preached at church at night to a full house.

October 2

Preached at tent at night.

October 9, 11:10 P. M.

Just arrived home from Kentucky where I was for three days in
an assembly of the churches. Preached two sermons besides
other talks and interpretations of messages in tongues. Had a
good time and pleasant fellowship with the precious people in
their assembly. See further particulars of the meeting in Evangel
of October 15, 1911. Gave some messages and interpretations
and while under the power the people saw the fire as it was above
my head and about me. The people were so wonderfully blest
that they asked the Lord to enlarge them and make then able to
ensure the blessings God was favoring them with. I stopped over
one night with Brother Mitchell at Tellico on my way up there.
Family well and happy when I got home.

October 10

Mary and Milton started for Indiana for a few weeks visit with
home folks.

October 15

Taught class in Sunday school and preached two sermons at
church afternoon and night.

October 16

Folded and wrapped and mailed paper. I am working at paper
most all the time these days. Big rain today. Homer and Iris in
school, Halcy working in Laundry.

October 23

Went to Sunday school yesterday and preached at the church afternoon and night. Two sermons. We are getting along very well but we sure miss wife and Milton. Weather has turned cold yesterday and today.

November 26

My work for a month has been without any special incident. Have been giving my time to publishing the paper and writing a book. Mary and Milton came home on the 18th of this month from their visit in Indiana. While they were gone I ditched and put drain or sewer tiling in the yard to carry off the waste water and leveled and terraced the yard and built a sidewalk except I have not got it graveled yet. I preached at church tonight. I had a very peculiar experience this afternoon in my room. The spirit of "go" came on me so heavy that it seemed I was almost beside myself. I walked and crawled and cried and prayed and writhed and twisted and groaned. I felt almost like the whole world was upon me. The band came before me with renewed force. Even now while I write at ten o'clock at night there is a peculiar feeling in my heart. It seems like I can hardly stand to wait much longer to start. My whole being is in a flame of love for this lost world. Oh God, help me! O God, help me! Oh God, help me! Help me!

December 14

I have busily engaged since last writing. Working on paper with all that publishing a paper means, teaching a Bible class at night. I am also writing a book for publication, besides preparing for the Assembly. I went out into the country over last Sunday where I preached three sermons and lectured Sunday school. I am working from 6:00 A. M. to eleven and twelve o'clock at night and some times till one.

December 26

The work continues except the school is discontinued. I preached the Christmas sermon at the church yesterday. Wife and I ate dinner at Brother Bryant's in commemoration of his 49th birthday. We have had rain, rain for weeks with occasionally a day without. Warm and rain now.

1912

January 18, 1912

Things went on in the common routine with busy preparations for the Assembly until the time came and the people came, about 75, and the work of the Assembly commenced. It was a great meeting. Much information gained and such good accomplished. Many good speeches made and much of the power of God demonstrated. During my annual address the Spirit came upon the audience so strong that I was obliged to discontinue for a spell while the people fell upon their faces and wept. At another time while I was speaking on the government of the church the power fell so strong that the people were held until after dark and I lay on the floor under the power of the Spirit for five hours. They appointed me on a committee to visit Elhanan Institute to investigate and arrange for a union of that institution with the Churches of God. I just returned late last night. It is located in North Carolina. I have taken a severe cold but I am asking God for deliverance as I am too busy to be sick. The Assembly selected me for General Overseer for another year by acclamation, also retained me as editor, although I asked to be released from both positions that I might be free to pursue other work for the Master.

January 26

I have spent considerable time in preparing the Minutes at the Assembly for the printer. Then since that was done I have been working day and night getting the manuscript of my book ready for the printer. On last Wednesday night, January 24, the pastor was selected for the church for another year. F. J. Lee. I was asked to speak on tithing which I did and inaugurated the plan to give all tithes to the church, not the pastor nor others promiscuously, but to the church, and some of the offerings too. I had 20¢ of tithes and I placed it there in the church with five cents offering for the seven deacons to take charge of it. This is, as far as I know, the first on this line since the days of the apostles.

February 20

At a deacons meeting held I think on the night of January 29, 1912, I was invited to address them, and in the address I gave a Scriptural outline for the financial plan for the Church. The plan is given in full in my book, The Last Great Conflict. They accepted the plan, adopted it for the local church and began immediately to put it in practice. On the night of the 15th of February, I started for Raton, New Mexico and after traveling for about 61 hours I arrived at Raton on the forenoon of the 18th to engage in a convention to commence on that date. Brother Barden met me at the station and conducted me to the place of meeting where convention was already in progress. The pastor, R. M. Singleton, met me and conducted me to the platform and in a few minutes he introduced me to the audience. I delivered three discourses that same day and three yesterday and after the night service I walked a mile through a blinding snow storm to my room alone. The snowstorm is still raging today and they phoned me not to venture out as none could get to the convention today. I am entertained in the home of Mr. Fulture, who are from Indiana, my native state. A fine comfortable place. I am shut in today on account of a western blizzard. Preached 6 sermons. In recounting the past I find I have been in the following states besides the Bahama Islands: 1. Maine, 2. New Hampshire, 3. Massachusetts 4. Connecticut, 5. Rhode Island, 6. New York, 7. New Jersey, 8. Delaware, 9. Maryland, 10. Pennsylvania, 11. Virginia, 12. North Carolina, 13. Florida, 14. Georgia, 15. Alabama, 16. Mississippi, 17. Tennessee, 18. Kentucky, 19. Ohio, 20. Indiana, 21. Illinois, 22. Arkansas, 23. Oklahoma, 24. Texas, 25. Colorado, 26. New Mexico. I will probably reach a number of other states before reaching home. Sister Flora E. Bower of Olney, Ill., is assisting Mrs. Tomlinson in the publication of the paper in my absence.

February 27

The convention closed last night at eleven o'clock. Last Sunday I was shut in all day by another severe snow storm. Yesterday afternoon at the business meeting there were seven additions to the church. Afterward two more ordained bishops and three evangelists. The Lord manifested His approval of the work. The church here is very much strengthened and blest. During almost all the convention we have had with us four Mexicans, three men who could only speak Spanish and one woman who could interpret. Very interesting indeed. I have preached 12 sermons since last writing. We are to continue this week in another part of the city in cottage meetings. On account of the rough weather there have been few people in attendance but much good has been accomplished. One received the Holy Ghost, one sanctified, four converted. Beautiful day.

March 4

Preached seven more sermons, three yesterday. I am still in Raton. Will leave probably in a day or two. Have had some precious services, Snow and bad weather has hindered some, but I feel that some good has been accomplished. Just received word from home that they are all well. Praise God.

March 7

Three more sermons, I expect to leave Raton this evening for Trinidad, Colorado. Brother Singleton expects to go with me. We expected to go this morning at five o'clock but he was not able, so we go tonight.

March 9

Preached three more sermons, at Trinidad and came to Pueblo, Colorado today. Done nothing here yet except prayed and read my Bible. I am tonight in an upper room just across the street from the mission. Don't know what tomorrow will develop. I am in God's hands.

March 14

Came from Pueblo to this place, Colorado Springs this morning. Done some work at Pueblo. Preached five sermons and four converted, two sanctified and three baptized with the Holy Ghost, and quite a number healed. Weather is cold. Word from home said they are 0. K. Will probably remain here for several days.

March 18

Preached four more sermons. Monday morning. Still at Colorado Springs. Been visiting homes and preaching. On the 15th we visited the garden of the Gods. It is wonderful to see what God has wrought, The view of Pikes Peak through the garden gate was wonderful. Beautiful weather now. I met Charles Stalker at Friends Church Friday. He sent a request for me to meet him again at the Peoples Mission this afternoon. I'll try to go.

March 22

Friday morning. Still at Colorado Springs, Colorado. We leased a nice church building for a year and held the first service in it Wednesday night, March 20, and organized the church. We are to commence for a revival tonight. I met Brother Charles Stalker had a blessed time with him for a little time. God bless him, how I love him. Preached three more sermons. Been having more snow and cold weather.

March 27

Wednesday morning. Preached five sermons. Have been visiting
and praying for the people during the day and preaching at night.
Brother Singleton left me last night and went home. I will expect to
stay a week or two yet. A card from home states that all is well there.

April 1

Monday morning. Preached six sermons. Yesterday was a great day
at the church. Saturday night the power fell and one and I guess two
got the baptism. During the service a man fell as if he had been shot.
The Lord gave me great liberty in preaching yesterday and the altar
was full of seekers at afternoon and night services. Some under the
power but none got through. The people are begging me to move my
family here and take charge of the work and stay with them. I have
so won their confidence that they all love me it seems. Still cold and
snow on ground.

April 8

Monday morning after a good day yesterday. Preached ten sermons.
The work is progressing slowly but seems to be continually
increasing. Baptized two in the lake Friday. Took the Lord's supper
and feet washing last night. All seemed to enjoy it very well. The
people seem to be drawn together more and more. I may leave here
for Denver this week. Last word from home stated they were getting
on fine. Still see snow on mountains. Pikes Peek is seen plainly from
Mr. Magdon's home where I stay.

April 12

Friday morning. I leave Colorado Springs this morning for Denver.
Three more sermons.

April 15

Monday afternoon at Denver, Colorado. Meeting the same night we
arrived. Brother Singleton came with me to pray for the healing of
a woman. He went back to Colorado Springs Saturday. I preached
three sermons yesterday. How God did honor His Word. Altar filled at
every service. I feel like I made lots of good friends. I have consented
to stay here with the folks this week. Meetings to be held every night.
Last Saturday was I believe, the windiest day I ever saw. The dust
was driven until the sun was hidden. I remain here to try to get the
church established. Don't know how I will succeed. Earl B. Crayton
and his wife seem to be jewels for the Lord. They have charge of the
work here.

April 22

Monday morning at Denver, Colorado. Preached ten more sermons. During the week at times the power fell so that some were prostrated. The preaching was in demonstration and power. Some times the congregations were bathed in tears, other times rejoicing and shouting over the truth. They were all crossed up when I came, but much has been accomplished in bring them together. Yesterday was a great day. I was nearly exhausted when I got in last night at about midnight. They have given me about $15.00 besides a lot of subscriptions and some for books. I go tonight or start for Omaha, Nebraska, D. V.

April 24

I arrived at Omaha, Nebraska yesterday at 3:45 P. M. after a ride of 18 hours from Denver. I came to Brother Hewitt's home at 3641 Haskill Street where Mrs. Jessie Hewitt received me with a glad welcome. I was so exhausted with toil in the meetings at Denver and traveling I did not get out early this morning, but I now feel rested and refreshed and good in my soul and body. Expect to go over to Council Bluffs, Iowa for meeting tonight. Don't know about the outlook for work here yet.

May 3

I arrived home yesterday. Preached at Council Bluffs, Iowa at night April 24. Left Omaha the night of April 25 and came via Kansas City to brother Ollie's at Rantoul, Kansas. Preached two sermons there and on April 29 came on to Baxter, Kansas to see Mama Kain and some of Mary's brothers and sisters. On the night of April 30, I started for home and missed the trains and laid over and hindered by the high water until I did not get home till May 2. Found my folks all well and happy and I was happy to get home, too. It was written me after I left Denver that Mr. Craton accused me of being false, but had won the hearts of the people and he injured himself more than he did myself. I suppose it came from jealousy. May the Lord deal tenderly with him.

May 13

On Sunday, May 5, I went with Brother McLain out in the country about nine miles and preached three sermons, organized the church and had a powerful time because of the presence of the Lord. Sunday, May 12, I went with Brother McLain to another place in the country about nine miles and preached one sermon and organized a church. Preached in church at Cleveland at night. Preached a funeral this afternoon.

May 20

Preached yesterday and last night at the church. I am constantly busy with the paper and in meetings. Preached five more sermons.

May 23

Preached to the young people at the church last night. I expect to start for Durant, Florida to conduct camp meeting Saturday 25, 1912. Homer delivers his graduation oration Friday night. I leave home under somewhat embarrassing circumstances on account of a shortage of means, but I am hopeful and happy. Folks well.

June 3

I am now at Pleasant Grove Camp Ground. I arrived here twelve hours later than I expected on account of the lack of good connection of trains. The meeting was on its way nicely. I preached at the first service and on occasionally. Spent much time in answering questions and mingling with the people. I delivered one discourse of about two and a half hours on the Church and its workings. How the power fell and how the people were strengthened and blest! I anointed and prayed for the sick until was almost exhausted. I preached about ten sermons. The meetings at times were wonderful in power and demonstrations. Brother Lemons rather conducted the meetings and did the baptizing. 28 I believe baptized, about 25 received the Holy Ghost, a number sanctified and converted and reclaimed, quite a lot healed and 34 joined the church. The Church of God was illuminated and people saw it as they never had before. I was not able to preach any yesterday because of being so exhausted the night before with praying with a large number of sick folks and preaching under such extreme power of the Spirit. This is Monday. The meetings practically closed last night but there are to be some meetings today and tonight, I expect to go to Parish tomorrow.

June 4

Tuesday morning. Held a conference meeting yesterday to consider the question of ordaining Edmond Barr (colored) and setting the colored people off to work among themselves on account of the race prejudice in the south. In this service Mr. Renaker of Orlando, Florida, who had been rejected the office of bishop because the committee thought him not qualified, became somewhat offended and gave a lengthy discourse against the church and its workings, complaining that we were attacking his moral character by rejecting his application. The church sit quiet and gave him audience until he concluded, when I arose and delivered a discourse in defense of the church and the brethren who had considered his case and found him wanting. He withdrew from the church and went off. I shook his hand and told him we would meet at the judgment and that there was no personal feeling in my heart against him, but that I must stand in defence of the church. I also told him I hoped he would see his mistake and any time he would get right and come to us with the right spirit we would gladly receive him with wide open arms. The ordination service followed and God wonderfully blest and honored the work as we ordained the colored brother.

June 10

I am at Parish. Have been here about a week and it has rained so much that we have done no good. I have only preached four sermons and these under quite a strain because of the incessant rain beating on the roof of the tabernacle. I regard the meeting as a failure but the folks have already asked me to make a date and come back again in the fall. I suppose I'll have to come although I have not fully decided. Expect to leave here day after tomorrow, Roy and Brother Haynes are with me here. The camp meeting at Durant gave me $79.25.

June 12

Two more sermons. Leave Parish this morning for Plant City, Florida. Sun shining bright but ground full of water.

June 14

This is Friday morning. Got tent up yesterday. Had the first meeting last night. Preached the introductory sermon. Good beginning,

June 17

Monday morning. Preached six more times. Tent nearly full last night for the first. People seemed interested and some came to altar. Great meeting among the saints at the eleven o'clock service. Did not close till two.

June 20

Preached six more sermons, Thursday morning. The meeting here is to continue right on under E. E. Simmons and others. I go to Wauchula today. D. V.

June 24

Preached eight sermons. This is Monday morning. Am at Wauchula. Great time yesterday. Three or four, I think, went through to Pentecost. Great crowds are attending the meetings. Sick are healed right in the presence of the congregations.

July 2

Preached 12 sermons. Rained so the meeting was hindered very much but four, I think, baptized with the Holy Ghost. Very large crowds on Sunday nights. Had a severe struggle with principalities and wicked spirits yesterday morning, praying for Nora Whidden, Brother Marion's wife. I fell on the floor desperate twice, with darkness and semiconscious on account of demon powers. I was so weak all day yesterday and last night, but the Lord gave me special strength last night to preach to a large crowd. I go to Arcadia today.

July 8

Monday morning. I am still at Arcadia. Held services twice a day since coming here and three times yesterday. Thirteen sermons. Wonderful outpouring yesterday.

July 13

Saturday noon at Valdosta, Georgia. Been here about an hour. Preached four more times at Arcadia. The service Monday afternoon was another wonder. Left the church in fine order, Left there July 10, stayed at Palatka Florida same night. Came to Melrose, Georgia July 11, drove out about five miles where the folks had gathered for a meeting. Went into a meeting, another at night and yesterday all day and again last night. Wonderful time yesterday. The power surged the people to and fro and the manifestations of the Spirit were marvelous. Four received the Holy Ghost and some converted. Left Melrose this morning and came to Valdosta. Brother and Sister Haynes came with me. (4 sermons) Roy and Lula were married Sunday evening at the meeting at Arcadia, July 7. I performed the ceremony. They will be on here in a few days, D. V. I met Brother Lemons here to my delight. I am exceeding tired and worn but my soul is at rest.

July 20

Saturday morning. Been here at Valdosta a week. Preached eight sermons. Two or three baptized with the Holy Ghost. I baptized nine in water. Nine joined the church, among the number was a minister from the Pentecostal Holiness church. Brother and Sister Haynes left last night for Atlanta. Roy and Lula will remain here until Monday. I go today to Benhaden, Florida for a few days. The Lord gave us some very refreshing showers. The saints all built up and blest and the church very much strengthened. Brother Lemons went back to Florida, his field of labor.

July 24

I am out in the country from Benhaden, Florida about three miles from the railroad. On account of the engine breaking down I never reached this place till about two o'clock Sunday morning. I did not feel able for service Sunday morning but when I reached the place of worship there was a large crowd there. The Lord took hold almost at once. I preached four times on Sunday. Had the communion and feet washing and it was a very impressive service. The bread was broken amid a shower of tears and it was taken by all with much crying and tears. The power was on the services till nearly midnight. That night I dreamed that I found myself riding on the back seat of an automobile and I finally discovered that there was no one on the front seat guiding it and it was gradually getting out of the road and was running very rapid. I climbed around and over into the front seat and got the wheel and my foot on the clutch just in time to prevent a wreck and turn it around a wagon and mule team. I run it on for some distance and finally stopped it and got out and went into a house and looked out and saw the machine running backwards and I run out and put on the emergency break just in time again to prevent another wreck. The dream impressed me very much. On Monday morning the people came to the meeting shouting, taking and singing in tongues and great power was on the meeting. I fell under the power and I seemed to get a part of the interpretation of the dream. The automobile represented the Holiness Baptist church as a whole. I finding myself on the back seat was the meeting I am in here now with Brother Cross who is pastor of two or three of their churches. These churches are considered the back churches but I am with them riding along. The climbing over and getting control of the machine was the whole body of churches coming into the Church of God and giving me the control or oversight of all. The machine running backward after I left it was them drawing back and revolting again, but I got possession again just in time to prevent their fall and wreckage. I await results and say nothing about this to any one but I am going to wait and see the results and developments. Every service has been freighted with God's power. One received the Holy Ghost. A number in altar. I left three or four men stretched on the floor last night at eleven o'clock. I leave here D. V. tomorrow morning about four o'clock for Woodstock, Georgia.

July 27

I am now at Woodstock, Georgia. Arrived here yesterday morning. Stayed in Atlanta the night before. I preached here at 11 o'clock yesterday and last night. The last night of the meeting at Benhaden, Florida was wonderful. I only slept two hours that night. The Lord waked me at exactly 3:30 as I asked Him to do. The meetings here yesterday and last night were wonderful. Some got baptized with the Holy Ghost in the meeting at Benhaden and every service here. Eight more sermons. This is Saturday morning. I leave here Monday morning.

July 29

Monday morning. Yesterday was wonderful. Set the Church in order with 45 members. 31 baptized in water. Ordained one bishop and five evangelists. I preached five sermons yesterday. Had the Lord's supper and feet washing. The discourse on the Church was wonderful in revealing truth and light interspersed with messages and interpretations, shouts, weeping, prayers, praises, etc. Six more sermons. I start home in a few minutes.

August 7

I am now at Ethelville, Alabama. I was at home two days and came on here August 1. The meetings have progressed nicely under an arbor. One baptized with the Holy Ghost. This is Wednesday, brother and sister Haynes are with me. Roy and Lula came yesterday. It is raining this morning. Ten sermons.

August 9

An incident happened yesterday that is worthy of note. I had been preaching very close during the meetings and yesterday was given a picture of the normal condition of a Christian. At the close of the discourse we had a few prayers and started to sing when three messages were given in tongues successively with the interpretations. These messages melted us all down. I was still down on my knees bathed in tears when I felt some one pull my arm and shoulder. I opened my eyes and it was Brother Simpson, the minister who invited me here. I yielded to his wishes expressed by pulling me up and arose to my feet, then he began to pull me toward the front of the platform. I did not know what he meant but I yielded to him. I wondered if he was taking me out there to publicly denounce me. When he got me to the stand he embraced me and broke down into tears and sobs. I still did not know what he meant, but he finally sobbed out he was a member of a lodge, but now he was saying goodby to it for he was going to belong wholly to Jesus. Another brother grasped my hand and confessed likewise and this with other confessions created quite a sensation. An altar service followed which found sinners, lukewarm Christians, those who wanted deliverance from tobacco and various things, and some who had been the worst enemies to our work, all broken up and crowded in the altar. One received the Holy Ghost while much was accomplished other ways. The meeting lasted fully four hours. This is Friday morning. Have preached four more sermons. Another serious incident took place the next day after our arrival here. I was sitting right where I am now in my room talking with Brother Haynes. I heard shots fired in quick succession. I turned my head and looked out of the window. The R. R. station is in plain view only about 100 feet away. I saw a negro woman running this way, and a man after her shooting at her.

Before I could scarcely realize what was the matter he had run up behind her and put the pistol nearly against her back and she fell. He then jumped on her head and stamped and cursed her. By this time they were only about fifty feet from me. The man was arrested by the sheriff and it was discovered that two were shot. It is thought they will both die but are still alive yet. Horrible, and I did not want to see it but it was done before I fully realized what was going on so I could not turn my head.

August 12, Monday morning

Preached six more sermons. The meeting closed last night. Today is to be spent in preparing to go on to Mississippi tomorrow. At the meeting Saturday I formally received about 200 members into the Church of God by receiving Z. D. Simpson who is pastor of five churches. The Lord manifested Himself blessedly as we kneeled and extended our hands over the Bible which was lying between us. The union was sealed and witnessed to and ratified by the Holy Ghost. Almost every one was bathed in tears and several talking in tongues. Ordained Brother Simpson yesterday as bishop. 12 new members added to the church here. I received a wire Saturday to come to Cleveland to preach the funeral of Sister Nora Lee, wife of our pastor. I wired back that I could get there today and they wired back that they would have to bury her yesterday. So I go on to Mississippi tomorrow, D. V.

August 20

We arrived in Oakland, Mississippi, Tuesday evening about six o'clock. We stayed at hotel over night. They came after us Wednesday and we came to Brother Morgan's that day. The meeting was to have commenced Thursday night, but it rained so we had no meeting till Friday night, August 16. Saturday night we had the meeting in the new tabernacle. We worked at it with our own hands all day Saturday that it might be ready for Saturday night. Preached five sessions. Great crowds are coming to the meetings. Four received the Holy Ghost yesterday and two today. This is Tuesday afternoon. Needed no preaching yesterday nor today. Power falls in a wonderful way in waves and waves.

August 21, Wednesday P. M.

Seven more received the Holy Ghost. Preached last night. About 30 seekers at altar last night. Altar full again today. People are coming for 25 miles. Crowds and crowds.

August 22

Midnight just home from service. Still crowds and crowds. Increasing every day. Wonderful meetings. Two more baptized today. Many affected and moved. I preached and cried today and everybody melted. Before I finished my discourse a big man came walking into the altar saying he had been compromising long enough and that he wanted the Holy Ghost. He pitched into the altar and others followed until the altar was full. Four more sermons.

August 24

Saturday midnight after service. Three more baptized with the Holy Ghost. Six more sermons. Great meeting last night but the meeting tonight was more quiet. Altar crowded day and night and lots of others would come it looks like if there was room.

August 25

Sunday night after service. Great crowds all day. Done but little today but preach, but the Lord wonderfully gave a door of utterance and the truth went out sharp and powerful. I preached two sermons Multitudes at meeting tonight.

August 28, Wednesday morning

Five more sermons. I preached about three hours yesterday and was on my feet for four hours. Organized the church with fifteen members. The Lord made me able to answer all questions. Outsiders as well as the saints fired in the questions. The Lord made me able for every emergency. Oh, but my body was tired and lower limbs stiff but I am all right this morning. Altar filled with seekers again last night.

August 29, Thursday morning

Preached four sermons yesterday. Had Lord's supper and feet washing. Eleven o'clock till three. Several more came into church yesterday and last night. One more received the Holy Ghost. Nice service last night. Two baptized with water today.

August 30

Baptized six in water. Preached one more sermon. Drove through the country twenty miles or more south and am here near Cascilla, Mississippi, this afternoon. Arrived here last night about eleven o'clock. Am writing today. Meeting to commence at Franklin tabernacle tonight. One more received Holy Ghost up at other place.

September 2

Monday night after meeting. Six more sermons. The meeting is progressing slowly. Good sized congregations but it has been hard to get their attention till tonight I find they are getting interested. Several in altar. One baptized with Holy Ghost.

September 5

Thursday night after meeting. Six more sermons, About eight baptized with the Holy Ghost. Have had some wonderful meetings. They want to engage me for a year ahead to hold them another meeting. I start for home in the morning. Roy and Lula and Brother and Sister Haynes stay and run the meeting on.

September 17

Tuesday night after meeting. I arrived home from Mississippi in time for breakfast Saturday morning, September 7, Found all O. K. except plenty of work. They were in a tent meeting at home and they would have me preach Sunday afternoon. I left home Thursday morning, September 12, and came to Dora, Alabama where I am now in meeting, eleven sermons, with Brother Kennedy. Quite a number are receiving the Holy Ghost.

September 23

Monday night after meeting. Preached eight more sermons. Closed the meeting near Dora last night and came to Empire, Alabama today where I am tonight. One the 21st of September, 1912, in a conference under Brother Kennedy's tent they appointed M. S. Haynes, M. S, Lemons and myself trustees to hold church property to be deeded to the church by Dr. Abbott near Arckadelphia, Ala. Am to go there tomorrow to receive it and take charge of it. Have had some wonderful meetings. Lots of people have been falling prostrate and lying under the power for a time. Jerking, dancing, playing organ under power, three at one time played and did not make a discord. Singing in tongues as well as shouting, talking in tongues, etc. I tonight preached in tent with M. S. Haynes. Large crowd.

September 26

9:30 A. M. on the car ready to start from Empire, Alabama for home. Tuesday morning M. S. Haynes, E. Haynes and myself were drove in a wagon through the country about 12 or 15 miles where we were presented with a deed for a plot of ground (3 acres) with a two story tabernacle already built on it new for a camp ground for the Church of God. Held meeting at Dr. Abbotts at night in his gin house. Came back yesterday to Kimberly and in meeting again last night with Brother Haynes. Preached two more sermons. I may not leave here till afternoon as this is only a coal company private railroad to main line.

October 9

Wednesday morning at Solway, P. O. Byington, Tenn. I came home the night of the above date and was at home a few days. October 3 I went to Knoxville, Tennessee. Preached there at night, the next day went to Jellico, Tenn. Preached there at night. Was in the Mountain Assembly which convened a mile out from Jellico. Brother and Sister Haynes came with me and Brother McLain joined me at Knoxville. I preached at the Assembly Saturday night at Newcomb, Tennessee. On Monday I went to London, Kentucky and preached there P. M. and at night. Came on here last evening for meeting. Brother Perry was here and preached last night. Sunday at the Assembly I was in the congregation and after Brother Parks finished his discourse on the platform he called for me and I went up and preached for an hour and a half or more after he had preached an hour and five minutes. A great crowd estimated at 1,500. The seats were taken out of the house and placed out doors in front of the house and a thousand people stood up while we preached. We had to stand on a platform in the hot sun and most of the congregation was in the hot sun most of the time, but they stayed right there and God wonderfully helped to deliver the truth. After the discourse I was called on to pray and anoint quite a number for healing right out in the hot sun. I was almost exhausted when I got through. Have not recovered yet fully. Nine sermons, since leaving home. I'll be here D. V. today and tonight.

October 17

I came home from Byington October 14. Preached eight more sermons. I did not go to North Carolina as I had expected. That meeting having been called off until later. Brother F. J. Lee has gone to Florida and left me in care of the church here now. I am busy, busy, busy. 0 God, give me wisdom.

October 23

The meeting last Sunday was full without preaching. I advanced a project to build an addition to the church house. The response was good and steps are already taken to carry out the project. Good meetings. Three more sermons. Lot in altar Sunday night. Quite an interest Good prayer meeting tonight. I am working in office.

October 27

After meeting at night. Directed the meetings last night and today. House nearly full at every service. Went to tabernacle to Sunday school A. M. Raised 81 dollars to purchase lot by the side of the church lot. I wrote Mr. Loomis about giving it and he wrote back he would sell it for 100 dollars although he valued it at much more than that. All of our people are taking great interest in enlarging the house and purchasing the lot. Good interest in the meetings and

God is blessedly working. Conviction is seizing the people and some who have grown a little cold are getting back to God. The power fell in waves in some of the services. Nearly the whole house bathed in tears at times. People are being revived. Homer at home yesterday.

November 6

Raised the balance of the money for the lot last Sunday. Sent the check off for the lot today. I preached last Sunday. Good meetings Saturday night, Sunday and at night. Fine Sunday school. I am busy in office, printing office and looking after the building of the addition to the church house.

November 15

Preached last Saturday night, Sunday and at night, also last Wednesday night. Four sermons. Powerful services in some respects. House full at every service. Sunday night crowded. Mailed paper today. Brother D. W. Haworth from Florida is here. The building of the church house going on. Homer reports good success under his ministry at Knoxville. Our old mission house at Culberson, N. C. was set on fire by enemies and burned down last Sunday night, November 10, 1912.

November 18, Monday morning

I paid the cost of the lawsuit that we had about two years ago to hold the church house. The amount was $29.06. The church may help me to bear it. The Sunday school is building right up. 135 yesterday. Brother F. J. Lee preached Saturday night and afternoon yesterday. I preached last night while he went to the tabernacle. At the close of the discourse the Lord broke in upon us in a marvelous way. The altar was packed, several got special blessings. About two sanctified, one baptized with the Holy Ghost. A great cry of intercessory prayer went up from the saints. Screams, falling on the floor, talking in tongues, shouts of joy, well it was wonderful.

November 28

145 at Sunday school last Sunday. I preached Sunday night. Had Thanksgiving service at the church today. Brother Flavius Lee had the A. M. Meeting. I had charge P. M. and preached three sermons and administered the Lord's supper and feet washing. Had a wonderful time. We had the feet washing in the new part. Have not got it seated yet, but used it some today. The old part of house was packed full and some in the new. Brother and Sister Haynes are here. The power fell marvelously. About 25 or 30 or 40 under

the power at one time, dancing, playing organ, talking in tongues, shouting, crying, screaming, fallings etc., etc. It was wonderful. Received six into the church. Want to finish the house tomorrow, all but the seats. Quite a snow yesterday. Cold today and clear.

December 19

I went to Virginia the 5th of December. Preached twelve sermons, returned home December 13. Had some glorious meetings. I preached at church last Sunday night and Wednesday and a funeral yesterday. Three sermons. Two more sermons. Mrs. Tomlinson took a baby girl to an orphanage at Cumberland Gap the 16th. Came home yesterday. Worked at church all day today and in office tonight till nearly eleven. 190 in Sunday school last Sunday. To dedicate church next Sunday P. M., D. V.

December 23

Dedicated the church house yesterday at five o'clock P. M. Commenced the service at 2:30. I preached the sermon. The Lord gave great blessing. As we formally gave the house over to God, the Lord manifested Himself in a great measure. A more complete account is given in the chronicles of the Church at Cleveland, Tenn. 227 in Sunday school yesterday. Great day all day for us. Glory

1913

January 2, 1913

Preached two funerals this week before the old year went out. I have been working day and night preparing for Assembly, working at the paper, correspondence, etc. Quite a number of people are coming to the Assembly already. Brother and Sister Mitchell are both bad sick.

January 18

Many things have transpired since I last wrote. The Assembly has come and gone. Sister Mitchell died and taken to Ohio and buried. Brother Mitchell still sick and set for me to come see him, but I was not allowed to go. The Assembly was an eminent affair and a great success. The Lord surely gave me great wisdom to direct the work so that everything went off smoothly with love for God and one another. I attributed all the success to the wisdom and presence of God. He shall have all the glory. I'll not attempt to describe the Assembly here. It is written in the records. To say the least it was wonderful. The order was so perfect in every way that it seems that God surely beheld the order with joy as he watched us in all our deliberations. I am now laboring under considerable strains. I was almost overtaxed during Assembly and my body has given down, but I am compelled to work right on as long as I can hold up. I am preparing minutes for printer, my paper work and the general work besides. Oh God, I have no time to get sick. The work must be done, please give me of Thy strength. I was selected again as General Overseer for this year. The selection was surely ordered by the Holy Ghost and it was so marked that everybody felt it was the Holy Ghost, I feel like exclaiming, Oh Lord, dost Thou notice me? How unworthy of thy notice! And Thou Thyself ordering my steps? It hardly seems possible that I could be recognized and placed in such an exalted position by One so great as art Thou. My spirit melts within me as I meditate upon this subject and yet know that it must be God ordering my life and work.

January 28

The Church here chose me for their pastor this year. Those who had a hand in it say it was surely the Holy Ghost that made the selection. I was not there. I preached Saturday night, Sunday and Sunday night. Three sermons. I am very busy working in office day and tight. I am writing at eleven at night. Brother Bryant has been arrested on a charge of using the mails for fraudulent purposes. Brother Mitchell would have been arrested but he is bad sick and they can't get to him. This makes it very hard on our work just at this time, but God will help us to pull over it. We are hoping that they will not be proven guilty.

February 3

Time is fleeting by. Went last Wednesday with wife out in the country to see Sisters Lawson and Stevison who are sick, also called on old Brother Felker. Brother Mitchell is still shut in and we are not allowed to see him. Conducted prayer meeting last Wednesday night and ordained W. G. Anderson, Yesterday was full. Taught Sunday school class, at 11 A. M. preached a funeral, at 2:30 married a couple at the church, then preached, and meeting last night. One profession. Five more sermons. Have been busy working in office, getting the paper off, etc. Homer and Halcy were both home with us yesterday. It delights my heart to know they are still the sweet children and full of the Holy Ghost. Milton is going to school, started the first of this year, 1913.

February 10

Wednesday P. M., February 5, preached funeral at church, meeting the same night. Meeting Saturday night. One sanctified and baptized with the Holy Ghost. Yesterday was full again. Sunday school, meeting at 2:30 p. m., ordination service besides. Last night had another ordination service. Five sermons. I have so much work, pastoral, editorial, correspondence, proof reading, Sunday school work, directing the church work, advising and talking with workers as they call at my office, etc., etc., until I have but a few hours for sleep. God is helping me I'm sure or I could not hold up under it. Praise Him.

February 17

I worked in office all last week. Led the regular meetings. The Lord graciously poured out His Spirit upon us yesterday. The messages came by the power of God. Seekers in altar at every service. One reclaimed and one sanctified. The power thrilled through the audience last night. Preached four sermons.

February 25

Monday, the 17th. Officiated at marriage of our Miss Mayme Williams. Preached funeral of a child burned to death in house that burned down. Tuesday preached funeral of a Mr. Weiss. Conducted regular meetings. Busy day and night. Preached four more sermons.

March 3

Preached three sermons. Conducted regular meetings, worked in office, etc. Am building a house for printing office and publishing house across the street.

March 10

Preached four sermons again and worked at my regular routine of work. The Lord has been giving some special refreshing showers. The young people's meeting last Tuesday night was wonderful. The sister's meeting Tuesday afternoon was also much blessed of the Lord. The regular services at the church have had special manifestations of the presence of God. Saturday night I think one or two were saved from sin and one received the Holy Ghost. At the Sunday school yesterday there were forty or fifty boys and girls at the altar for prayer. It was a glorious scene. Much weeping and praying as the teachers and older ones were trying to lead the children to Christ. There has been much dancing, talking in tongues and exhortations under the power of the Spirit. Every service is a revival and freighted with God's presence. I went to Chattanooga to try to adjust a difference in the church there between the pastor and others and T. R. Austin and others. Did not reach a final settlement. The matter is to be brought to Cleveland April 8, 1913.

March 20

Nearly eleven P. M. Preached seven more sermons. The regular meetings and one funeral. Have been working day and night. Folding and preparing my book. Having fine meetings. Last night was a special down pour of the Spirit, several at altar. Went out about eight miles to pray for the sick.

March 24

Preached four more sermons. One at the funeral service of our good old sister N. J. Lawson out at Union Grove. Good meetings at the church. I am overrun with work. I am about forty or more letters behind with my correspondence. About twenty or twenty-five yet unopened. This is about six P. M.

March 31

Preached two sermons. Great meeting last night. One baptized with the Holy Ghost at home while we were at church. Several at altar. Some blest.

April 8

Preached three times. Had a great time Sunday night at the church. The Power fell upon us in a wonderful way. Two reclaimed. A number at the altar. Had business meeting last night. Had a meeting here at the church in the interest of the church at Ridgedale church to consider some difficulties. Have not been able to fully adjust matters yet. Some of us go to Chattanooga this evening, D. V. More about it.

April 14

One funeral service last week. Preached four sermons. Last night was a great time at the church. Altar full of seekers. Some got blest. Several have received the Holy Ghost about in town at the different meetings in the last week or ten days. D. W. Haworth and his family came last week, April 8, from Durant, Fla. They are locating here but have not found a place yet. The church at Ridgedale are refusing to accept our advice in regard to the matter pending.

April 20

Preached four sermons, one funeral service. This is after meeting at night. Great meeting this afternoon. More quiet tonight. Good service.

May 6

Work has gone on as usual. Went to Chattanooga one day for brother Bryant's lawsuit, but it was put off for six months. Five sermons. Preparing to get paper printed next time at new office. I had Sister Cotton here for three weeks visiting my church members, etc.

May 12

Monday morning. Preached the funeral of another of our faithful mothers on the 8th out at Union Grove. House full of people and very attentive. Saturday night at the church the presence of God was manifested. Wife's youngest sister, Maud, came in from Kansas Saturday evening. She had never been in a meeting like this. When the altar call was made she came with others. She was converted and another sanctified. Good time yesterday. We dismissed the meeting at the church afternoon and all went down to the tabernacle to the Sunday school rally. Good time last night at the church after I preached quite a number came to altar. One professed religion and others got blessed. Glorious meeting. Three sermons.

May 27

I went to Durant, Florida the 14th instant to conduct the camp meeting. I just arrived home today. I preached thirty sermons from one text. Acts 4:32, first clause. Wonderful meeting. Indescribable. 12 baptized with the Holy Ghost evidenced by the other tongues. Quite a number renewed and the saints wonderfully edified and built up in faith. Brother McLain was with me to pray for the sick as usual. Brother Buckalew was also there and rendered valuable service. About 400 campers, including men, women and children. Great crowds came to the meetings who did not camp. The last day some estimated it at 6,000 in attendance. They came on foot, horse back, buggies, wagons, and automobiles. God gave me great liberty and boldness in preaching. Weeping, shouting, visions, dancing, music under the power as well as music and singing in every service. The people were carried by the Spirit from weeping to shouting and vice versa, like the waves of the sea. Their voices many, many times sounded like the falling of many waters. The preaching was under the power and demonstration of the Spirit. I give God all the honor and glory.

June 2

Preached two sermons yesterday. Had the meeting in the grove at the baptizing pool yesterday afternoon and baptized 13. The Lord gave us His presence and blest His Word as well as the people who were baptized. Large crowd and good time.

June 9

Preached three times. Nothing special more than the common work at office and in meetings.

July 1

Nearly midnight. Preached twenty sermons. I left home the 17th of June for Kansas City, Mo. I was there until I just arrived home this evening. I find all well at home. Homer at home, but dear Roy Miller has passed away and was buried two days ago. Brother Payne has been holding tent meeting in South Cleveland nearly ever since I have been away.

July 9

About six P. M. Had a great time at the Fourth of July meeting at Church. The Lord wonderfully blest and poured out His Spirit. Raised over two hundred dollars for the payment of property. Commenced tent meeting near the church house on Saturday night. Large crowds and good interest. I have preached seven more times.

July 14

About five sermons. Great meetings at tent. Some getting through to the Lord.

July 20, 11:30 P. M.

The Lord has been giving us great meetings and tonight was the greatest in some respects. Some converted or sanctified or baptized with the Holy Ghost every night. Six I think have been baptized with the Holy Ghost up to date and the saints are getting greatly revived and blest and the altar is full of seekers at every service. Old time power falling. I have not been preaching much but have charge of the services all but the sermon. The Lord gives me great liberty in raising money, making altar calls and rallying the work along. Preached about two times. The tent meeting closed tonight on account of Brother Payne having to take it and go to another place, but we will continue the meeting in the church house.

July 28, 11:10 P. M.

Preached five sermons. One week ago tonight the power fell marvelously at the church. Some swept into the shower that I never saw in before. People laughed, cried, shouted, leaped, danced, talked in tongues, got under conviction, fell into the altar, got victory and I don't know what all else. Meetings all last week. Prayer meeting in our house at 9:00 A. M. and at the church at night. Some baptized with the Holy Ghost now and then. The meetings still going on this week. I am so hungry for the gifts and greater power that it seems I can never preach any more until they are given me. I am almost desperate about the more power. As I sat on the rostrum yesterday just before preaching, I felt like slipping out at the door without saying a word and going to the woods or some where and stay till I received the special help from God I am craving. I did not go. I stayed and preached, but I am still desperate for more of God's power for service.

August 3

After meeting at night. The Lord has blest in the services today. Five more sermons.

August 10

After meeting at night. Had special prayer at our house every morning a little past nine every morning last week. Thursday morning I think it was that I became so desperate that I suppose I acted like I was beside myself. I fell into a spirit of agonizing prayer that lasted I think for more than an hour. I feel just like the gifts of the Spirit must be given in their fullness or multitudes will be lost that otherwise might be saved. It seems that I can hardly stand it. I am desperately desperate about it. Others are anxious but it does not seem like any one is desperate like I am. I feel rather lonely about the matter but must press on. I preached two sermons today with fairly good liberty, but it does not satisfy me. The folks are better satisfied with me than I am with myself. What to do I don't know. I am troubled about the matter all the time. I must now stop here. I must have these gifts in their fullness. I must know I have them as well as I know I have the Holy Ghost. My heart is stirred. I pray God to stir me more and more until I can't rest day nor night without these wonderful manifestations. My heart goes out in agonizing cries, 0 God, 0 God, almost constantly. What WILL I do? God help me.

August 18

Monday night near midnight. At one of our morning prayer meetings last week the power fell and Iris played the organ under the power and some danced and great blessings fell. Preached six sermons. Two funerals. My heart is constantly going out to God for the gifts, I feel that the Church is perishing for the last of them. I am so desperate about the matter that I am turning every stone possible to do my part to meet the conditions God requires. Some time during prayer I had got a little vision of Brother McLain and myself passing near our baptizing pool and I got him to baptize me, so last Saturday morning we were called to go and pray for Tom Priest who was sick and this called us by the place, so on our return I asked Brother McLain to baptize me. He was much surprised, but I insisted and although I had been baptized twice before I got him to baptize me. I have so many perplexing questions that I feel I must have the gift of wisdom and knowledge and others as well to make me able to meet every demand and advise correctly. I am praying and fasting and my heart almost bursts out of my bosom apparently with agonizing cries to God. Besides all this I have to attend to my correspondence which is heavy, keep up the Evangel work, pastor the church, and have the care of all the churches, and try to keep some of the unwise ministers straight. All this and more. Oh God, please help me!

September 4

Nearly midnight Thursday night. Preached eight times. Two funerals. On September 1, Wife and D. W. Haworth presented me with a new desk. I had been using an old board table with an orange crate fixed up for pigeon holes and a few boards put together for shelves. Made the picture of it yesterday. Had a wonderful time at prayer meeting last night. We kneeled to pray about 8:20 and were not able to get off our knees until after ten. Some down under the power and nearly every one effected more or less. Much intercessory prayer.

September 9

Preached three more times. The meetings at the church over Sunday were very impressive and powerful. Meeting running at the tabernacle and quite a number are getting saved, sanctified and filled with the Holy Ghost. The meeting is in the care of some of our boys, Roe Cry, Charley Grissum and Homer. Quite a revival spirit manifest.

September 15, 12:30 Sunday night

Four more sermons. Funeral this morning, married a couple at 3:00 P. M. in the church and then meeting following and went to tabernacle at night.

September 23, Tuesday morning

Two sermons. Eleven taken into the church Sunday night. Mary's sister Julia has been with us a few days. Homer has gone to Knoxville again to school. We are making preparations for a great time at the Assembly.

October 3

Six more sermons. Went to Rome, Georgia last Monday to see Brother Buckalew on some church business. Working in office constantly almost. Am preparing for Assembly, etc.

October 12

After meeting at night. Seven more sermons. My work has been in the office and my regular routine from day to day. Many things have been reported that tends to discouragement, but God gives grace and victory and courage right over everything. Last Monday night we disfellowshipped about twenty-five members for using tobacco and refusing to quit it and a few for other offences. Some saw they were going to be turned out and asked to be dismissed. Lots of reason for encouragement from many places.

October 20, Monday night

Two sermons. Things going on about as usual. Praying for the sick nearly every day and some times three or four times a day. Preparing for great things at the Assembly. The Lord makes me able to meet every bill as they come due but the grocery bill and we are paying some on that. Good reports of work on the fields.

October 28

Preached two more. One funeral.

November 2

After meeting at night. Two more discourses. Quite a number of
people have already come in for the Assembly. The Lord gave us
wonderful meetings today. I am taking every preparation I can to
make the Assembly a success.

November 26

I have been so busy with my work that I have neglected my
journal. This Assembly has come and gone. Have had Assembly
folks in our home until today, the last have gone. Eight left today
and Mary and Milton have gone as far as Chattanooga with some
of them. The Assembly was a great success. I suppose between
two and three hundred visitors. There is no language that can
fully describe it. The Holy Ghost sat His approval on me as
General Overseer again. It was wonderful. The workers all showed
a willingness to work and God displayed His power marvelously.
Three more sermons. On the night of the 24th instant the
church selected a pastor F. J. Lee for another year. I asked them
to release me so I could engage in other work. The publishing
committee selected C. H. Shriner as office editor and that releases
me of much care of the paper although I retain my position as
editor. I am expecting to travel this year and establish churches
and the work in general. The Assembly has cost me personally
about $75.00. I am expecting the Lord to give me means to pay
my bills some way.

December 1

Preached three more times. Quite a number of our people
quarantined on account of the small pox and our congregations
were small yesterday, but God was with us and we prayed for
those who were absent. Yesterday closed out my year as pastor,
so I am looking to God for plans to do the most for Him in the
shortest time.

December 17

Left home the 6th instant and came here to Augusta, Georgia
where I am now. T. L. McLain came with me. I went over into
South Carolina eight miles and preached once. Will remain here
now but a few more days. Preached eight sermons.

December 27

We are out in the country from Hephzibah, Georgia. Came here
the 21st instant. Have been spending much of our time in prayer

and the study of the Bible. Having meeting in a school house at night. We are royally entertained in the home of John Goodin. Have a room to ourselves where we can read, write and pray. Eight more sermons. We expect to leave here Monday for Langley, S. C. This is Saturday night after meeting. The last word from home all is well. Brother McLain retired to rest.

December 30

Two more sermons. Am at Augusta today. Come in late last night. Expect to go on to Langley, S. C. tomorrow. I feel very bad in my body on account of a deep cold, but I am working right on. When not preaching I am usually writing or engaged in prayer or otherwise. No time for idleness in the great harvest field and the harvest so ripe. Brother McLain is not well either.

1914

January 1

I am at Langley, S. C. Came here yesterday. Held meeting last night. I preached.

January 6

Came home Saturday, January 3. Have been working with my mail, etc., in office ever since except of course attended Sunday school and meeting. Dear old Brother Felker died and was buried while I was away and I did not get to preach his funeral according to his request. I was very sorry. I officiated at the marriage of a couple at the church in Augusta while there.

January 19

I left home January 10 and went to Nauvoo, Alabama. Then January 13 went to Dora, Alabama, 14th to Empire, Alabama, where I met with Brother Trim and wife. The 16th went to Creels and the 17th came here to Kimberly where I am now. Fifteen sermons. I expect to go home tomorrow. Brother Trim expects to go to Siblyville. Have been having some wonderful meetings.

January 24

Came home the 20th. Have been working in office writing and preparing for going again. Preached at church Wednesday night. Went out into the country to pray for a sister who was sick. Preached a funeral too on Wednesday.

January 26

Preached at church last night. Am at my desk again today. I was much exercised all last night about the gifts of the Spirit. My soul is so hungry for deeper things.

February 11

I went to Knoxville, Tennessee, January 31 and left there February 6. Preached six times. Was with Homer some. He is faithful to God and His service even if he is in the university studying. February 7 went to Chattanooga, Tennessee, Birmingham, Alabama and on to Kimberly, Alabama. Came home again yesterday. My work has piled up again in the office. Busy day and night. Had meeting at Kimberly on Sunday and after sundown walked with G. T. Brouayer about seven miles to Belltonia to overtake George C. Barron. We got into his meeting just before it closed. He went back to Kimberly next morning where we investigated him about a case against him for fornication. He claims innocency and we are still continuing the investigation.

February 16

I went to Chattanooga Saturday night and stayed with Halcy. Yesterday I preached at the church and last night again and came home last night. Two sermons.

March 2

On February 19 I left home bound for Arkansas, arrived in Monroe, Ark. the next day. Preached four times. February 24 I left Monroe, Ark. and arrived in Kentwood, Louisiana, February 26 where I am at this time. Preached four times. May remain here this week.

March 9

Nearly midnight at Kentwood, La. Have just got in from meeting. Organized the church tonight with over thirty members. Preached 15 more sermons. Baptized 9 in water. Several reclaimed, some sanctified and some filled with the Holy Ghost. The saints were joined together in love, fellowship and unity. God's blessings were wonderfully poured out. The Lord gave me great freedom in preaching the Word. We leave here D. V. tomorrow morning at 9:37, bound for Pitts Ark.

March 14

Arrived at Pitts, Arkansas March 11. Went out about four or five miles and preached that night. Came back to Pitts next day and remained here until now. Worked hard here and the people came to the service freely, but there has been no response. Closed the meeting last night and go D. V. today to Jonesboro, Ark. Eight more sermons.

March 17

I am at Jonesboro, Arkansas today. Expected to get off to Wheatly about eighty miles south, but the train left here earlier than expected and I got left. Brother and Sister Haynes got on and went, but as I got left I rented an upper room where I am busily engaged in writing and praying. I'll try to go tomorrow.

March 23

Six o'clock P. M. At Wheatly, Arkansas. I arrived here the 18th. Have preached day and night ever since, but seen no visible results. Eight sermons.

March 26

Four more sermons. At Wheatly yet. Ordained W. A. Capshaw evangelist yesterday. Have worked hard a full week and it does not seem that we have accomplished anything more than just to give out the Word. Brother and Sister Haynes and myself start this morning for Hollister, Mo. Brother Capshaw and little Jessie will remain here and continue the work a few days. Last I heard from home they were getting along very well except Milton could not go to school on account of the vaccination law. 2:45 p.m. Now at Newport, Arkansas. Arrived here about 10:00 P.M. and have to stay here till seven o'clock tomorrow morning before I can get a train for Hollister, Mo. I have secured a room and spending my time in writing, planning and prayer.

March 30

I am at Cedar Valley, Mo. this morning. We arrived at Hollister Friday. P. M. and a brother met us and brought about ten miles out from the Railroad. Held three meetings over Sunday. Rained and hindered some, but the Lord gave us great victory and liberty. Three sermons. We are to start back to the Railroad this morning to take the train for Carthage, Mo. Sold several books here which will leave the truth that I cannot stay to give out. Conflict and Roy's.

March 31

At Carthage, Mo, this morning. Nice pleasant morning. I expect to spend the day in writing and prayer. Expect to go to Kansas City tomorrow.

April 1, 12:00 Midnight

Arrived in Kansas City this afternoon at about three o'clock. Brother McMurray met us at the station and took us on the street car and brought us to 2515 Troost Avenue where Sister Diehl received us into her fine palatial home and fed us bountifully and gave us nice upper rooms. Wonderful contrast to what we had in Arkansas. We have spent much time in prayer tonight. Those we have met seem delighted to have us here. Have not heard from home as I expected. Hope to hear soon and that all is well. We are to commence meeting tomorrow night.

April 13, Monday morning

Preached 12 times. Held meetings in a private home. 2515 Troost Avenue. I am still here in Kansas City. Good day yesterday. Several new ones in. They are preparing to get a public hall where we can reach the people better. Beautiful morning. Folks all right at home when I heard last.

April 20, Monday P. M.

8 more sermons. Went down in what they call the North Bottom from Thursday till last night and held meeting in a mission. Had small attendance but good interest. I wired Brother Lemons to take my place at Empire, Alabama yesterday and I've just got word that he went. I have sent for Brother Perry to come here and take charge of the work here in my absence. Letter from home says they are all well. Beautiful weather. Will have to start for Florida next week. Aim to stop at home a few hours.

April 29

Arrived home this morning at 6:30. Preached six more sermons at Kansas City. Left there on the morning of the 27th. Got things arranged at Kansas City so I think the work will go on until I get back. They seem determined to have me back there to continue the work. I find my family well and happy in Jesus. I expect to leave tomorrow for Florida.

June 13

Just returned home yesterday morning from Florida where I labored for forty days. Was at Midway out from Wauchula twenty miles eleven days, 18 sermons. At Wauchula ten days, 11 sermons. Parish three days, five sermons. Conducted the first camp meeting at Wimauma and dedicated the ground and new tabernacle, all paid out of debt. This lasted ten days. Wonderful meeting. Lots of people blest. About 20 baptized with the Holy Ghost, Acts 2:4, 19 sermons. Tampa two days, one sermon. Lenden three days, five sermons. Lulu two days, two sermons. The Lord gave liberal blessings and not a few souls were blest in these meetings, yet I did not see the results that I desired. I feel myself an unprofitable servant indeed. Brother W. S. Caruthers, state overseer for Florida, was with me at most of these places. Several of our friends came in last night and we had a good song and prayer service. Family all well and Homer at home. Have lots of office work to do now while I am at home.

June 24

Weather exceedingly hot. Have been at home about twelve days except a short trip to Ooltewah with F. J. Lee to pray for the sick. We walked over Whiteoak Mountain and back after dark. Quite a task for us. Have preached three times and prayed for sick folks several times besides my office work. I expect to start for South Carolina tomorrow to be gone a few days.

July 1

Just returned from South Carolina yesterday. Had a great time over there. Won lots of friends and organized another church with 26 members. (5 sermons) Was in a severe rain, wind and electric storm and got wet and my clothes soiled and some of those in my suitcase too. Nearly as soon as we got out of the buggy the horse broke loose from the buggy and ran away. Got scared at the lightning and thunder. I find lots of office work piled up again for me. I am cramped financially again but believe God will still stand by us. I've made a few trips and did not get my Railroad expenses. But I am giving my life, my all for the glorious Church of God. It is a hard battle against all the oppositions and criticisms, but I know I am right and expect to push on till Jesus comes or calls. The reformation must win. Prophecy must be fulfilled.

July 6

Preached at tent fourth of July. Preached Sunday too. I am home for a few days, Three more sermons. We are keeping Sister Haynes and her children while Brother Haynes is in Kansas City holding the work together there.

July 14

I am now at Knoxville, Tennessee. Came here last Saturday, the 11th, Having meeting under a tent. Preached three times Sunday and taught a Sunday school class. Five sermons up to five o'clock P. M. The altar filled with seekers. Prospects look encouraging. Homer leads the singing. Large attendance Sunday night. Very good last night. Heavy rain and storm this afternoon. Blew the tent down. Don't know whether we can have a service tonight or not.

July 16, Thursday afternoon

We have been hindered some in the meeting because of the rain but we had a little meeting last night. I came home to Brother

White's and wrote till midnight after which I retired, but was not able to sleep for several hours on account of a heart hunger for a renewed and deeper experience. Ruins and wreckage appeared in visions before my eyes unless we are able to press on into the fullness of the blessing of the gospel of Christ. Oh, how my heart was wrung and twisted in suffering as I tossed on my bed and agonized and groaned in prayer to God for His favor and help. I feel less than the least and my ability for preaching seems at times to be taken from me, but it is a marvel even to myself as I seem to be inspired to write. Last night and today I have written on the subject, "The Doctrine of Balaam." I have written 3,486 words and as I rehearse it I seem to be instructed and edified as if was reading after some one else. I think I see that I may probably add about 1,500 more words yet on the Balaam doctrine.

July 20

Monday morning. Seven more sermons. Preached three times yesterday. Altar services good. Some got the baptism. Great crowd last night. God gave great liberty in preaching. Brothers Kelley and Koon with me over Sunday. Gave out hundreds of tracts, papers and Echoes. People seemed greatly interested.

July 25, Saturday P. M.

Still at Knoxville. Five more sermons. The meeting still going on with increasing interest. Altar full of seekers every night. Some going through and receiving the Holy Ghost besides other good that is being done. Brother Lemons came by to see me as he stopped on his way to Jefferson City. I greatly enjoyed his presence for a few hours as we talked over matters of interest to the work in general.

July 30

At home. Came home from Knoxville last Monday. It rained the meeting out on Sunday evening. I left it in care of Homer and Brother Kelly. Two more sermons. Have been at work in office this week. Go to North Carolina D. V. tomorrow.

August 10

This morning finds me at Brother Whitmire's near Toonigh, Georgia. Monday morning, I left home July 31 and arrived in Murphy, N. C. the same day in the afternoon. I was not expecting any one to meet me at the Railroad as I expected to go out on the mail hack, but as I walked down the platform I heard my name called, but as I could see no face that I recognized I waited a moment, but soon I was in a buggy riding out through the mountains to go 25 miles to the camp meeting at Tusquittee. I preached seven sermons there. Brother and Sister Anderson were there. We had a glorious time the few days I remained. On Wednesday the fifth of August I came here to be in convention with state overseer C. M. Padgett. Had been having good meetings until last night we were rained out. A few who were at the house had meeting but we did not go. Seven sermons. One day I stood for about three hours answering questions and explaining Scripture. I expect to start tomorrow morning for Dora, Alabama to meet Alabama state overseer, George T. Brouayer, to adjust some matters there.

August 11

Two more sermons. I start in a few minutes for the train.

August 13

Now at Birmingham, Alabama, 7:15 A. M. Arrived here a few minutes ago from Dora, Alabama where I went yesterday and stayed last night. Spent about six hours last night in investigating the case of William Allen and Mrs. Clemmie Lawson, charged with fornication. Examined both of them very thoroughly and other witnesses too. Mrs. Lawson confessed they were guilty, but he declared they were not. A plain case of lying and hypocrisy on the part of one or the other and the evidence was strong against Allen. They both claimed salvation so it leaves them in a bad light. We advised the church to suspend them both until after the Assembly in November and even then an indefinite time awaiting for more proof or developments. We feel that the Lord gave great wisdom in dealing with the matter.

August 17

Monday morning. I am about four miles south of Buhl, Alabama. Came here the 13th. Brother Brouayer and wife and others came with me from Dora. Yesterday was a great day. I preached about 1 ½ hours. Altar full of seekers. Much prayer and great rejoicing among the saints. Preached four more sermons.

August 23

Sunday morning. Have been laboring hard all the week. Preached I guess nine sermons. Great liberty. Multitudes of people. Altar full of seekers nearly every service. Up till after twelve nearly every night. I'm making lots of friends and of course some enemies. All well at home last report. Weather very hot. I wet my clothes every time I preach, have to hang them all out to dry every morning, I expect to leave here tomorrow.

August 24

Monday morning. Preached two sermons yesterday. I am about to start to the train bound for Kentwood La. Nice weather but very warm.

August 28

Preached three sermons. Great liberty and the saints refreshed. I start to the train in a few minutes, bound for Evansville Ind. Friday morning at Kentwood La. Copy of letter written wife on the train August 28, running I suppose a mile a minute north through Mississippi. 12:00 noon Friday. Hallelujah. Dear wife: I know you will be much disappointed to get this instead of your own, but it seems the best I can do. It was a little hard to decide to not come by home, but seeing I was there days behind any way and I could save about $5.00 by going direct I finally decided to pass on this time and try to love you a little harder when I do some. I guess you remember of reading the letters you sent me from Kentwood, La., about the trouble there. Well, the Lord helped me to fix that all up as sweet as you ever saw. The saints there have had a three days feast. One man heard of me being there and came 18 miles to see me. He had heard of me and was a sinner. The first message he heard pricked him in the heart and he fell into the altar and cried through to God. I kissed him goodby this morning and he was so full he could hardly contain himself. That is worth my trip down there if that had been all. Then getting the saints so blest and the trouble you read about adjusted, I feel amply paid for the sacrifice of a little time at home and you will feel paid too I know. I would have spent two or three days at home if it had not been for that trip but it is certainly one of the best trips I ever made in such a short time. They gave me just about money enough to have paid my way from Tuscaloosa, Alabama and back which makes me nothing out of trip except the sacrifice of a few days at home. Thank God. Hallelujah. You may now write me to the address I gave you at Evansville, Ind. Very kindly and sincerely, Husband.

September 2

At Evansville, Ind., Wednesday morning. I arrived here last Saturday. Six sermons. Besides answered many questions and gave Bible instructions. I am here in meeting with Brother and Sister Trim. Will only be here a day or two more. Wife was not well when I last heard from her. Hope she is well now. I'll go home in a few days, D. V.

September 5, 1:30 A. M.

Just closed a meeting here tonight at Bompas Creek, Olney P. O., Ill. Came here for just one service. I left Evansville, Indiana September 3. Ordained three deacons tonight. Had sacrament and feet washing. I preached three sermons tonight besides other instructions. Fine meeting. One more sermon at Evansville. We start in a few hours to Orchardville, Ill. to be with them over Sunday.

September 6, 11:00 P. M.

At Orchardville, Ill. Preached four sermons last night and today. But really did not get to finish the sermon tonight. I suppose I was a little more than half way through when a woman came in at the door excited and called for a certain woman saying that her son had been cut and nearly dead. Of course, that stopped the service. I had noticed a few minutes before that there was a shot fired and I suspected there was trouble, but I held my congregation fairly well, although several seemed to feel that there was trouble brewing. I don't know the particulars, but the tragedy I understand took place right in front or nearby the meeting house. After the affair the brother of the young man that was killed came in the house and with a large open knife in hand cursed and threatened our holiness people with infamous blasphemy as if we were to blame for it. His mother done her best, it seemed, to stop him, and after a little time somebody got him away but the quarrel seemed to go on for some time afterwards. No officer near, but we met the officer hastening to the scene of the tragedy as we were coming away. The wounded man did not die at once but after we came to our stopping place we heard over the phone that he was dead. I was aiming to make it to the train nine miles away tonight so I could get the train at 3:30 tonight, but all of this coming up got up such a stir so I'll not be able to get away till morning. I start home D. V. as soon as I can tomorrow morning. It will delay me much but I can't prevent it.

September 17

I arrived home the 8th. Found my family well, Thank God. Preached two sermons at Church Sunday. Many of our people have been handling poison serpents at the tabernacle. The power of God was demonstrated marvelously. I am working day and night preparing for Assembly and other office work.

September 23

I was 49 years old yesterday. Spent the day in laboring for the Master. Writing, praying for the sick, etc. The pastor, F. J. Lee, has gone away and left the church in my care. Preached three times.

September 27

> After meeting at night. Preached five sermons, one funeral. I am called about over town praying for the sick besides my office work and preaching. I am working day and night preparing for Assembly and the paper interests as well as my correspondence and official duties.

October 4

> After meeting at night. Two sermons. Meetings seemed to be somewhat effective for good today. I baptized four in water. The Lord blest, the presence of the Lord was strongly manifested in the afternoon service. Was hindered about getting to the night service on time by a spell that Sister Lemons had.

October 11

> Done office work, prayed for sick, held the regular service, etc. At the service this afternoon just the time I was expecting to preach Sister Ward was taken suddenly ill. She was taken out of the house to the cottage close by and I called all the saints to prayer in the church and I and a few more ran out to where she was and we all held on to the Lord until she was completely delivered so we had a good service any way. The service tonight was fine. Songs, testimonies, shouts, dances, manifestations in different ways. Several forward for prayer. One saved just before the service. Great time of freedom. Mary went to Sunnyside tonight, has not got in yet. The Assembly is nearly here. I have traveled since last Assembly 9,192 miles.

October 18

> At night after meeting. This has been a glorious day. The manifestations of God's power have been glorious. In praying for the sick the power fell every time. One converted at a little prayer meeting, One sanctified at home. The regular services at the church were wonderful. Can't describe it. Shouts, praises, talking in tongues, preaching, dancing, crying and weeping over souls, love of one another displayed. Good attendance. Busy, busy day and night all week in office and looking after the work in every way.

October 26

> Worked all last week in office preparing for Assembly. Preached a funeral yesterday. One sermon.

November 15

Have been so busy I could not or did not take time to write. The Assembly has come and gone. It was wonderful and beyond description. God made able to manage everything with wisdom and love. There was a greater display of love than I ever saw. In three of the services "like as of fire" was witnessed by many. I delivered three discourses besides having charge of all the work. Harmony prevailed over every tendency to separate. The Holy Ghost set me in as General Overseer again. This time it was made plain that I should continue in the position until Jesus comes or calls. Tears form in my eyes as I write. I am unable to express my gratitude to God for strength and care bestowed upon me. I go deeper in to humility as I launch out into victory. God is faithful and I want to be. O God, make of me what ever pleases Thee at any cost. Don't mind my shrinking if I should shrink. Put me through for Thee regardless of myself. I don't want to hinder Thee in making me like Thyself. The description of the work of the Assembly and the way I was made Overseer is recorded in the 1914 Echoes from the Tenth Annual Assembly. Oh, how I love everybody!

December 12

My work has been one continuous round of office work ever since the Assembly. I was made editor and publisher of the Evangel. I have also been preparing Sunday school literature for next year, besides a heavy correspondence. I work from early morning till late at night, sometimes as late as one o'clock. It is after midnight now I see as I write this.

December 25

Homer and Iris and little Milton are with us at home today. There is no decrease in my work, it rather increases as time goes by. This has been a wet muddy rainy Christmas.

1915

January 20

Work about the same. The Sunday school literature has been a success in one respect and a defeat in another. There has been a much larger demand for it than we anticipated and prepared for, so we haven't been able to near supply the demands. Have had to return several orders. This has been a source of embarrassment. I feel very much worn because of constant toil and limited time for sleep, and no time for rest only when I am compelled to sleep.

February 20

The work for the past month has been much the same. The constant toil in preparing copy for the Evangel, Helper, Sunday school literature, reading proof, writing letters, attending to all the work of the General Overseer, besides praying for the sick both day and night has left no time for recreation or rest except while I sleep. This has been blessed, through only a few hours each night. I sent T. S. Payne to Trion, Georgia to investigate Mr. J. H. Newton who has been giving us some trouble on account of some reports of having a wife and children at Mize, Ga., and claiming to be a single man. Brother Payne went on February 13. Mr. N. refused to go with him to Mize, Ga., so we believe him to be guilty of some crime in some way. Today I sent W. E. Gentry to search for R. L. Cotnam against whom are some reports that leave him in a bad light. I sent M. S. Lemons to Virginia February 9 or 10 to investigate the matter of Walter Barney who was placed in jail, accused of man slaughter because he let his child die without calling a doctor or giving medicine. T. L. McLain to Kentucky about two weeks ago to attend to some matters in the church there. The church as a whole is moving on nicely and constantly increasing.

March 24

I have recently prepared and enclosed a place for an office in the building at 2524 Gaut Street where I moved my office furniture last week, March 17, 1915, after having my office in an upper room at home for about ten years. My work has so increased and callers so much more frequent that it demanded a larger and more convenient place. We are now sending out the second issue of the Sunday school literature. I am still working day and night and my work is constantly increasing. The work as General Overseer takes much of my time besides the paper and Sunday school literature. Also called to pray for the sick, but I am compelled to push this off on others most of the time much as I regret to do so. W. S. Gentry resigned his position as overseer of Alabama on the 20th instant and this throws still more work on me. My daily prayer is that God will give me health and strength to work hard for Him. It is wonderful what He makes me able to do.

April 20

Once more I write a few lines to say that my work is a daily round of office work, praying for the sick and people's souls. The Lord has kept my health up remarkably well under the strain and pressure of the work. The paper has increased to 4,000 printed and the demand the last two weeks has been even above that number. Brother Gentry has accepted the reappointment as overseer of Alabama which brings me some relief. He went back to his work this morning. Homer is home now and working in the printing office. We are a happy family all working hard for the Lord.

May 14

My heart is almost broken because I am not able to do more. Calls and calls for meetings and to assist in matters of business. Have just sent George T. Brouayer to South Carolina to adjust some matters there. Have a special call to Florida now, they say they can't get along without me, besides to hold their camp meeting beginning next week. I ran over to an all day meeting last Sunday at Dividing Ridge. Preached twice. Preached a funeral this week. Have preached a few times this year, but hardly enough to mention. I am still working from sixteen to eighteen hours a day. Some times I almost give out and then the Lord seems to stimulate me and on I go again.

May 17

I went to Mineral Park yesterday and dedicated a church and preached twice.

June 8

The saints at Wimauma, Florida informed me that they were
without a leader for their camp meeting and that I would have to
come. I did not see how I could go, but under the circumstances
it seemed I would have to so I rushed off on the 19th of May and
came home on the first of June. Had a great meeting but my work
at home piled up and I have not got out yet. I preached about
twenty-five times. I am having some great problems to meet just
now, but God is giving me grace, wisdom and love.

July 9

Another month has past since I made any notes in my journal.
Have kept up the regular routine of office work, besides some
problems in connection with the Church affairs. Have been
dealing with a problem at Kentwood, Louisiana that is not solved
yet. Have two cases in Florida and Alabama that have been very
perplexing. J. W. Buckalew and V. W. Kennedy. Don't know how
the end will be. I called a council consisting of M. S. Lemons, W.
F. Bryant, George T. Brouayer, W. S. Gentry, F. J. Lee, J. L. Scott,
and Efford Haynes on Wednesday, June 16, for advice about the
matter. Since then I have followed closely their advice. God is
helping me to love the erring and yet take a firm stand for the
right. His grace has been unfailing

July 26

The two last Sundays they came after me early in the morning
and took me several miles in the country to a tent meeting. Of
course, they had me to do the preaching. Preached twice each
Sunday, four times. My office work is still going on as it has been.
Have to work day and night.

August 7

Mary, Homer, Iris and Milton left home Thursday morning August
5, to go to Indiana to be gone three weeks. They have only been
gone two days, but almost seems like months. I have all the
office work to do and it has already swamped me till I don't know
whether I will ever see out any more or not. This is Saturday night
and I am so worn that I am compelled to leave the office at about
ten o'clock without my week's work up. O God, help me and keep
me able to work and give me wisdom and strength. I have many
perplexing questions to meet.

1916

January 28, 1916

Well, here I come again after an absence of several months. During this time I have waded through some of the hardest places of my life, but thank God in every conflict I have come out more than conqueror and I am still on top. Since last writing I passed the age of fifty, went through the great Assembly, was continued as General Overseer and publisher of the paper. My work is still too much more for me, but the Lord helps me and still I go on. I have done much more than I ever thought I could and greater things are just ahead. The office work has kept me busy day and night and it seems there is no end yet. The paper has reached a circulation of 6,200 and the Sunday school literature is gaining in favor with the people. Homer is still in Indiana. Wife and Iris came home and have been helping me faithfully. We have recently purchased a big temple at Harriman, Tennessee for the next Assembly. The great Church of God is growing and prospering in power and numbers. Multitudes more are looking this way. Calls for workers and preachers come from every direction, far and near. My nerves are strained to the uttermost nearly all the time with responsibilities and work. God alone has been sustaining me both with health and wisdom. He shall have all the glory. Hallelujah!

March 18

I don't write much in my journal any more for two reasons. First, my work is one common routine from week to week with the general editorial and office work. This keeps me busy from early morning to late at night. Second, my time is so taken that I scarcely have time to take on the extra few minutes every day that it would take to prepare interesting notes. A meeting last Sunday night is worthy of note. The young people had gathered early and the leaders had asked me to speak and conduct a reconsecration service. We were not through when the pastor came in so we closed

the young people's meeting rather abruptly and gave way to the
pastor. After a few songs and a few prayers the pastor stepped to
the pulpit apparently to preach, but just as he commenced to speak
the spirit gave a short message in tongues through me, followed
at once by the interpretation. This was repeated a time or two and
the people became much effected at once. A sister gave a few short
messages and the interpretations followed quickly. These messages
and interpretations continued occasionally until many were in tears
and some almost screaming. The large house was about full of
people and many were effected. The pastor gave a chance for all to
come to the altar that wanted to and the whole front was filled with
seekers and many carrying earnestly to God for help and mercy. I
was so under the influence of the Spirit that I stayed in my place
and the cries, tears and prayers continued for near two hours while
many got blest. It was a great service. I believe every person in the
house felt the presence of the Holy Ghost.

May 15

Here it is summer time again. My work has been a routine of office
work since I last wrote, with many perplexing questions, but victory
has always been the result. I was at Harriman, Tennessee a week
ago making some preliminary arrangements for the November
Assembly. Preached three times in the Temple. Yesterday I was at
Copperhill and raised three hundred dollars and dedicated their
church house to the Lord. All day meeting and reached the end
at ten o'clock at night when all stood before the Lord while the
dedicatory prayer was said. Came home this morning. Find my
work still piled up before me. I'm still on the run.

May 24

Went to Chattanooga last Sunday, May 21, and dedicated their
new church house to the Lord. Had a fine time.

July 14

I went to Chandlers View on the Fourth of July to adjust some
difficulties that had arisen between them and J. S. Llewellyn.
We were successful in the matter although it took much prayer,
wisdom and love. I preached in Knoxville both going and coming.
Today we are getting a loan of $1,200 at the Bank to relieve
Homer of a debt he owes Mrs. L. C. Fitzsimmons. Homer is at
Culver, Ind. I am spending my time in the regular routine of
business. Office work, praying for the sick, etc. S. W. Latimer's
little boy has been here for a week. He was about to bleed to
death when he brought him. The blood has been stopped and
he is getting stronger. On the 19th and 20th of June a few of
the brethren met here to talk over the divorce and remarriage

question and try to get together on it, but our efforts seemed to be in vain although we believe there was some good accomplished. I have many perplexing problems to consider and deal with of late. God is helping and giving wisdom, but oh, how I feel the need of help from Him in the great position of responsibility I occupy. God help me and give me love, grace and wisdom.

July 25

Last Sunday I went out seven miles from town and dedicated the Kinser tabernacle. Had all day service. Large crowd. The power of the Lord was gloriously realized.

August 1

Preached at church last Sunday and Sunday night. Pastor was out in the country holding a meeting.

August 10

Preached at church again last Sunday, also at night. Had a wonderful demonstration of God's presence at night. The work is getting greater and heavier on me. 0 Lord, hold me up and help me.

August 14

Mr. Casen's little girl died in our home Friday night and they buried her yesterday, Sunday. I conducted the funeral service at nine, went and prayed for Sister Logan who was sick, hurried back and went to the church and taught Sunday school class at ten and preached at eleven-thirty. I am still working hard day and night, and then can scarcely keep up. I have had to quit answering calls to pray for the sick.

September 23

I was fifty one years old yesterday. Am still working hard day and night besides my regular work of the Evangel, Sunday school literature work and Overseer's work. I am now preparing for the Assembly. This is no little task of itself.

October 5

I am still working day and night. I went to Harriman, Tennessee September 30, last Saturday, to look after the interests of the Assembly which is to convene in next month. I preached morning and at night on Sunday. To my surprise on last Monday night the church here at Cleveland selected me as pastor by acclamation. I never saw the like. As I hardly see how I can take the pastorate on account of other matters and press of work, I have not yet accepted the position, but I am giving it some attention and will decide probably before long.

November 13

The great Assembly at Harriman, Tennessee has come and gone. The press of work is so great I am unable to make much note of the proceedings here, the most important matters are given in the paper and the minutes. I have been preaching and preaching and giving no record of the sermons. The power falls wonderfully at the services. I have accepted the pastorate, although as I told them I do not see how I am to do the work justice with all the other work pressed upon me. The publishing committee has put me in as editor and publisher of the paper and Sunday school literature again. We are planning to purchase a printing plant and do all the work ourselves. It does not seem favorable to move to Harriman now.

December 26

I have been preached two or three times a week since the Assembly, besides doing all of my other work. On Sunday, December 17, the message was powerful and it was so effective that many were much affected and the service continued till some time after noon. Last Sunday we had a great time and many were melted to tears while the message was given to the children. The message Sunday night was owned and blest of the Lord and after it was concluded the power began to fall and many danced and shouted for joy while some handled fire, red hot coals, blazing coals, hands on stove and in the blaze. Wonderful time. Music under the power, etc., etc. In our Sunday schools were reported 289 besides visitors. Have taken in some new ministers too. Have not been able to install our printing plant yet, but hope to do so soon. Our work is still heavy. We are at it constantly from six in the morning till ten and eleven at night. God is giving strength and making us able for it.

1917

January 3, 1917

Last week I preached funerals one day. Married a couple, did all my regular work. Sunday night we had a watch-night service at the Church. Had a wonderful time. No sleepiness in the congregation. Can't describe the meeting, it was so wonderful. One joined the church. One reclaimed. It seems that I cannot get to bed any more till near midnight or after.

January 22

Well, I could not possibly keep up and do the work I am doing if the Lord did not hold me up. But it is wonderful how my strength holds up, and the work I do. I can hardly tell all I do. I have my regular office work, editing, publishing the paper, Sunday school literature 150 to 180 letters every week to answer or attend to, pastoral work, making peace some times among members, praying for the sick, preaching three and four times a week. Funeral of Sister Luda Clark today. Preached twice yesterday. I can't take time to give a detailed account of my work in my journal as I used to do. I work from 16 to 18 hours every day and have to hurry in everything I do. God gives wisdom, grace and strength. My heart magnifies the Lord for His wonderful help to me. How I love Him.

February 21

Another month has passed since I wrote on these pages. My work still continues and is really increasing on my hands. I have had to secure another helper in the office. Last Sunday I held a funeral service besides my regular Sunday work. Monday my body gave way a little under the strain but I am at myself again now. Thanks to God. Am having to build an addition to my office to make room for extra machinery and office help and equipments. Good word from the churches and Sunday schools generally. The work all over is on the increase.

February 26

This is Monday night. The Lord wonderfully poured out His Spirit on us yesterday at the meeting. Preached the funeral of five-year-old Edna Sample today that said, "I'm holiness." "I don't believe in it," referring to medicine. She wanted us to pray for her but told her mama that she was not going to get well. Funeral at church.

May 28

Have preached several funerals, besides the regular services. Have had meetings at night at the new Sunny Side tabernacle every night except Sunday nights for nearly a month. Six or eight have received the Holy Ghost. I have preached nearly every night besides having all my regular office work to do. The first of April we commenced doing our own printing of the paper and Sunday school literature, etc. I had to build an addition to the office at a cost of nearly $700, and now I am getting a new press at a cost of about $1,100, besides the outfit I got of Brother Llewellyn for $1,250. But our work is moving on nicely. Employ seven regular hands, besides one or two days in the week I employ from four to six extra. I shipped Shriner's press to him on the 25th inst. One week ago last night we had one of the most wonderful meetings we have ever had in Cleveland. Only one got the Holy Ghost, but much other good accomplished and the power continued to fall in waves for hours.

June 29

Have been having meeting every night at the tabernacle in South Cleveland nearly all this month. 25 or more converted besides a number sanctified and filled with the Holy Ghost. We have had some very interesting street meetings at five or six different places in the city. Had the brass band with us a part of the time. At some of the street services people shouted and danced and talked in tongues besides many good testimonies and the songs and preaching. I am running my business, preaching nearly every night and up till midnight in the revival and preaching, three times on Sunday. It is really marvelous to me how I am able to do so much and hold up and be as strong as I am. Scarcely ever get more than five hours sleep in twenty-four, and every moment of my time is full for eighteen and nineteen hours every day. Have been running a wagon from my home to the tabernacle to take the workers. As high as thirty have rode at a time.

November 10

As it has been several months since I have written anything here, many things have transpired. We moved the meeting up to the church and the revival went right on till the first of September. About thirty additions to the Church and about the same number received the Holy Ghost. At the quarterly meeting the first of October, they pressed me so that I accepted the pastorate again for another year. The fourth of October the Elders met in council here and November 1-6, the Assembly at Harriman, Tenn. This was indeed a wonderful time. The other records show the happenings mostly so I will not take space to describe it. But God made me able to manage everything in my department as moderator. I feel somewhat worn over the strain, but I work every day and night just the same.

November 21

Work, work, work, I have about gained back my strength since the Assembly and feeling well again. I have at last secured the services of a short hand writer, Maud Pangle, who commenced work the 19th instant. I can now dictate my letters, then, she puts them in typewriting. I now have in my employ five in the printing department and five in the office, besides myself and some additional help one or two days in the week.

December 19

Another month has past and the year will soon be gone. My work is ever increasing, but God is making me able for it. One week ago tonight at the church I solemnized the rite of matrimony for Ransome Clark and Amy Lawson, Today I was called to the Woolen Mill to preach during the noon hour. This came with all the other work I had to do. I ran off down there, delivered a message and hastened back to my work. We got the minutes ready for distribution about two weeks ago. Work generally going good.

1918

January 2, 1918

The watch night meeting at the church was fine. Weather very cold and rough. The Bible Training school started yesterday. I opened the school with a lecture and Bible lesson and prayer. Dedicated the school to God for all the future. Only five yesterday, but there are ten today and still more are expected in a few days. Sister Nora Chambers is teacher under my directions.

June 26

I see I have not written here for a long time. Many things have transpired that are recorded elsewhere. The Bible School closed April 5, and the Council of Elders followed for several days, little Thelma died, the other work going on and increasing all the time. I am now about to finish up another addition to the Evangel office in order to get room enough to take care of the work there is to do. We have started a Junior quarterly and printing 9,000 Evangels every week. My pastoral work, office work, editorial work and all I have to do keeps me busy day and night. I must say too that I planned and made a Sunday school Secretary book and there is quite a demand for it. The office force consists of ten regular employees besides wife and I and two or three extra on Thursday each week. I am considering putting on two or three more on account of the increase of work. The churches are increasing rapidly, several every month. Revivals and camp meeting are reporting good success. Homer got to come home only a few days and was called back to New York in the war service. He is now in Pennsylvania. The war has spoiled all his plans and mine too, concerning him for I hoped to soon have him helping me in the Church and school work. All for this time. Should not wait so long again.

September 27

Much has transpired since the last writing. The work in the office
is increasing and I have added one more regular man in the office.
We are about to complete an addition to our dwelling house so
as to make more room for our Bible school students. I believe
I have had some of about the hardest trials to wade through in
the last few months of my life. But God has given grace and I
still have the victory. About a month ago a government officer
came in to make some investigations and took a sample of every
thing we have and some of our record books that has caused us
much inconvenience. He promised to have them back in a few
days, but they are not back yet. Homer was home a few hours
about two weeks ago, but we heard from him yesterday and he
stated that he with his company would probably sail for France
today or tomorrow. We feel very serious about it, but we have
the consolation of knowing he is trusting in God and we believe
the Lord will take care of him and bring him back to us. Milton
has started to school again and Iris is taking a course of music
lessons besides helping me so faithfully in the office. I am very
busy now preparing for the annual Assembly, besides my other
regular work. I work from 14 to eighteen hours every day.

November 13

We were deprived of having the Assembly on account of the
Influenza epidemic that has been raging for more than two
months. Thousands and thousands have died of the plague.
Some of our people succombed but not many. We are printing
10,000 Evangels every week. We held the Council, October 22-29.
The Church work is going right on as if we had the Assembly.
Overseers appointed, pastors appointed, and no block in the way.
The Bible Training School opened November 11 with five scholars.
Many having been kept away on account of the influenza and will
be in later. We have had cases in our home for about six weeks.
Only Iris and Milton have been down of our own family, but
six or more friends that came in and took down. I have prayed
for at their homes as high as thirty a day. Many handkerchiefs
have been prayed over and anointed sent to the sick. Telegrams,
telephone messages, letters came in by scores calling for prayer.
We have never known such an awful time before. The government
closed all churches, and public gatherings of every kind. We
missed four Sundays, but commenced again last Sunday.
The announcement came that the world war had closed and
preparations are being made for terms of peace. We do not know
what will be next. I will not be pastor here the coming year.

December 27

Many things have transpired since I last wrote. A few more students entered the Bible School. One of them, Mrs. Bennie Terrill, was taken sick about a week ago and only lived about four days. She died in our home. Three sick at one time, Blanche Koon and Mary Rowell were the other two. The town authorities have closed all public services again so we cannot have Sunday school or meeting. It is reported there are a thousand cases of influenza in town now. Many dying. Whole families sick and in some cases nobody to wait on them. Public schools shut down. Our office work much hindered because most of them have to be out so much, either sick or have to wait on the sick, or help bury the dead. I ordered machinery a week or so ago, to be shipped today, to equip a book binding department in our office. This outfit will cost about $350.00 installed. I also ordered on the 23rd instant a fine typesetting machine at a cost of about $3,700 installed. The Church is growing and the work is spreading in spite of all oppositions and discouragements. I am convinced now that I had a case of the influenza, I was very sick and went down to the house and layed down, but was called up in about fifteen minutes to attend to some business. The second time I went to bed and had to get up again in a few minutes. I thought, well, if I haven't time to be sick I'll just stay up. So never went to bed any more only at night. But I had the same symptoms and was affected just like all that have the disease. I was sick about two weeks but God held me up. Thanks be unto Him. I never missed a time of going to the table, but several times I could scarcely eat, and several times I only ate apples. While I was sick I prayed for many sick. I never told anybody how I suffered until after it was all over. I have preached many funerals, prayed for hundreds and on the go day and night all times of night. This has been an awful time and not over yet. Homer has been in France far some time, but since the war has closed we are looking for him to come home soon. We are anxiously awaiting his return. The year has nearly come to a close, but it has been a great year in many respects. My dear wife has never taken the influenza although she has had the care of fourteen or more cases. God has sustained and held her up. Thanks to His name. He is so good to us.

December 31

I have surely done my best the past year. I do not know how I could have done any more unless my capacity could have been enlarged. I have strained and forced myself to accomplish what I have. But with all this I feel that what I have done has been too little for my Lord. I finished the year by preaching the funeral of Lee Stanley, a promising young minister in the Church. The influenza epidemic is still raging and quite a number of the Church people are dying, but not so many, it seems, in proportion as others. Our office work is getting to be enormous. We now print 11,000 Evangels every week and we expect to have it increase rapidly the coming year. Goodby to the old year. For the new I go to another book.

1919

January 1, 1919

Early in the morning of the new year I have very good health. Wife is in good health. The children are scattered. Milton is at home going to school. Iris is working hard helping me in the office. Homer is in France, in the army. Although the war is over, they are holding thousands of the soldiers for guard duty or something. Halcy is at her home in Chattanooga. Little Thelma is in heaven, the best place of all. I want this to be the greatest year of my life. My heart cry is, Lord increase my capacity so I can serve Thee better and do more for Thy Church, and humanity in general. Give me both wisdom and knowledge, so I can be fully prepared and made fully able to meet every emergency and not make a single mistake in any decisions in my official capacity.

January 31

Wife went to the bedside of her dying father three weeks ago tonight to Elwood, Ind. Later he was moved to near Cambridge City. We received a wire message today that he is dead and will be buried next Sunday. Work going on here about the same as ever. Very seldom I get to bed at night till midnight, then up at five in the morning. I feel very much worn tonight at ten, but I do not have time for sleep at all, only I have to sleep some.

February 20

Wife came home last week very much worn but was well except some cold and hoarseness. Work going on as usual. Still scarcely ever get to bed till nearly midnight and up again about five in the morning. We are sending off about 13,000 papers every week now. Had a new experience yesterday. Held a funeral service for three corpses at once, all died in one home, two sisters and a baby. Clara Maples, May Tibbs and her baby. Influenza the cause.

March 10

Have recently installed a new Intertype machine in the Evangel office at a cost of about $3,700. We are printing 14,000 this week. The work is still on the rush.

April 21

Everything moving on nicely in the home and office. Homer came home on the 11th from France, having been discharged from the army. We have had all of our children with us two or three times since he came and we enjoyed it fine. The children presented us with some chinaware for our wedding anniversary. The Bible school closed April 4 with nice exercises. The school was small in number on account of the war and influenza epidemic, but it was a success. Two, A. D. Evans, of North Carolina, and Earl Hamilton of Tennessee, were awarded diplomas. The office work is still increasing. We are printing 16,500 paper each week to supply the demand. Took in a new office girl, Minnie Johnson from Alabama. We now have five men and ten women, regular office helpers, with wife and some others helping some at odd times.

August 12

Nearly four months have sped away so rapidly that I can hardly realize it has been so long since I opened my journal to write. Many happenings since I last wrote. Probably one of the greatest is the erection of a building for the Evangel office and Bible school room. It is not yet completed, but we moved into some of the rooms Saturday, August 9 and yesterday, August 11. I am having quite a test of faith for the money to complete the building. No one knows my heaviness and apparent perplexities. I tell it to God only and He is blessedly giving me grace. The Elders in Council advised me to put up the building when they met in April. So I am doing my best. I have borrowed money largely on my own responsibility. I am trusting God to make me able to meet it. I am also serving as Sunday school Superintendent this quarter at Church. Commenced July 1. Having a fine Sunday school. Have been a hundred and up to 135 every Sunday. Sam C. Perry and J. L. Scott have been discontinued from their ministry in the Church and are giving us some little trouble. They are opposing the Church and its government and doing all they can against us, but God is wonderfully with us and blessing us. He is pouring out his Spirit in a wonderful way at the church services and prayer meetings, both in this town and other places. Two Sunday nights in succession I had charge of the services at the church and the scenes at both meetings beggars description. It was wonderful. Large crowds and wonderful outpourings. Waves and waves of blessings poured out. Last Sunday night following the great outpourings we called for a collection for home missions and in a few minutes we had about twenty dollars.

August 20

I am out early this morning. Retired about twelve last night and out at the office this morning early enough to have a light to write by. I am very heavily burdened this morning about the work. The responsibilities are very heavy. The capacity of our printing plant is too small to get all the work done that is required. Many of our people from a distance have work here they want done and it seems impossible to get it done. We are printing the paper each week, preparing two grades of quarterlies and Home class quarterly for the Sunday school besides lesson leaves and picture cards for the children. Then we have the text books to prepare and print for the Bible school. I feel like raising my hands to heaven and crying out to God for help. Our new building is not yet complete and the financing of this is a heavy burden as well as all the other departments with the limited means at hand. 0 God, please help me this morning. Besides these responsibilities wife and daughter are to go on a trip tomorrow to Kansas for a family reunion, and on top of all of these and a thousand other cares I have the care of all the churches. I feel almost crushed under the load this morning, but I must roll it off on my Saviour who has promised to bear all our burdens for us. I'm sure God will help me as all of this work is His. I did not put myself in this position, I was forced into it, yet I accepted it willingly to do my best, and this I am doing. Lord, please help me this morning to bear up under the load.

November 17

Here I am, still alive and writing again after a silence of almost three months. Many things have transpired since last writing. Have just passed through the greatest Assembly that has ever been held. Descriptions of it are given in the Evangel of November 15, 1922. Personally the past few months have brought the bitterest opposition against me that I have even known, This opposition, however, brought no danger to my life like previous years, but the opposition has been more far reaching in extent, but the Lord has wonderfully sustained and given grace. The greatest victory was won at the Assembly that has ever been known. Each Assembly brings stronger ties and great evidences that God has set me as Overseer of the Church. Gleams of light, angels, Jesus, were witnessed by many either in vision or reality around and over me at certain periods to force the people to know I was in the place God designed. I have often longed to be free from the great responsibilities incident to such an exalted position, but as long as God will give grace I will not shrink, but go on boldly trusting in Him. The reports, work of the Assembly and everything went through with a sweep. We now have the Bible school here in the building, the correspondence course is under full sway with away over two hundred students. All the churches, the publishing house to operate with its twenty employees to keep busy, and 25 overseers of the states, besides the home and foreign mission work. All of this under my direct supervision. I still work day and night and my good wife sticks close to me in everything and bears her part of the responsibility, she having fed from one hundred to one hundred and fifty every day during the Assembly and keep forty or fifty in the house at night. Besides all of the above, she is teacher of a Sunday school class of boys, superintendent of the Home Class departments and I am superintendent of the Sunday school. And very frequently I am called to preach at the regular services on Sunday.

1920

February 20, 1920

Another three months have sped into eternity. Things unexpected have transpired. The most impressive was the death of our daughter, Halcy Olive, the 14th of January. This was so sudden that the shock was almost unbearable. And after this long it is almost more than we can stand at times. She died the 14th, was brought home from Chattanooga the 15th and we kept her remains with us in the home till the 16th, when we held her funeral at the church before a large crowd of sympathizing friends. Homer came home from New York, having married a wife only a short time before. God's grace sustains and comforts or it seems we could all be unable to endure. I preached the funeral of Brother S. R. Lee at the church and today of an eleven year old boy, Clarence Fortner, one of our little Sunday school boys. These services were both very touching. My work is still pressing. Work about 18 hours a day. Some part of the office work is going on from six o'clock in the morning till midnight or after. We are sending out 16,000 or more papers every week besides the other work. Have employed 23 hands besides myself and then we are unable to keep the work up to the notch. The church work and the Sunday school work are both prospering wonderfully everywhere we have touched. The drive raise money to pay for the publishing house has brought in over $4,000. We have purchased a plot of ground, about two acres, for the auditorium, also about 15 acres prospectively for the orphans home. I am still Sunday school superintendent. Mary is Superintendent of Home class work and teacher of boy's class. Iris is head clerk of B. T. S. by correspondence. Milton is in school. We are indeed a busy family. But God is with us. We are just now about to launch a new enterprise for the Church Exchange and Indemnity department. This as a department of the Evangel Office. This will add much additional responsibility and work. It will mean the handling of thousands of dollars.

March 16

Yesterday we dedicated the new auditorium site and land to the Lord. Good service, good attendance. I preached the sermon and prayed the prayer. The work of preparing for the foundation and basement commences this morning. From my office as I write I look out of the window and see the men and teams. Beautiful morning and fine weather.

June 16

Three months have fled away since I last entered a few words here. They have been months of interest, anxiety, responsibilities and progress. The work of General Overseer, the responsibility of which is growing greater, the Evangel office which includes the work as editor, superintendent and manager of the printing and publishing department, manager of the Exchange department, superintendent of the Sunday school which increased to over 200 part of the time, gave much attention to the building of the auditorium and have financed the whole of it up a date and paid out for material and labor $8,288.18. The frame of the auditorium is nearly to the top except the rafters and roofing. Our dearest daughter Iris married to Avery D. Evans at 8:30 tonight. Very impressive ceremony, decorations fine, prepared by friends. The wedding at the church. I am still working from about 5:30 in the morning to eleven and twelve at night. During this time I called on a special drive to finish paying for the Evangel building which went over the top the 6th of June. The whole cost was $6,367.10 with an over plus paid at of $108.97. The Lord has given me favor with the bankers and business men until I can get anything I ask for. I have borrowed thousands of dollars at the bank with no security, and have used hundreds with no notes given. Just my word. This is God's work. It is wonderful.

1921

September 2, 1921

I can hardly believe that more than a year has past since writing anything on these pages. The facts are that I have been pressed all this time beyond measure and could not snatch enough time to even think of it. So many things have transpired that it seems useless to try to go back over the time and give the information. I suppose almost every thing is recorded in the Evangel, or the Assembly Minutes and the books and papers in the Evangel Office. The past has been the hardest year of my life it many respects. Since the Assembly I have filled the place of General Overseer of all the Churches, distributed the money to the ministers since January 1 this year, Editor and publisher of the Evangel, business manager of the publishing house, superintendent of the Bible Training school, both the Home school and by correspondence, preached a lot of funerals, performed a number of marriage ceremonies, started and superintended the orphanage and children's home, financed the debt on the auditorium, preached a number of times for the pastor when he was sick or gone, superintendent of the Sunday school, which has grown up to 313 last Sunday. I have worked on an average of 18 hours a day and then I feel that I am falling behind all the time. In the office and publishing house I employ from 26 to 30 employees all the time, including the managers of the different departments, stenographers, bookkeeper, B. T. S. clerks, filing clerks, mailers, book makers, machinests, press feeders, etc., etc. The payroll is from four to five hundred a week. Just now we have a tremendous drive in the interest of the Evangel, both to pay out its indebtedness, meeting the current expenses and rallying for new subscribers. The strain has been intense, often more then I could stand but for the grace of God and the strength He imparted. And now the Assembly is almost here again, and it seems impossible for me to get ready for it because of the great work I have to do. The Council is to meet the 20th of this month and the Bible school opens the 26th. Then in November comes the Assembly. I work in the office day and night and scarcely take time to go over to the town. I do my city business almost wholly by telephone and messenger service. I have instituted and directed a number of city Sunday school drives, and one tremendous orphanage drive, besides overseeing B. T. S. drives for students and preparing dormitory and school room for them. I will be 56 years old this month and the work and responsibility is increasing with each passing week instead of becoming lighter. My health has been and is now extremely good. Wife is the same good faithful wife and helpmate in everything that she has always been, and I have thousands of friends and lovers that stick to me in everything. I should add that I have prayed for many sick folks and prayed over and anointed hundreds if not thousands of handkerchiefs and aprons for the sick people.

1923

February 19, 1923

In looking over this record I find nothing written in 1922. This seems to surprise me but what I remember the happenings and work done I conclude it is no wonder; there has been no time and things came so thick and fast that they could hardly be recorded, yet I am sorry that the record could not have been kept daily. I am now at Nassau, N. P., suddenly dropped down here on steamer from New York City—from snow and ice and cold wind to a land of summer and flowers. Avery and Iris are with me. We are here for a convention—Milton Padgett, overseer of all the Bahama churches. Arrived a week early because I had to take this boat in order to get here in time for the convention to commence the first of March. Now to drop back and come up again. Following the last writing came the great Assembly of 1921. This was the greatest Assembly we have ever had, but one mistake was made that has put a blotch on the Church that I would not have had on it for anything—adopted what was known as a constitution. My heart has almost broken over it many times, although I did not become awakened to what we had done until about the following February. When I came to myself I was frightened. Last year was an awful year. I was editor of the Evangel, manager of the publishing house, with Iris' help prepared the Sunday school lessons, Superintendent of the Bible school, both the home and by correspondence, and superintendent of the Sunday school at Cleveland. All of this time I did my work with an aching heart because four or more men, all of whom I had always considered my best and most to be depended on friends, rose up against me and made it awful hard for me. These men, I hate to name them, but feel I must, were M. S. Lemons, J. S. Llewellyn, J. B. Ellis and T. L. McLain, and I might also add W. F. Bryant. I can't tell all they did against me, but letters filed came in from places where they had been tells of their opposition in personal talk and influence.

It is definitely known that J. B. Ellis and J. S. Llewellyn took me quite often as a target in the pulpit. Their influence turned a few others. While I was working and wearing my life away for the Church of God, they were wire-working and planning against me so they could oust me from my positions at the Assembly. I was so brokenhearted much of the time that I could scarcely do my work. One time during the summer it developed in proof that J. S. Llewellyn instigated a strike among my publishing house force which I believe caused a loss to the house of not less than $3,000, besides the disgrace and trouble it brought. He denied it, but the proof was too plain. One of the girls told me at the time that some of the elders put them up to it, and she told others plainly that it was he. Later on though, he so intimidated her that she denied it. I think that was awful for an elder, a bishop and a member, and who I once considered my friend. Paul said, Alexander, the coppersmith did him much harm, and I can say the same of these men. The Lord reward them according to their works. I took abuse from J. S. L., both over the phone and to the face, worse than was scarcely ever if ever given to a criminal. He declared he would have me out of that office if it cost him every cent he was worth. He said this in a rage. Such as this went on until the Assembly. At the Assembly I was told that these men spent much of their time in wire-working and trickery and political chicanery of the basest sort to try to turn the Assembly against me. They came in on the blind side of the unsuspecting Assembly and secured the passage of such measures that grieved the Holy Ghost and the people, too, (the minutes of the Assembly for 1922 will show) took the divine appointment of the General Overseer out of the hands of God and ignored the work of the Holy Ghost and did some other things that I could not bear for I knew they were wrong, and by them ignoring the Holy Ghost and reappointed me General Overseer. I offered my resignation in protest of their dastardly acts, and the acceptance of the Assembly of their plans and measures. But the people who had been so duped and still did not understand begged me so hard that I finally consented to remain General Overseer, but I did it with a broken heart—I only accepted for the sake of the people who did not understand the evil works of those men. When I offered my resignation, which I did in as mild a manner as I could, M. S. Lemons rose up in a rage and there before 2,000 people bemeaned and spoke against me in terms probably worse than criminals are accustomed to hearing. He threatened to put me in the penetentary and used abusive language foreign to a gentlemen, much less a Christian. He has never offered an apology to this day. This raised a storm of criticism against him and there was such a commotion I was forced to call order and have him sit down as well as the rest. This was awful. Previous to this time, so I was informed, J. S. Llewellyn spent two hours and a half in vilifying and abusing me and my family before a committee meeting in joint session with the twelve and seventy. And the surprising thing to me has been and still remains that there was none to protest against his abuse, but let him go on till he run down, and when some rose to talk he broke in on them so that they gave it up. And when the measure that was so obnoxious to me was before the house for consideration. I called the Assembly to prayer as has always been my custom, and while we were in prayer J. S. Llewellyn ran up to me in a rage and shook his fist and pointed his finger almost against my face and said, "How dare you block this measure in any such a way." You dare not do it, you shall not do it," and walked away, white with madness. I took all such abuse without resentment—without talking back, without trying to defend myself. All of this happened at the Assembly after I delivered my annual address that brought a flood of applause and tokens of approval far in excess of any that had ever been delivered. For two hours, I suppose, amidst shouts, music by the brass band, and songs, cheers and weeping, about 2,500 people marched by and shook my hand and many of the men fell on my neck and kissed me and wept for joy. One precious old mother kissed me too. My hand was sore for two months from the tight grips of love. Nobody suggested such a move, and nobody ordered it. It was voluntary and spontaneous. It was wonderful, but it so enraged those men that they worked harder against me. Some time, during the enraptured overflow, two or three good brethren ran to me and literally lifted me up above their heads as a display of God's power. Still these men were not as careful about touching God's anointed as David was, but continued to do everything against me that was in their power and are still at it. But in the face of it all J. B. Llewellyn was put in editor and publisher of the paper. He did not want the Faithful Standard so I took it over to try to make it go and moved it to New York, thinking we might get it printed there, but have not yet had enough money to do it, so we are waiting and working to get up a stock company to make it go.

It was on the 9th of December that I took wife and Maude, my stenographer, and went to Knoxville where I dedicated their new Church house, then on to Morristown, Tennessee and dedicated another. Then we went to Canton, N. C. for a convention. Brother George T. Brouayer met us there. God gave us a good convention. This was December 21-25, then on to Kannapolis for December 28-31. Lillie Duggar joined us at Asheville. From Kannapolis we went to Middlesex and then on to Bogue. These conventions were great and plans were made to put this gospel into every country in the state this year. From Bogue we went in boat to Morehead City where we took train for Norfolk, Va. We were with the church there three or four days and then took boat for New York City. We were in New York about three weeks. Iris, Avery and Milton were there and we were with Homer and Marie and little Halcy. S. O. Gillaspie came from Illinois to meet us there to counsel about the magazine. We finally decided it best for mama and Milton to go back home as Milton was so dissatisfied with the school in New York and homesick besides. Maude and Lillie also went home and Iris and Avery came with me here. Mama and Maude will probably join me again later back in the states. I expect to travel all this year. I will be here (Nassau) till about March 6 or 7, then to Miami, Florida and back up the states again. May God be with me in every place.

February 26

I am still in Nassau. Have preached twice in Nassau, and these were wonderful meetings. The power fell in both services and to describe the wonderful manifestations would be impossible. At the service Friday night there were many seekers at the altar and some were slain under the power. It was said one was reclaimed and others were baptized with the Holy Ghost, probably four or five. It was impossible to learn just what was done. Yesterday at Fox Hill, about six miles out, I preached twice and delivered a Sunday school sermon on the lesson. Great meetings. Great manifestations of the power of the Spirit.

March 12

I am now in Miami, Florida. The convention at Nassau was a wonderful success. I delivered two discourses a day, Every service was wonderful. One, Stanley Ferguson, a colored minister, told of walking on the high places of the ocean a distance of twenty miles to get from one island to another to carry the gospel there. One time he carried some little children, one on his back, one in his arms and his packaged of clothes on his head and one place he had to leap through the water from one high place to another, that by guess, but he finally landed save but exhausted. The natives are enduring severe hardships to get the gospel to their people on the islands. At some of the night services there were fifteen or twenty at the altar. Several were slain under the power at different times. Quite a number got through to the Lord, but I was unable to get the number. Brother Milton Padgett, the overseer, has proved to be a wonderful man, both for his ability to handle the island people and work and in his love and loyalty to me as General Overseer.

We left Nassau March 6 on the steamship Miami. About one
hundred or more of the saints were at the docks to see us off. As
we moved away they sang, "God be with you till we meet again."
The waving of handkerchiefs continued as long as we could see
them. The last night of the convention was more wonderful. The
handshakes, the goodbys, the tears, the shouts, the last message
were all beyond description. Many kissed my hand, both men and
women. Cannot describe the scene. We landed in Miami about
9:30, March 7. Had meeting that night. Have had meeting every
night since our arrival, either at Miami or Cocoanut Grove every
night except Saturday night. Preached three sermons yesterday
besides two missionary talks or lectures and taught a Sunday
school class. I was about worn out when I got to my room nearly
eleven o'clock last night. Some came over sixty miles to the
meeting yesterday, and I think they staid over for the afternoon
service at Cocoanut Grove. I am billed to preach at Cocoanut
Grove three nights this week. These meetings are all for the
whites. The convention for the colored people opens Thursday,
March 15, and runs over next Sunday. We are staying with Sister
French who was baptized with the Holy Ghost in my meeting at
Cocoanut Grove thirteen years ago. W. H. Cross, the pastor here,
is taking all the interest he can in our comfort, conveyance to
and from church in his auto, and in the meetings. About fifteen
in altar yesterday. March 21. The convention at Miami for the
colored people was a grand success. Three meetings a day. I
spoke twice or three times a day. As many as 25 at altar once and
others at other times. The power fell wonderfully in almost every
service. The Lord put me through with great power in preaching.
O, how the people loved me! They showed it in many ways. I found
Brother Richardson, overseer over colored people, to be a fine
able man for the place. He is also a true friend of the Church and
myself. We had our last dinner in Miami with Sister Padgett.

Went from Miami to West Palm Beach in a bus on Monday,
March 19. On to Rivera for meeting at night with the white people
and next day also. Had two fine services. On Tuesday night for
the colored at West Palm Beach. Great and powerful meeting.
This morning left West Palm Beach in a bus and run out about
eighteen miles and then took a boat up the canal and across Lake
Okeechobee to Moore Haven where we are now for the night. This
was a wonderful trip through the Everglades, Saw aligators and
snakes and wild ducks by the hundreds. Eighty-five miles trip.
Will go in bus from here to Fort Myers tomorrow—75 miles.

May 21

Here I am behind again. Had fine meetings at Fort Myers, one meeting at Jacksonville, Florida and then to Hazlehurst Ga., March 29, Had a great convention there. The messages were wonderful. One special one consumed about three and a half hours and the people shouted, danced, and almost everything at intervals during the discourse because it was so uplifting and inspiring. Quite a few were baptized with the Holy Ghost in this convention. From Hazelhurst we went to Augusta when we had another fine time. At Augusta we stayed in an old Revolution days house where I think nine men were hung during the revolutionary war. Brother Latimer was with us in the Georgia meetings. Next week to Colombia, S. C. The convention there was wonderful too. Scarcely any way to describe its greatness on account of the presence of the Lord. Went to Rock Hill for one service and then to Greenville, S. C. This also was great. J. W. Culpepper was with us in South Carolina. Our next convention was at Lynchburg, VA., April 26-29. Was at Danville one service. This was another great convention. J. A. Davis was with us in Virginia. One service at Roanoke and onto Pulaski for convention. Came down by Cleveland Saturday evening and wife and Milton got on train and we went on to Chattanooga. On Sunday, May 6, I dedicated their new church house, raised $300. The power of the Lord fell and He gave us a great day. Went up home Monday, was there Tuesday and Wednesday. Those men who have been so hard against me tried to make it hard on me and they declared I should not leave any more to fill my appointments but I stated that I was General Overseer and I would go right on. They claim I am defaulter of $14,000, but I am not. They are giving me all the trouble they can, but I go right on and let them misrepresent me all they want to. God will look after them. I am busy with my work holding conventions. I came on to Pratt City, Alabama and the Lord stood by me in the very first service, the power fell and the convention was wonderful from start to finish. Came here to Cascilla, Miss., May 16. Convention opened the 17th. Closed last night. This was more than wonderful. Scarcely any way to describe these conventions. God puts the messages through me wonderfully. I am surprised at myself some times. The power falls in every service. I held congregation one service for two hours spellbound, except while they were shouting and dancing. Iris and Avery are still with me. Mama and Milton are at home. I win the hearts of the people every place we go in spite of all the wire-working those men do against me. And I hear that they are boasting that they are going to have me out of the place as Overseer and clear out of the Church, and I hear that they are working day and night to get people turned against me. But it seems the harder they work against me the more the dear Lord blesses me, and the more the people love me. I don't know what the results will be, but I know God is with me up to date and He is giving me great meetings. Multitudes are wonderfully blest. There seems to be no way to describe the manifestations of the Spirit as He operates on the people all through the services, through the preaching and all. The people cry, laugh, shout, dance, run, jump, talk in tongues, give interpretations, whole congregations fall on their knees and faces at times when the presence of the Lord seems so great. If every meeting could be described it would make books to tell it all. Only at home two days, May 9, 10, since the 9th of December, 1922. Traveled nearly 5,000 miles.

September 10

My time has been taken up with so many duties and there have been so many responsibilities upon me that I have not been able to keep up my diary. I am now at Nashville, Tennessee and will try to make note of some happenings since the last writing, I arrived home from Kentwood, La., where I was engaged in convention which was wonderful, on June 10. A council of the 12 elders had been called for June 11 giving the 70 and others the privilege of attending. We met according to arrangement and quite a number were present. I made some statements and explanations of matters in question including the alleged auditor's report that tried to show I owed the church $14,141.83. I stated that I was not short that amount and explained in detail my reasons for not accepting that report as dependable. At the same session charges were presented against three of the elders, M. S. Lemons, J. B. Ellis and J. S. Llewellyn. This aroused quite a feeling and interest among all present. Detailed information can be found on other records. After a hearing from both complainants and defendants, the matter was referred to the General Overseer and nine of the elders for consideration. In this council which was not open to the public, it was decided to postpone action on this subject until "the cloud was lifted from the General Overseer," which had been hanging over him for several months because of certain reports and accusations that had been circulated against me for several months. It was agreed to bring up these charges against these elders later on, but this was never done. T. S. Payne openly avowed that he would do it himself if no one else did, but this also failed. Later, developments proved that seven of these nine men did not regard their word as of any worth.

When the time came to consider questions relative to myself, I vacated the chair because requested to do so and because of a message and interpretation advising us to submit ourselves one to another. I explained that there were no provisions for such action on my part but I would submit to the request, as I wanted to do my part in obeying the message. I did not want to appear to be stubborn. They selected another and proceeded with the business behind closed doors in my absence. I was to go back to the chair later, but they finally dismissed the council in my absence and dispersed without giving me any more privileges. Other records will show the proceedings and results. I regard all of their proceedings as unjust and illegal and I have utterly ignored the whole thing except to take action as recorded elsewhere, but this was done because they became so corrupt in their proceedings and work. Having no other recourse for adjustment I, with others, prepared a declaration of independence, dismissed these men from all their positions to which I had had a part in appointing them and this started a revolution to save the Church of God from wreck and ruin. Some day this act of loyalty to God and the Bible will be regarded as a heroic act. Amidst all of the corrupt actions of the Elders led by J. S. Llewellyn, George T. Brouayer and S. O. Gillaspie remained true to me. They are regarded as the Caleb and Joshua of this revolution. Other records will show the call for the twelve to come together again July 24 to complete the work of the council called for June 12, and the refusal of the ten to attend, also the action of the General Overseer and George T. Brouayer and S. O. Gillaspie, loyal elders. Other records will also show the council of representatives and revolutionists at Chattanooga, August 8, 9, 10 and the proceedings of said council, etc. Continuing their corrupt actions they proceeded to impeach George T. Brouayer, S. O. Gillaspie and myself even after they had been dismissed from their positions of elders and judges and been notified of same. Then later F. J. Lee and M. W. Letsinger had the "gall" and audacity to call for my credentials and try to revoke my ministry and they themselves both carried credentials signed by myself. Such inconsistencies are viewed by wise men as absurd and ridiculous.

It was on August 22 that myself and wife left home and came to Nashville on train where we were met by Brother Brouayer who took us to Louisville in automobile for a convention there. We arrived at the convention hall about nine o'clock the night of August 23. We were ushered in, dirty and worn as we were, amidst shouts, hearty handshakes, and honor by C. H. Randall, overseer of Kentucky and those in charge. We were soon informed that W. F. Bryant and J. B. Ellis were there trying to create more trouble and

seemed bent on hindering the progress of the convention. Next day
I was on the program and they were there, but the Spirit lifted me
so far above the opposition and cross spirit that they had no show
and then never showed themselves in the convention any more.
The convention was wonderful. On the last night of the convention
I delivered the message under the power of the Holy Ghost, and
at the close there were wonderful demonstrations. An attempt to
give a description would be futile, but during the demonstration
I saw a woman pointing with her finger as if at some object just
over my head and her eyes glaring as if beholding some wonderful
object. I glanced to one side and saw a man apparently pointing in
the same direction with his hands but his eyes were closed. Later
on in the service the sister described what she saw—a blue-like
mist extending downward from the ceiling and a convoy of angels
beholding us while the demonstration was going on. Everybody
seemed to feel the presence but it is not known that any others
saw the angels. For myself I seemed to have a kind of sacred
fear to look up, All this time the demonstrations were wonderful.
Messages, interpretations, weeping, screaming, shouting, tongues,
dancing, leaping, running and almost everything imaginable, This
continued till a late hour in the night. The next day wife and I with
Brother Marlow and wife went out about fifteen or twenty miles
over the river into Indiana to see Sister Mamie Woodward and
her husband. She used to help me in the office with the Evangel.
Tuesday Brothers Brouayer and Gillaspie and wife and I went to
Terre Haute, Indiana for another convention, This also was fine and
God honored us with His presence and power. From there we went
to Akron, Ohio for another convention. On the way across Indiana
we stopped at my old home and place of my birth. Arrived in time
to take dinner with my youngest sister, and my half-sister was
there, saw some of my other relatives and wife's relatives too. Could
not stay long. It had been about 13 years since I saw any of them.
The convention at Akron was fine. Great demonstrations and glory
displayed. The first night I preached I think there twenty or more
in the altar. Fine altar service, but I do not know the results, On
this trip many were healed at the different places. Made the whole
trip from Nashville and back in auto. Brother Gillaspie left us at
Louisville and Brother Brouayer left us here yesterday. The services
here Saturday night and all day yesterday were fine. Last night I
stood on the porch of a house and preached to a large congregation
assembled on the porch, in the yard and street while the street cars
and autos whizzed by. We are to have a similar service in another
part of the city tonight and then we go home tomorrow D. V.

November 3

I am now at Alva, Florida. Only one more day of a meeting here, then we go home to get ready for Assembly. It was October 5 that myself and wife and George T. Brouayer and S. O. Gillaspie left Cleveland for this trip through North Carolina to visit and established churches. Went in auto. Our first stop was Knoxville, then Canton, Asheville, Gastonia, Springhope, Selma, Bogue. Then came on here. At every place the Lord met with us and wonderfully blest us in our work. I scarcely ever had such liberty in all my life. We made good at every place in establishing the saints and getting them settled down to working order.

1924

February 28, 1924

Much has happened since my last writing, and my time has been so taken that I have not had time. But I am now at Moundsville, W. Va., in the home of Brother and Sister Montgomery and will now go over the past few months briefly and try to catch up again.

We arrived home from Florida November 8, 1923, and began immediately to prepare for our Assembly which convened November 22-27, 1923. This Assembly beggars description but some of it is told in the following issues of the White Wing Messenger and the published Minutes. The calendar year was closed out in office work in Cleveland, Tenn. Office in my home. The record shows I traveled 12,457 miles last year, 1923, and delivered 218 sermons and discourses. My office work help me at home till January 11 when I visited the saints in Atlanta, Ga., and preached four times for them. God gave great liberty and many were blest by my going. While there W. M. Murphy, who used to be a minister in the Church but resigned because he did not approve of some things then beginning to show, decided to come back and join us in this mighty revolution.

My next trip out was to Dayton, Tennessee where I found Brother Byerly and a few saints battling away against odds as they had to give up their place of worship because they had refused to support the ten elder faction. I preached for them three times and helped them considerable, and got them started up grade for the Master, and they were much encouraged.

My next run was Somerset, Ky., with Brother C. H. Randall as pastor. 0, the Lord so wonderfully blest there that the services cannot be described. One special incident might be mentioned. Once while I was preaching I stopped all at once and sat down and stated, I will sit down while the Holy Ghost takes the stand. Immediately a message flashed through Brother Randall in other tongues. This was so like clock work that some mention was made about us having it made up beforehand to do that, but it was the Holy Ghost for neither of us knew anything about such a thing until it was done. Only four sermons there but the saints were edified and wonderfully blest. They often shouted out, cried, danced and rejoiced during the discourses. And I was so demonstrative under the power of the Holy Ghost that I was a wonder to myself. This was February 1-4. One man saved wonderfully.

I came back by Harriman, Tennessee, February 4-6. While there the Lord did wonders. They would not let us in the church house, but the meetings were in homes. But the people packed into three or four rooms so there were good crowds. The last night an incident is worthy of mentioning. In the forepart of the service several shouted and rejoiced. Finally all quieted down but two sisters, they danced to the piano played a few moments, then danced together out to the center of the room when Sister Duggar stopped suddenly and stood like a statute with her hands stretched out like a cross with her eyes closed. The other sister danced about a few moments, then got my Bible and laid it on the floor at Sister Duggar's feet and acted as if she wanted her to stand on it, but all motions showed that Holy Spirit was trying to show that we should stand on the Word of God, as our only rule of faith and practice. After a few minutes demonstrating this, she (Sister Aiden) ran into the other room and snatched up a little baby off the bed and brought it in her arms and showed by the demonstration of the Holy Ghost that we should be as submissive to the holy Ghost as that little child was to her, and stand on the Bible as our guide and keep low at the feet of Jesus. When this was over she took the babe back to the bed and ran back to Sister Duggar who was still standing with her eyes closed. Sister Aiken picked up the Bible, opened it and turned a few leaves, handed it to Sister Duggar who came straight to me with the Bible open and handed it to me right side up for me to read. She ran her fingers over a few verses like lightning and I caught the place, took the book and closed it. When all was over I arose to speak. I understood that the message was to come from those Scripture verses, 2 Cor. 7:1-4, which I used for an hour under the power and demonstration of the Spirit while the saints laughed, cried, shouted, danced and I don't know what all else. It was wonderful. My work there helped to encourage the saints wonderfully. One brother told me after the meeting was over that he laughed so under the power of the Spirit that he lost his breath a few moments. And it seemed that the Lord took me further out of myself than I had ever been before in preaching. Wonderful does not do justice to a description, but it's the best word I know to use.

My next trip was to Illinois, February 9-21, where I preached five times at Eldorado, six times at Johnston City, once at Olney and twice at Lawrenceville. A description of these meetings is also out of the question. Can't be given in full detail, neither can the demonstrations of God's power be expressed. At Eldorado God gave me great boldness and liberty and won the hearts of many. They are already anxious for me to come back again. They say the fire was just getting started. Brother Gillaspie was with me there a part of the time. Think we will soon have a good church there. We only had cottages for services but they were large and commodius and a lot of people were present. The meetings were wonderful in power. At the Sunday morning service especially the Lord came into our midst until everybody present were more or less affected by His power. Can't describe the service. It seems tame to say people wept at times until there were scarcely a dry eye in the house, at other times there was great rejoicing. All the meetings were wonderful, but this seemed to be the deepest in power of any. From there we went to Olney for one service. Only a few came to the service as the night was very bad weather. The Lawrenceville saints gave us a hearty welcome and the two services were wonderful in power and demonstration.

When I arrived home much office work was awaiting my attention. Piles of letters to answer, besides other important work in the interest of the Church. Of course, they would have me to preach at home once.

My opposers are very better but our work is prospering as the records show. We now have 170 ministers on our list lined up to help us in this great revolution. Just as I was about to go to the train to come here the sheriff came into my office and served an injunction on me stating that the full injunction would be served the next day on Brothers Lawson and Hughes. This means that J. B. Llewellyn, Lee and their clan are entering a lawsuit to put us out of business in working for the Church of God. I only had time to phone Brother Lawson and Brother Hughes and give them a few brief words of instructions and encouragement and hurried to the train which I took at 7:16 p. m. The Scripture the Lord gave me immediately was Acts 4:17-20. This shows the early apostles were enjoined and gives their answer. I laughingly told the sheriff I guessed he would get to take me to jail for we would be obliged to go on with our work for the Church of God. I tried to console my wife and children and urged them to be brave as they had always been. My soul was full of rejoicing and has been ever since. I do not know what will befall me but I know the Word of God is not bound and all this will turn out for the furtherance of the gospel and this makes me happy.

When I stepped off the train at Parkersburg on my way here I was caught in the arms of friends who came to the train to meet me. They covered me with kisses and escorted me a short distance to the home of Brother Jackson where some of the saints were gathered awaiting my arrival. I spent about thirty happy minutes with them and two of the brethren accompanied me to the station to catch the train for this place. They told me there was quite a number ready to join me in this revolution. I am to stop there as I go back and give them a good boost. My time here will be short as I will be obliged to run back home and give attention to the meaning of that injunction.

March 29

I am now at Nassau, N. P., Bahamas, arrived here yesterday morning at six o'clock. Brother Eneas met me at the boat and brought me to Brother Scott's home where I stayed last year. The meeting opened at 9:30 and at eleven I was on the floor delivering the message. I am to be here five or six days.

When I left Moundsville, W. Va., I came back by Parkersburg where I stopped over one night and delivered one message. House was crowded and 0, how the Holy Spirit displayed His power both in giving out the Word and in healing. The joy and glory were so great at times that it seemed the saints would almost be swept into heaven itself. 0, it was wonderful.

When I arrived home I found our church people all tied up with that injunction. They were doing their best to get released. Avery, Jesse and Brother Lawson with their lawyers were working faithfully. I went to work with them and in a few days we got some relief but not full liberty. The bill was demurred by our lawyers, but the court not knowing the case refused to throw it out but gave us some relief, I spent seven days in Chattanooga working on the case and one or two days in Cleveland. We were to go before the court Monday March 24, which we did at Athens, Tennessee, but our adversaries had prepared a petition accusing us of contempt and cited us to court at Cleveland, Tenn., April 14, so I boarded the train and came on through Cleveland and on here for this convention. I stopped over at Miami, Florida for one service while I waited for the boat. And that was indeed a wonderful service. 0, how the power fell. I had to stop often during the discourse to let the people shout. And when I finally closed the message I believe they shouted and demonstrated fully thirty minutes. The meeting did not close till almost midnight. There seems to be no way to describe these meetings, I can say they are wonderful, but that is a tame expression. 0, how the saints here love me. They are solid with me in this revolution. Visions, prophecy and messages encouraging me to push on and that victory will finally be ours by the help of the Lord. I have not heard from home since I left, but they were going on with their work the best they could with joy and happiness when I left Cleveland. I may be here till next day, then I go to Miami for over next Sunday, then home.

March 29 or rather 30, for it is 12:30 at night

The service tonight beggars description. The power began to fall in the early part of the service and kept up occasional showers until finally the big shower fell and I think lasted continuously for one hour. I believe there were 100 or more people dancing at one time and this steady fall seemed to have no intermission. Brother Eneas said he never saw it on this wise before. I think it was ten o'clock before I preached and this was for an hour under the mighty anointing and demonstration of the Spirit and power. 0, it was wonderful, and even at that late hour several came to the altar. The power still kept on us until many left the house at midnight still under the power. Some danced and talked in tongues on the street on their way home. 0, it seems the meetings get better and more powerful every place I go. I must lie down now for a little rest and get ready for tomorrow—Sunday.

March 30

0, this has been a wonderful day. The leaders are constantly saying they never saw it on this fashion before. The power is so great, and more people were present tonight they say than ever had been before. The house was packed and jammed and probably as many on the outside, and a good-sized house. They told me six got the blessing tonight at the altar. I preached three times today. 0, what power, what demonstrations, what joy and glory, no possible way of describing. The wonderful scenes cannot be described, but it seems that hundreds are shouting and dancing, running jumping, falling under the power and—well, I can't tell it. It is now midnight, I must lay down for a little rest.

March 31

This has been another great day in Nassau. The morning service was taken for counsel, advice and instructions, but the Lord set His approval so wonderfully upon all that was done that the power fell until we were unable to close the service till one o'clock. The afternoon service was not so long but it was powerful. We closed at four o'clock to form outside and get a picture made of the convention. This over we had a funeral.

A sister in the church had died and I asked the brethren to conduct the funeral in Bahama style which they did. We all went to the house of the deceased, the hurse [*sic*] was there, and immediately the corpse was carried out and placed in the hurse. It happened that the deceased had only one relative a cousin, she was put into a carriage behind the hurse. Two long columns of women were formed in the street in front of the hurse. At the head between the two columns was a man to lead the way as a vanguard, then a man was at the rear between the two columns as a rearguard. Then the march commenced. All walked. There were only the two vehicles mentioned above. The men followed the carriage walking in two columns. I walked with the men. As we marched through the narrow streets the sisters sang as they walked—such songs as "Nearer my God to Thee." "Sweet by and by," and others. All along the streets people stood on either side listening and watching. It was a very sacred and impressive scene. The distances was almost three-fourths of a mile or quite. At the cemetry the people around the grave sang as the pallbearers carried the corpse from the hurse to the grave, there the sexton and his men took charge and lowered the coffin into the grave. There was no box in the grave, no vault, nothing but the coffin. Then the minister took charge, read some Scripture from 1 Cor., 15th chapter, spoke a few words and at his conclusion several picked up dirt and threw into the grave, others dropped leaves and green sprigs on the coffin as the minister repeated some words of ceremony, a prayer was offered, both by a brother striding by and the officiating minister. Then as the sexton's men filled up the grave the people sang beautiful hymns. When this was over the line of march was formed again and they sang again as they marched away from the graveyard. The whole ceremony was very impressive to me. A holy sacredness prevailed over the entire company and the spectators on the sides of the streets. The streets are very narrow but the funeral procession holds sway as they march while all traffic and business stops.

I am writing again at midnight. The meeting tonight was wonderful again. At the close of a short message and an exhortation and an altar call the power began to fall as the seekers fell into the altar and never ceased for fully an hour and a half. Altar services probably 100 or more shouting, dancing and singing almost constantly. A few times the waves seemed to subside a few moments only to break out with more force. Several were saved or sanctified or filled with the Holy Ghost or all three, but there was such a crowd and so much powerful demonstration that no one could tell the number. But about all I can tell, it was a wonderful service with good results. They still say they never saw it on this fashion before, and I have to almost say it too, for it seems it is a little ahead of any of my former meetings in some respects. 0, how good God is to stand by me so wonderfully in my work every where I go. Wonderful! Wonderful.

April 2

The convention closed last night, but I cannot go till day after tomorrow as the boat does not go till then. Yesterday was wonderful again on up to the close last night. I do not like to mention their names but yesterday morning soon after the convention opened Milton Padgett and T. S. Payne, two of our avowed enemies, came in. We went on with our work as if they were not present except we could tell that the Spirit was displeased by them being there and doubtless some messages were given that would not have been given had they not been present. For instance, the Holy Ghost plainly referred us to 2 Peter, second chapter from which the Islands overseer gave a wonderful message and made it clear that we did not want to be bothered with false teachers, but our object was to save souls. After the service closed I shook hands with them as I went out and passed a few words with them. Poor Brother Padgett looked awful bad. How my heart pitied him. He did not come back to the afternoon service but Brother Payne came back with two or three of his crowd. For about two hours the power fell and the Holy Ghost demonstrated so wonderfully until we could not get started on the program till four o'clock. It was told afterward that Brother Payne had boasted that he was going to take a chance to speak against me, but any how, the Holy Ghost kept him from his purpose and he left about four, 0, the demonstrations were wonderful and a description is out of the question, Almost every saint in the house, probably every one, was used in the drama in some manner. Of course, I had my part, yet not so much as others. The night service was fine. We finished up the program and closed a little before eleven. Brother Stanley Ferguson, overseer has displayed an ability in directing the convention far above what I thought he had. Surely God anointed him for the position and service. All the saints are fine and those on the program filled their place high honors. After service last night a letter was handed me from Brother Payne which read as follows:

Nassau, N. P., April 7, 1924. Mr. A. J. Tomlinson: Since the people here are in the dark as to the trouble existing between us, will you do me the favor to allow me the privilege of explaining matters to them as I see it. Let us give them both sides of this matter so they can decide for themselves. Please give me a written reply to this note. T. S. Payne.

By such a note as this one would conclude he either thinks I am a fool or crazy. But this alone has lowered him in my estimation of him more than a thousand present, and by such I conclude he is not worthy of an answer or notice until be repents of his wickedness. He has sent twice already this morning for an answer, but each time I have replied, "No answer." These precious people got his side of this smutty question through their black degraded literature and went down before God and God gave them the revelation that they (ten elders) were wrong and for them to stick to A. J. Tomlinson. This they have done and for this vile man to even attempt to inject poison into precious innocent souls is nothing less than a heinous crime when they are living happy, victorious lives and their ambition now is to work for the salvation of souls, I have a righteous indignation against a man that would have the gall and brass to even attempt such a thing. These people on these islands are fine intelligent people and have a blessed Christian experience and for an American to come over here and throw off on them like that is too much. Poor old brother Padgett has been overseer of the islands for several years, but now because he stood out against me in this revolution the Islanders have thrust him aside. They are loyal while he has rebelled against the right, and thus he has lost his standing with them, and he is the cause of it and will have to suffer for it. He promised allegiance to me just before the final break came and then turned traitor or sold himself to the ten rebellious elders. I am through with him until he repents. Poor fellow, how I love him yet, but he is out of my reach at present. I have two more services with the loved ones before I leave Friday. I want them to be blessed services.

April 3, 11:00 p. m.

Tonight was my last service. Great time again. It was stated that about 30 souls have been saved and eighteen additions to the Church. This is fine for a week. I have been told that Brother Payne is slandering me in his meetings until even the sinners are disgusted. They said there were only five in his first service, and only a few any time. While he was speaking evil of me I was happy in getting souls to God. I am to take the boat for America tomorrow, but our people are so settled and established that nothing can move them from their steadfastness.

April 5

I arrived in Miami this morning. T. S. Payne came on some boat with me and not surprised we were given the same state room on the boat as the Lord had showed me. He went to bed before I did and got up and got out before I did and we talked but little. I preached at the eleven o'clock service and 0, how the Lord did bless with gospel honey. I preached again tonight and the power fell wonderful two or three spells, and one time I think I waited fifteen minutes, and, well, after I was through there was a continuous shower for quite a while. How we all feasted on the Word and Spirit. I am writing at 1:25 tonight, The power and demonstration of the Spirit were so great and wonderful we could scarcely close the service. Tomorrow is Sunday and I wonder what will happen.

April 30

I did not get to write up the Sunday meeting, and have not written until now. The Sunday meeting at Miami was wonderful. I gave a Sunday school talk in the morning, preached at the midday service which lasted till about three o'clock afternoon, then at night again, Both services beggars description. The power fell upon probably fifty or one hundred at a time. The attendance was immense. I left Miami Sunday night about 12:50 for home. I had to hurry home to prepare for our court trial.

On April 14 our case for contempt was heard, Brothers Hughes and Lawson were both exhonorated and the court fined me one cent on account of some point of law about the paper. The other case was tried Tuesday and Wednesday. The trial was only a preliminary hearing but we were given more liberty. The court records will tell, it is also given in the White Wing of May 3. The court gave as his opinion, besides his decree, that I was not guilty of the charges contained in the bill against me. The next hearing of the case will probably not come up till next October, but the depositions will have to be prepared which will take much time from my conventions and meetings of which I am sorry.

I was home on Easter Sunday and delivered the Easter sermon, and the Lord wonderfully blest. 356 in Sunday school, and I am still superintendent, had a big dinner at the tabernacle, and all day meeting. I also delivered a short missionary lecture afternoon. Last Sunday, April 27, I was again the preacher and 0, how the power fell. A regular refreshing shower when quite a number were greatly exercised in running, dancing, shouting, crying, and I can't tell it all. Service continued till nearly two o'clock afternoon. I preached again at night, but it rained and not so many out, God blest much.

Monday April 28

I went to Nashville and preached there that night. 0, how the Lord poured out His power and blessing, I had to stop while the people shouted and danced. Well, it was wonderful. Yesterday morning Brother Brouayer, Brother Kimlin and myself left Nashville bound for Texas in Brother Brouayer's auto car. It came a rain soon afternoon and made the road muddy and slick. We came to a place in the road where there was a slick metal culvert across the road and the wheels sank in the mud so they could not pull over it, so we had to pry it up and while we were working at it in the mud Brother Kimlin got sick and went off in the woods and made an awful loud noise vomiting. Brother B. and myself worked on and paid no attention to him because it was coming another rain and we wanted to hurry up and get out before the storm came up. After it was all over we have had several laughs about it over an expression I made, saying, Brother Kimlin enjoyed it so he just left us and went off in the woods and shouted (vomiting) while we worked, thus breaking fellowship with us. We laughed innocent laughs over it until we almost split our sides and l cried so I had to wipe tears freely several times. Last night we stopped at Hollow Rock, it was raining and I hunted for a place to stay, at last I got into a big boarding house, and when the land lady came to meet me in the hall she took a big laugh at me the first thing because I was covered with mud and dripping wet from the rain. We got in alright but was awful dark, but we washed up and she gave us a good supper, although Brother K. was not able to eat. We came from there to Brownsville where we are tonight, April 30. Have made slow time on account of bad roads. But we are getting along very well and happy in the Lord.

May 6

We came through Memphis, Tennessee on May 1. Stayed at Brinkley, Arkansas that night. The next night, Friday night, we stayed at Akradelphia [sic], Ark., then Saturday we came on here, a distance of 258 miles in one day. The Whole trip measure 806 miles from Nashville, Tennessee to Point, Texas. Had our first meeting Sunday afternoon. Not very many present but at night the house was packed, and the message fell on me. The only text I felt like using was some letters on a board nailed on the end of a bench in the church house—"This side up." It seemed very appropriate for the occasion and the Holy Spirit gave great liberty in the delivery. I think I spoke an hour and a quarter or more under the power of the Spirit of God and the Spirit demonstrated it all the way through. Some times the whole house roared with laughter and other times everything was as still as death, while at other times the saints shouted and at different times the tears flowed freely. This was the beginning in Texas. Can't tell what the outcome will be. Word from home tells of matters going on very well. Praise the Lord.

May 13

I am now at Temple, Texas. Did some good work at Point, the work there was successful. Gained a number for this way. Came on here and arrived Saturday, May 10. Brother Hurley had the meeting going and we fell in and are here yet. I preached here Sunday afternoon and then went to Belton about ten miles distant and preached at night to a large congregation. 0, how the Lord did pour out His power and blessings. Home was still all right the last I heard. My adversaries were trying to get a case against me through the Grand Jury, but had failed up to the last word that came. But no knowing what has happened by this time. I spend my time writing during the day and in meeting at night. I am to discourse on the Bahamas tonight. Will leave here in a few days for Slaton, Texas,

May 18

This is Sunday afternoon at Slaton, Texas. We came from Temple to Abilene in the auto, but it broke down and we left it there for repair and came on here on the train, arrived here yesterday morning about daylight. T. S. Payne, my adversary, arrived in the community and was endeavoring to poison the people against us, and some of the people wanted us to go to the same church house where he was, but we declined. Some of our friends told us he wanted us to come over there and discuss the trouble, but we told them we could not do it on account of the injunction we are under, and that we believe he wanted to draw us into it to get us cited up for contempt of court. So we refused even to go. Had a nice service last night at a private home and a large crowd gathered together. Many in the house and probably as many out in the yard. The service today was wonderful. The power began to fall while the people were coming in and went right on for about two hours, so we did not commence the service nor close it. The power played on me during the entire service. A kind of light or glory flame was seen playing up and down above and on me. It would come down on me and then rise suddenly and disappear, then it came down again after a short interval. This was repeated several times. Brother Brouayer gave a Scripture lesson or message under the power, then I followed him with another continuing the same subject. This was given with much demonstration and power. 0, how wonderful! The tears flowed freely all about from the eyes of the congregation. All that were there were convinced that we are of God. We feel sure that the fire and influence has started here and at the other places that will sweep Texas. 0, I say, hurrah for Jesus and His power and glory. We go about 12 miles out for service tonight.

May 19

Monday afternoon. I must say that I was danced about over the house yesterday by the power of the Holy Ghost so easy, 0, so blessedly. My feet and all were completely in His control. Service was announced for last night at a school house and after the crowd arrived it was learned that one of the trustees raised objections, but after being detained a while we went about a mile to the home of a friend and when it was learned that the crowd was too great for the house they made seats out in the yard and a wall out of a semicircle of cars filled with people and the front porch for a platform. Got the service started about 9:30 and it lasted till after eleven. I think I preached about an hour and the people listened attentively and the saints shouted and rejoiced in the truth at intervals. I was told today that T. S. Payne was about two miles away delivering one of his notorious messages against me. I was happy while he was doing it, and this was about the same time I was preaching the gospel and blessing the people. Poor man, he is foaming out his own shame. He will regret it some day, but it brings happiness to me. Praise the Lord.

May 29

I am now at Canton, Ohio, been here four days. I left Texas the night of May 21 after the service, arrived in Cleveland, Tennessee about 6:30 A. M. May 24, left there 7:20 P. M. for this place, and arrived here the next evening 7:10. I made my way to the place of meeting. They were singing when I opened the door. They gave me a glad meeting and within fifteen minutes I suppose I was up delivering the message. And it was truly wonderful when the Holy Ghost poured out upon us. The word went forth with power while the saints shouted and praised God. Every night since it has been repeated. The power of the Holy Ghost falls upon every service. Oh, it is wonderful. I am making my home with Brother J. A. Henson, writing letters in day time and preaching at night. Weather is cool, damp and rainy.

I left Brothers Brouayer and Kimlin and Sister Shepherd Taylor in Texas to continue the work there. Haven't heard from there since I left. The few hours at home were full. Had to look after business pertaining to the lawsuit and other business, spent a little time in my private office, but got but little done that needed my attention. I did not have my shoes off for four nights. God is wonderfully with me, praise His name. While my adversaries are hounding me down every way they can, God takes care and gives me favor with the people every where I go. I have traveled nearly 10,000 miles since January 1 and been in ten states and the Bahama Islands, preached at twenty places or more. Good results every where I go.

June 16

I am now at Lynchburg, Va. I went from Canton, Ohio to Akron and held services in tent Friday and Saturday nights, Sunday and Sunday night. 0, they were wonderful. Brother Wilkerson took me to Toledo Monday and we had a nice meeting in the home of Sister Gretsinger. Very good attendance. Several of my opposers were there but the Lord gave me good freedom in the message. Left Toledo about one o'clock the same night and arrived home the next night about eleven o'clock. Helped, in meeting every night while at home. Maude came and helped me with my office work for a week. Got my mail pretty well caught up. I came here last Thursday, June 12. The meetings have been wonderful. Whole congregations have been affected by the power. The meeting Saturday could scarcely stop for the power was so great. We managed to have two short recesses, Yesterday, Sunday, was great. The meeting started at ten and continued till one, under the power all the time. We immediately got in cars and trucks without waiting for dinner and drove 2 miles to Altavista for dedication services at three. The house was full and the power and demonstrations were wonderful. Did not get away till nearly six o'clock, then hurried back to Lynchburg for services at night. Got a little lunch and went right into service again. This is now Monday morning. Must hurry off now to service again. 0, it is wonderful and that is about all the description I can give, Tongues, shouts, praises, songs, preaching and often I have to stop preaching several minutes while the people dance and shout. A brother saw another sheen of light envelop me while I was in prayer. O, wonderful God.

October 13

Well, here I am several months behind again with my writing. In looking over my notes I find I arrived home from Lynchburg, on June 18, then on the 24th I started for Emlenton, Pa., above Pittsburg, Pa. Then on July 2 I made for New York City to see Homer on some business. I was called home before I was ready on account of that lawsuit Llewellyn and Lee started against me. I came home July 6. Since that time I have had to remain at home constantly except going to Chattanooga several times on the court business. Our óposers took depositions of 16 witnesses. Then we recessed for our Assembly September 10-16. This was a wonderful event in history. The minutes and articles in the White Wing

Messenger give a description of that great meeting, Then followed the taking of depositions of six of our witnesses. Then we recessed again till November 6 when we are to commence again. I have had to spend several days in Chattanooga since that time and will probably have to go back some more yet, My notes show that I have traveled 13,719 miles since January 1, 1924. Would have covered several thousand more if this lawsuit had not hindered.